BLACK SATURDAY

BLACK SATURDAY

An Unfiltered Account of the October 7th
Attack on Israel and the War in Gaza

TREY YINGST

FOX
NEWS
books

HarperCollins books may be purchased for educational, business,
or sales promotional use. For information, please email the
Special Markets Department at SPsales@harpercollins.com.

Fox News Books imprint and logo are trademarks
of Fox News Network, LLC.

FIRST EDITION

Library of Congress Cataloging-in-Publication Data has been applied for.

ISBN 978-0-06-342005-2

24 25 26 27 28 LBC 5 4 3 2 1

To my parents, Jerry and Debbie Yingst, you supported my dreams to be a foreign correspondent when no one else did. Thank you for teaching me to be empathetic to all humans regardless of race, religion, or background. It has made me a better journalist and human.

And

To the journalists who risk their lives in Israel and Gaza to tell the world what is happening. You are heroes and must always be protected. And to all journalists unjustly jailed around the world—like our colleague Evan Gershkovich—we are with you. We will not rest until you are home.

CONTENTS

Prologue 1

1 Something Is Happening 7

2 "We Are at War" 17

3 Momentum 27

4 The World Would Be Watching 39

5 The Battle in Sderot 47

6 "This Time Will Be Different" 67

7 Hamas Is Here 81

8 Kibbutz Be'eri's Houses of Horror 95

9 An Information War 113

10 The Army Isn't Coming 127

11 "We'll Meet on the Beach in Gaza" 143

12 The Ground Invasion Begins 153

13 In the Heart of the Battle 169

14 Front Office or Front Line? 187

15 Taken to Gaza 201

16 Nowhere Is Safe 211

17 "He's Alive!" 217

18 In the Tunnels 223

19 Cease-fire 235

20 To Start Reporting 249

Epilogue 257

Acknowledgments 263

Notes 267

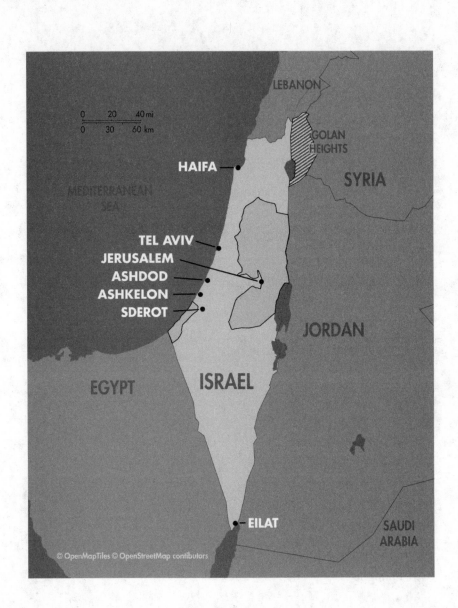

LEBANON

GOLAN
HEIGHTS

HAIFA

SYRIA

MEDITERRANEAN
SEA

TEL AVIV
JERUSALEM
ASHDOD
ASHKELON
SDEROT

JORDAN

EGYPT

ISRAEL

EILAT

SAUDI
ARABIA

0   20   40 mi
0   30   60 km

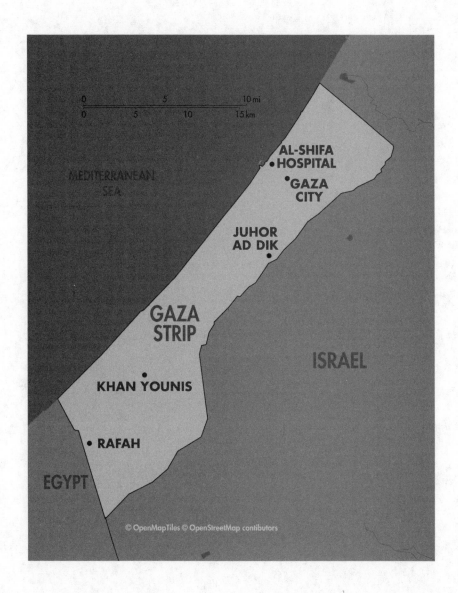

0 5 10 mi
0 5 10 15 km

MEDITERRANEAN SEA

AL-SHIFA
HOSPITAL
GAZA
CITY

JUHOR
AD DIK

GAZA
STRIP

ISRAEL

KHAN YOUNIS

RAFAH

EGYPT

© OpenMapTiles © OpenStreetMap contibutors

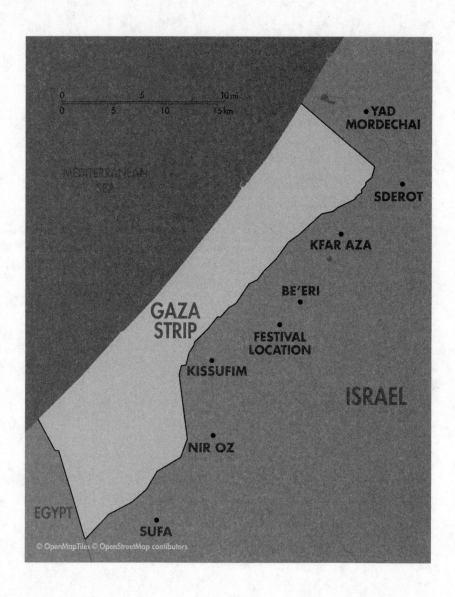

0   5   10 mi
0   5   10   15 km

MEDITERRANEAN
SEA

**• YAD
MORDECHAI**

• SDEROT

• KFAR AZA

• BE'ERI

**GAZA
STRIP**

**• FESTIVAL
LOCATION**

• KISSUFIM

ISRAEL

• NIR OZ

EGYPT

• SUFA

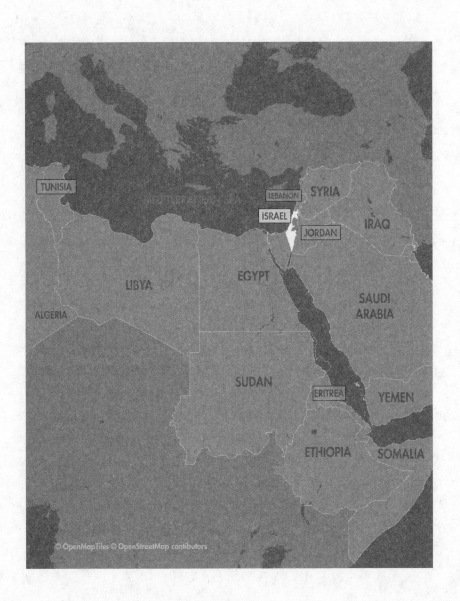

BLACK SATURDAY

PROLOGUE

My team and I were riding, late at night, through the lightless Gaza Strip in an open-air army Humvee, wide open to rocket-propelled grenade (RPG) fire from the darkened buildings above, hoping against hope we were going in the direction of the border with Israel. I was wondering what I was doing with my life.

This embed—a correspondents' attachment to military units in armed conflict—already dangerous enough, had become by far the most dangerous thing I'd ever done. On what was supposed to be a two-hour assignment, we'd been off the grid—no cell, little GPS—for more than four hours. We hadn't been able to check in with New York, and our bosses would be worried.

I hadn't been able to text my dad, in Pennsylvania. Since my mom died in 2022, he's been even more focused on my career than before. He, of course, would be concerned as well.

And now we were lost in the war zone in Gaza.

I'd been embedded in order to visit Al-Shifa hospital. The Israel Defense Forces (IDF) had bombarded and partially occupied it. I'd seen sleeping soldiers on the floor of the cafeteria, go bags stashed behind an MRI machine, a gaping hole blown in the wall through which we entered the complex, so dark that as we climbed through it, I couldn't see my hands. It was critical for me to report on that scene—beyond the front line of Israel's war against Hamas.

Now, though, I was questioning my choices.

Exposure to danger like this had become a repeating pattern. Exactly four years before, to the minute, I had been reporting from Gaza City because I'd gotten trapped there when a conflict broke out between Israel and Islamic Jihad. Tonight I was back, and the situation was even more perilous. Going in, we had ridden through the war zone in an armored personnel carrier (APC), on roads and paths cleared by the Israeli military—and that had been tense enough. Then, after the hospital visit, the officers at the staging area hadn't been able to find us an APC for the trip out. Our only option: open-air Humvees with a bunch of young soldiers. And though I knew the soldiers were trying to keep us safe, they kept doing everything wrong.

As the tires spun in mounds of sand and dirt, they told us to keep our seat belts on, but Sean, our security member, muttered to me and Yaniv, the cameraman, not to listen. Stay unbuckled. If we got hit or ambushed, we'd need to be able to bail quickly. The soldiers argued about which way to go, took dark streets not yet fully under the control of the Israeli military, and turned the headlights on, then off, then on again.

My focus went into hyperdrive, as it always does when I'm in danger. I could see better. Hear better. Smell better: decomposing people buried under the rubble, the stench hitting me in the face.

Body tense, I gripped the Humvee's metal cage. With each bump, my left shoulder slammed the ammunition box mounted on the vehicle's edge. It seemed more and more likely that we'd never get out . . .

How did I get myself into this? What am I doing?

* * *

At this point, the war had been underway for nearly forty days. Two and a half weeks earlier, Israeli ground forces entered the strip to take the battle to Hamas in the aftermath of the October 7 attack and massacre. Active ground fighting was unfolding in numerous locations.

Even before October 7, it had been a year of even greater tension and conflict than usual between Israel and Gaza. A Palestinian territory lying between the Israeli border and the Mediterranean Sea, block-aded by Israel and governed by Hamas, an Islamic fundamentalist or-ganization avowedly dedicated to Israel's destruction, Gaza has been a frequent source of operations carried out against Israel by Hamas. For its part, Israel has frequently assassinated leaders of Hamas and smaller organizations.

On January 3, 2023, militant forces in Gaza made their first attempt of the year to target southern Israel. National Security Minister Itamar Ben-Gvir, who has a history of taking extreme public positions regard-ing Palestinians, had visited the area known by Jews as the Temple Mount and by Muslims as the Al-Aqsa Mosque compound. Hamas had warned that such a visit would ignite the region, and indeed a rocket was launched from Gaza that day. While the fire fell short and didn't lead to a major clash, the day set the tone for the year.

Tensions further escalated just a few months later, in the spring of 2023, giving us the first major sign that the year could see a larger war. A four-day conflict erupted between Israel and Islamic Jihad in an op-eration the Israelis called Shield and Arrow. The death of Palestinian prisoner Khader Adnan after an eighty-seven-day hunger strike drew rocket fire from Gaza in early May. Rather than respond immediately, Israel waited a week before targeting and assassinating Islamic Jihad commanders. That move was as much about deterrence as it was about sending an internal message that attacks against Israel won't be toler-ated.

That short conflict was relatively intense—but it never drew in Hamas. Some analysts said that was because Hamas was looking for-ward to a more stable political future in Gaza and the territory on the West Bank of the Jordan River. Observers online even went so far as to say Hamas was changing as an organization, becoming more moderate.

To many, that idea seemed like a fantasy. Hamas leadership routinely made threats against Israel. They held rallies calling for the destruction of the Jewish state and jihad (holy war) against Jews. And Hamas had often made serious miscalculations about Israeli responses.

Tension between Israel and Gaza is the rule, not the exception. Multiple skirmishes and limited conflicts can erupt during a single year. The sparks have varied: sometimes prisoners on hunger strike, sometimes clashes at the Al-Aqsa Mosque compound and rising tension around the Muslim holy month of Ramadan.

The fire, though, was always the same: rockets launched from one of thousands of positions in Gaza, followed by heavy Israeli bombardment of Gaza, coupled with artillery and naval shelling. Sometimes, as in the fifty-one-day war in 2014, a limited Israeli ground component was added to the equation before a cease-fire solution was arrived at: more money into Gaza, aid projects, extended work permits for the Palestinian population.

Such interactions had become routine. Still, the months after the Shield and Arrow conflict saw bloodshed on a scale uncommon even for Israel. Two thousand twenty-three became the deadliest year for Israelis and Palestinians in decades. The state of tension and conflict was becoming categorically different.

*   *   *

How did I get myself into this? What am I doing?

Simple: I always wanted to be an international journalist. Every day after school, in our rural part of the suburbs of Harrisburg, Pennsylvania, my twin sister, Aly, and I walked across two fields to our grandmother's house. An avid traveler and adventurer, she had ventured around the globe. She had stories, coins, and gifts that piqued our interest in far-off lands.

I was also fascinated with Indiana Jones and Egypt. My grandmother promised that when I turned sixteen, and she turned eighty-two, she'd take me there. She made good on that promise.

In November 2009, my grandmother and I were at the end of a riverboat cruise down the Nile when I went to her cabin and found her very pale and looking like a deer in headlights. She asked me to find our local guide. It turned out that she was having a heart attack, ultimately a stroke. In Aswan, Egypt, five hundred miles from Cairo—not a place you'd expect the best medical treatment.

But my grandmother survived the ordeal. She lived into her nineties. And it was on that trip that I started to journal, to write notes of our adventures in this faraway land. When she died, I buried those notes with her—with the exception of one page. It described seeing the Pyramids of Giza.

I took that page back to Egypt and floated it on the Nile.

*   *   *

And now I was stuck. Literally, stuck in the sand, under immense threat. And emotionally, trapped by the necessity of putting myself in danger to get these stories, knowing there was no other choice.

Sean pulled out his phone and got a ping of GPS signal. My anxiety spiked. We were about a mile off the exit route, in an unlit, destroyed neighborhood full of tall buildings. "Maybe don't tell New York about this," he whispered in my ear.

As we contemplated the possibility of being targeted at any moment, few words were spoken. I scanned the buildings and piles of rubble for militants who might try to ambush us. So did Sean and Yaniv.

I started thinking of all the things I would miss if I died. I realized that for the first time in my life, I was truly contemplating death. But just in case we made it out unharmed, I was also making a deal.

No more embeds, I promised. *At least for a while—maybe the whole war.* That's what I told myself.

1

SOMETHING IS HAPPENING

Trey, something is happening in the south." Yonat's urgent voice blared through the speaker of my phone. It was 7:03 a.m. on October 7, 2023.

As my producer, Yonat sometimes called me this early, but her tone jolted me awake. I sat up. "What?"

"There are rocket sirens all over. I'm not sure," Yonat said. "They're firing on central Israel."

This had to be something significant—Hamas and Islamic Jihad don't launch rockets without a reason—but, phone to my ear, waking quickly, light filling my Tel Aviv apartment, I had no idea what. I'd covered the region for years now. There were no clashes this weekend at the Al Aqsa Mosque compound, no hunger strike developments in Israeli prisons . . .

No particular reason to think anything was going down.

*   *   *

I went to X, formerly known as Twitter, to look for information—the maps showed rocket fire all over Israel. I hadn't seen anything like this since the war in 2021. Sure, there had been smaller rounds in between, but this much fire at one time was unheard of. Especially with no prior warning.

Six minutes after waking up, I was on the phone with Greg Headen, vice president of news coverage at Fox News. Since the summer of 2018, I'd been working at Fox as a foreign correspondent based out of the Middle East.

I got to the point. "Israel is under attack. We don't know what happened, but there are sirens all over the country. It looks like a surprise attack. I'd like to take the team and head to the south."

There was a beat of dead air, so I filled it. "We'll report from Sderot and go from there."

Sderot is a town of nearly 30,000 people that sits along the border with Gaza. Down Route 4, it's an hour south of Tel Aviv during the week, even quicker on the weekend. We frequently use it as a base for reporting during conflicts between Israel and Gaza; you can see into the strip. Plus the city is filled with bomb shelters.

Headen has decades of news experience. A former producer, the former Miami bureau chief, and a former head of the Fox News Foreign Desk, he has an eye for news. He knows when it makes sense to move and when it makes sense to stay put. He had come to Israel with Fox News president Jay Wallace after the eleven-day conflict in May 2021 to see the Gaza border. Both former field guys, they like to see operations firsthand. I'd first met Headen in 2018. If I ever need anything, he is the guy who answers the phone at any time of day.

After a couple of questions about safety and logistics, he said, "Okay, let's do it."

"Copy, thank you. I'll keep you posted."

*　　*　　*

Nine minutes after getting the call from Yonat, I was on the office group chat:

7:12: Yalla, just spoke to NY

7:12: We will go to Sderot now

7:14: Same plan as always. Meet in parking lot of Sderot ASAP.

Can someone grab the black bag from outside my office? My vest and helmet.

I also called Yonat. "We've got the green light from New York."

I told her to round up the crew: Yaniv, the cameraman on call that weekend, and Yoav, the engineer. She and Yaniv planned to drive together from Jerusalem, an hour east of Tel Aviv. Yoav would meet us later on his motorcycle.

A seasoned war producer, Yonat is used to breaking news and knows Israel and the complexities of its society. She grew up in southern Israel in a kibbutz, or communal settlement, in the Negev Desert and then served as an officer in the army, as every Israeli is required to do. After a stint at Israel's Channel 2 (now known as Channel 12), she joined Fox News just before the Israeli disengagement from Gaza in 2005.

Producers in conflict zones have to maintain extensive military and government contacts while coordinating daily live shots and coverage on the ground. Yonat is one of the best-sourced producers in the entire Middle East, with an intricate understanding of the stories we cover. The whole team has a deep, personal understanding of the region— one that I simply don't have, even after six years of being based in the Middle East. I live there, but it's their home.

We made plans to meet in Sderot, at the parking lot next to the entrance to the town. We would coordinate by phone on the drive down.

Sirens were sounding all over Tel Aviv as I went upstairs to pack a bag and put on my boots. It was a warm morning, with blue skies and a few clouds. A bulletproof vest was sitting next to my TV. I grabbed it: I wear a vest whenever we're in a situation that might involve gunfire or shrapnel; I tend to keep one in my apartment or car in addition to one in my office. Today I had only the light one at home, not the best protection from shrapnel but better than nothing. I went out onto my balcony.

I watched as two rockets slammed into the sea. Another one was intercepted overhead by missile defense.

As booms echoed through the city, I began reporting, speaking into my phone for a video to post to social media. I post often to bring a new, younger audience to Fox. I'm a big believer in meeting your audience where they are: often that means online. This morning, I described what I was seeing, in real time: "Right now there are rocket sirens sounding in Tel Aviv. You can hear behind me interceptions. Those booms in the distance. I can see off in the distance, some of these rockets are landing in the sea. Others are being intercepted by Israel's missile defense system, the Iron Dome." That's the Israeli counter-rocket, -mortar, and -artillery system formally known as C-RAM. It uses radar to track incoming projectiles and then fire intercept missiles at them.

Israel was obviously under attack. But it wasn't yet clear that this was any different from other attacks—aside from the unclear context and the significant volume of firepower. At this point, I assumed that the Israelis had targeted a senior figure in Hamas or Islamic Jihad. That can send the region into an occasional round of conflict.

Whatever it was, it must have been a big deal. This was more than just a large amount of rocket fire—the factions in Gaza were clearly using both medium- and long-range rockets. I didn't have time to think about it further. I needed to get to the south and start reporting from the Gaza border.

*   *   *

Driving my black Jeep Wrangler, I didn't encounter much traffic. It was early in the morning on Saturday—the Sabbath—and rockets were flying, so even those who would otherwise be out were either still asleep or sheltering. At the end of my street, I took a left and headed for the highway.

Overhead I saw more rockets being intercepted: white trails of smoke from the Iron Dome interceptors, then puffs of smoke followed by more booms. I drove south toward Sderot with my left hand on the wheel; with my right, I refreshed my X feed and learned that the Israelis had ordered residents along the entire length of the Gaza border to remain in their homes due to a "security incident." If the fire was this heavy in central Israel, where I was driving, the border had to be extremely active.

At this point I figured Hamas had to be involved. This wasn't just an attack by Islamic Jihad and other smaller factions. This amount of fire had to be coordinated and approved.

As I drove, I also looked at my WhatsApp archive folder for feeds with my sources in Hamas. Nothing. I checked signal for other regional sources. Again nothing.

While I hadn't realized it when I first woke up, my best source in Gaza—Nael—had already texted me from Gaza City at 6:39 a.m., when the attack began. Nael is the former Fox News local producer, known as a "fixer," in Gaza; I developed a friendship with him during our years of working together. He had moved to the United States a few years earlier to raise his young family there; he only happened to be in Gaza right now because he was visiting his parents in Gaza City.

Nael has spent his life in journalism. A complicated man, he and his wife, Nancy, wanted a better life for their sons, but Nael felt guilty about leaving his parents in Gaza. He's also a brave and loyal friend. In 2019, when I was trapped in Gaza, as conflict erupted between Israel and Islamic Jihad, Hamas accused me of spying on behalf of Israel. Nael put his name and safety on the line to defend me. I'll never forget him yelling at the Hamas intelligence officers who tried to threaten and intimidate me.

He loves the craft as much as I do, and in classic fashion, it turned out that while I slept, Nael had been first with the news:

6:39 a.m.: Good morning, the first text read. Rockets now from Gaza. Also followed by two videos he'd taken of outgoing rockets.

Then, at 8:07 a.m., he texted again: Qassam leader: We are starting operation called Aqsa flood.

I couldn't make sense of that, so I told Nael to be safe and kept driving. Thirty-six minutes later he sent me a photo—it looked like it had been forwarded—of Hamas militants holding a kidnapped Israeli. The man was shirtless. The faces in the photo were drawn over with digital ink to conceal the identities.

The rocket attack was unusually intense, and the trigger still wasn't clear.

An Israeli held by Hamas fighters? That didn't fit.

*   *   *

I continued racing south, running a few red lights on empty streets before making it to the highway, all while staying in touch with Yonat as I drove.

The team and I were trying to figure out what exactly was going on.

The incoming rocket fire south of Tel Aviv was getting heavy, and I pulled over with other cars to take cover. It was more rural here, with trees lining Route 4, which connects the suburbs of Tel Aviv with the southern areas. Nearby I saw a family lying in the tree line as rockets were intercepted overhead. One of the women cried as a man who appeared to be her father covered her with his body. I snapped a few photos on my DSLR, fumbling with my phone to take a video.

Boom: a huge rocket interception. I looked up around the edge of my car for falling shrapnel. During rocket attacks, you're taught to get out of your car and lie on the side of the road. I've always stayed close to the car, hoping that if a rocket lands, some of the shrapnel will hit the car, instead of me.

Why were they launching so many rockets? I still couldn't find any report of a targeted assassination by Israel. It was about thirty minutes since I'd started my drive south, and nothing online indicated that the Israelis had done anything to provoke this barrage.

Back on the road, I called my dad. When something big happens, I know he'll be watching the news or he'll get a call from someone telling him to turn on the news. I never want him to worry.

"Hey," I said—trying not to sound like I was worried. "There's something serious going on. Hamas launched a huge attack against

Israel. We're heading to the south now, but I just wanted to let you know."

"Okay. Well, be careful, Treybird, and keep your head down."

"I'm sure the Iron Dome will intercept a good amount of the fire," I assured him.

"Can't depend on that. It just takes one little piece—"

I interrupted. "You're right. I'll be careful. I love you."

My dad watches every single one of my reports, then sends notes and suggestions. He's always been my biggest supporter—he even used to come shoot with me when I had my company News2Share, which I cofounded in college; he came with me on a trip to Ferguson, Missouri, and a trip to Ukraine. When I got the job at Fox, he came to visit and was with our crew getting teargassed on the Gaza border and in the West Bank as we covered clashes between the Israelis and Palestinians. He's always been not only understanding of my work but more than encouraging. Especially since my mother's death, in 2022, the news and my role have given him something to look forward to.

Now I was close to the city of Ashdod, about fifteen miles northwest of Sderot. Here it seemed the missile defense had been overwhelmed or wasn't working properly. Large black plumes of smoke filled the skyline to the east of Ashdod and told me that rockets had clearly slipped past Israel's missile defense system, slamming into buildings and roads.

I called Yonat and Yaniv, who said they saw the smoke I was talking about, so we agreed to meet near the largest plume. I figured we could do a few taped reports about the rocket fire with the smoke behind me. I saw fire trucks headed in that direction and followed them, stopping only one more time to film from the side of the road.

Arriving behind the fire trucks at an industrial area off the highway, I saw a factory engulfed in a huge blaze. But I didn't see Yonat and Yaniv. I was getting frustrated, worried we might not be first to the story. We had to keep moving. I parked and got out of my car in a dirt lot. Pacing back and forth, I called Yonat again. She didn't answer; it just kept ringing. *Where are you? I'll send you my pin again,* I texted her.

It took me about ten minutes to find Yonat and Yaniv; Yoav would meet us later. The firefighters had jumped out of their truck but quickly realized the blaze was too big to fight with the men they had. I still had on my light bulletproof vest: I grabbed my blue flak jacket and helmet from the back of Yaniv's car. Black smoke continued to spew from the building. We didn't have much time.

I did a few "pieces to camera"—quickly taped reports—with the smoke behind me, one fifteen seconds long, another thirty seconds. We planned to feed these reports to our editor Uri in the Jerusalem bureau, through the LiveU, a backpack that uses cell signals to transmit our video; he would then send them to New York. If we didn't have any compelling live imagery later, I could use this taped report to show the audience what it had looked like earlier in the day.

We finished our brief reporting and pushed on toward Sderot. By now we'd seen one video circulating online: Hamas fighters in the city. We assumed that the army or police would have taken care of them by the time we arrived.

*   *   *

Yonat jumped in my car for the last leg to Sderot, and we followed Yaniv. She was visibly frazzled, something I'd rarely seen.

Having reported on attacks against Israel over the years, and having lost friends along the way, Yonat knows the toll that terrorism takes on the population. Her best friend was killed during the Sbarro Pizza restaurant bombing in Jerusalem in 2001. She's long since lost count of how many similar incidents she's covered.

Yet today she was shaken. "There was no warning. Nothing," she told me. "This is a nightmare."

She read updates off her phone, confirming initial fears that this was an outright infiltration—far more significant than even a major air attack or act of terrorism. The Israel Defense Forces (IDF) were releasing small bits of information indicating that an attack was indeed underway, but we didn't need statements. By now we could see it, smell it, hear it. The radio buzzed in Hebrew. Residents in communities along the border with Gaza, shocked and terrified, were calling in to Israeli radio and TV stations to give updates. Occasionally, Yonat translated a few sentences for me.

"Have you talked to your parents?" I asked.

"They're in the shelter, I think." Living in southern Israel, Yonat's parents are used to rocket fire. But this was different. "My dad has a gun," she told me. "My brother is checking on them."

Yonat's identity is focused on journalism: no husband, no kids, only work. A deeply empathetic person, a highly strategic thinker, she's not only my producer but also a confidante, giving me advice about women and friends.

Yonat knows more about my life than most people do.

I drove, still checking my phone, and looked over at her. "Sorry," I said, attempting not to swerve.

I tried to keep my eyes on the road.

2

"WE ARE AT WAR"

As we drove toward Sderot, the effects of what was really happening unfolded around us in real time. We couldn't fully grasp it yet, but the rocket attack's unusual intensity was serving in part as cover and diversion. The astonishing fact was that at more than thirty locations, more than 3,000 Hamas fighters, along with numerous Palestinian civilians, had broken through the fence between Israel and Gaza.

Within hours of the first rocket fire into Israel, the entire border had been breached. Using rocket-propelled grenades, small arms, and hand grenades, the best-trained, deadliest militants from Gaza infiltrated southern Israel and engaged in a massacre of the civilian population, slaughtering people in their homes and overwhelming the relatively small number of Israeli soldiers at bases along the border.

With gun battles now unfolding across southern Israel, the Israeli army was nowhere in sight. At HaKirya, the central military base, in Tel Aviv, officials were still trying to make sense of what was happening and contacting the bases along the Gaza border: the Zikim base, under attack; the Nahal Oz base, under attack; the Re'im base, under attack.

While driving, I kept monitoring buzz on X. A news anchor for Israel's Channel 12 was also trying to make sense of what was happening, though much of the country wasn't watching TV because of the Sabbath. That moment was later also written about in the *Times of Israel*.

"I can hear gunfire," Kibbutz Be'eri resident Dvir Efrat whispered into her phone just after 9 a.m. Be'eri is a small farming community of just over 1,000 people along the Gaza border eight miles south of Sderot. Like many of the kibbutzim, it has a more liberal population than much of the rest of the country.

"We have terrorists roaming between the neighborhoods causing chaos," Dvir went on. "We are really scared. I don't understand the situation; there are already several casualties. I'm with my partner in the safe room."

She explained that his community had a small group of men trained to protect the kibbutz—nearly every community among the border had a similar volunteer force. But that morning, most had already been overrun. "We need to send forces, police, the army," Dvir begged. "The kibbutz has a nearby army base, they should send people who can handle the situation." She and the other residents of Be'eri didn't know that local army bases too were already overrun by Hamas gunmen.

Another resident of Kibbutz Be'eri, Eli Messika, called in to Channel 12 with more details. "There are wounded here," he said. "There are burning houses."

This was a scenario long considered impossible. The latest and most advanced security technology—including drones, above- and below-ground fences and sensors—was deployed on the Gaza border. Now it had failed.

Israel's worst nightmare was underway.

"Please send troops," Eli Messika begged.

*   *   *

Driving with Yonat, I could only wonder how far-reaching this attack might be. I thought especially about the possible plight of kibbutzim in a region I'd come to know well, north of Kibbutz Be'eri, right along the northern border with Gaza. Back in 2018, on my very first day on the job in Israel—I was Fox's new correspondent, learning as fast as I could—I'd been part of a team reporting from that very area. Not far from Kibbutz Kfar Aza, we were also only yards from Gaza's border. A cease-fire was supposedly in place; in fact we were within range of snipers. Across the border, black smoke plumed upward.

The fill-in correspondent was on camera, and the Jerusalem bureau chief was getting me oriented. Picking up a stick, he drew a map of the Gaza border in the dirt.

"We're here," the bureau chief told me, pointing with the stick. Then, barely moving the pointer: "Gaza City is here."

Driving toward Sderot on the morning of October 7, I replayed this moment with the bureau chief and thought of how exposed the kibbutzim were to Gaza.

I would later learn that by the time Yonat and I were in the car together, residents of that kibbutz were in a horrible state of shock and terror. Hamas gunmen had entered the community.

* * *

Like so many others in Israel that morning, Chen Almog-Goldstein, her husband, Nadav, and their four kids were huddling, terrified, in their bomb shelter in Kfar Aza.

The shelter doubled as the bedroom of their eldest daughter, Yam, twenty. The only one with a cell phone, she was reading aloud the urgent instructions coming from the kibbutz group chat and alerts from the army. Two months away from completing her army service, she was also calling and texting army contacts for help—to no avail—and taking over as commander of the family.

She ordered her younger sister and two younger brothers to get under the bed. The shelter door wouldn't lock, so her father, Nadav, used a cable to tie the handle.

When an explosion rang out, they opened the door, thinking that an Iron Dome interceptor had hit the home. But it had been a Hamas explosive—taking out a wall.

They ran back inside, re-cabled the door, and huddled again.

A strange and awful quiet fell around their house. It was punctuated only by occasional gunfire.

There was nothing to do but wait.

Where, Chen kept thinking, *is the army?*

* * *

Everyone under attack that morning had the same desperate question. Yet mobilizing a defense against what would soon turn out to be the most devastating surprise attack in Israel's history—coming from a quarter that Israeli officialdom had long ruled out as a ground threat—was taking time.

At about 8 a.m., Israeli defense minister Yoav Gallant had arrived in haste at the country's military operational center, HaKirya, a tall gray building surrounded by heavily fortified walls in the center of Tel Aviv, as I later learned from Gallant himself. He went straight down to "the pit," which, with its maps, secure communication lines, and battle-monitoring tech, serves as the underground nerve center for all IDF operations. It was up to him to mount, from a standing start, as rapid and powerful a defense as possible.

Gallant, sixty-four, former commander of Shayetet 13, Israel's elite naval forces, then of the Gaza division, ultimately all of southern command, was nine months into his new position. A stoic man with a weathered face, he'd spent most of his professional life not in the cabinet but in the field. He speaks in a decisive, firm, military tone, often pausing between sentences to choose his next words strategically.

On the wall of his office is a pyramid chart with wanted Gazan militants. When one is taken out, Gallant uses a Sharpie to mark an X over the face.

Since taking the job of defense minister, he'd spent a lot of time preparing for threats against Israel from places like Lebanon and Iran; today he'd planned on spending a quiet Saturday cycling in the mountains. But, hearing the sirens and noting the intensity of the rocket fire, he and Israeli chief of staff Herzi Halevi had agreed by phone that something unusual was going on, and they'd both hurried to HaKirya.

Gallant and Halevi's first meeting that morning was with the head of the Israeli Security Agency, known as Shabak or Shin Bet; top military officials were also in attendance. It was clear that Israel was at war. By 9 a.m., Israeli prime minister Benjamin Netanyahu had joined the room.

Gallant assessed the unfolding threat as a military man, not a politician. With Israel under attack, he believed they needed to be prepared for the attack to expand and change quickly. Hamas had probably coordinated in advance, he believed, with Hezbollah, the Iran-backed Lebanese militant group with reportedly more than 100,000 rockets and precision-guided missiles. Even lacking prior coordination, Hamas would certainly hope Hezbollah and other proxies would join the attack. An offensive from Lebanon, in the north, would be deadlier for Israel than an attack from the southwest by Gaza.

The country had to brace for a multifront war, Gallant told the others. "Send forces to the north—recruit everybody," he said.

*   *   *

Even while launching the attack that morning, Hamas had taken credit for the operation. The organization's military commander, Mohammad Deif, said in an audio message that Hamas was firing more than 5,000 rockets into Israel that morning. He called the attack "the day of the great revolution." As Defense Minister Gallant had predicted, Deif called on the rest of the Arab world to join in. "Our brothers in the Islamic resistance in Lebanon, Iran, Yemen, Iraq, and Syria, this is the day when your resistance unites with your people in Palestine," the Hamas commander said. "Today, the people are bringing back the revolution and reviving the March of Return."

The Israeli military would later estimate that around 3,000 rockets were fired into Israel during the first four hours of the attack—a number hard to process, given that during the entire fifty-one-day war in 2014, around 4,500 rockets were fired into Israel; a similar number rained down during the eleven-day war in 2021. To have 3,000 confirmed in the span of a morning was nothing short of shock and awe. Hamas and Islamic Jihad were using sheer volume of fire, mostly of homemade rockets and mortars, to initiate the war and, just as importantly, to distract from the stunning infiltrations on the ground.

Hamas officials also released the name of the assault, Operation Al-Aqsa Flood. The name refers to the Al-Aqsa Mosque compound, which Jews call the Temple Mount. It is also the third-holiest site in Islam, a traditional flashpoint for regional conflict.

*   *   *

As Yonat and I continued toward Sderot, I was still communicating with Nael, who was able to act as a second source—from his family home in Gaza City—confirming much of what we were hearing in Israel. But even though he was in Gaza, and as well-connected as anyone, he too was having difficulty making sense of what was happening.

We found the first route into Sderot blocked. So: change of plan. Yaniv, Yonat, and I pushed farther south, toward Gaza's northern border, near Kibbutz Yad Mordechai.

I was familiar with the area. My previous team——the bureau chief, the field producer, and the cameraman—used to have lunch once a week at a gas station nearby. Now, as we approached an intersection, we saw a small group of people there, civilians and officers. We stopped. They warned us of shooting in the distance. We could hear it.

Now we had a decision to make: go forward, stay put, or get to Sderot the back way. As the correspondent on the team, it was my call.

I thought back to when I'd first arrived in the region, five years earlier. I was taught how to get around areas like this, driving through fields and dirt roads. Something in my gut told me not to push it today.

We could also head toward the coast and drive to Zikim; we had numerous options and places to go and report from.

In the end, we decided to stay put. That was a good call, because we quickly learned that we really didn't want to be heading into the chaos that people were fleeing. Around 9:20 a.m., casualties began flowing into our intersection: wounded civilians, soldiers, border police officers. The intersection was quickly becoming both a meeting point and a triage station, as paramedics arrived from the southern cities of Ashkelon and Ashdod. We jumped out of the car, set up, and tried to start reporting but suddenly found we had to deal with people trying to stop us from filming. Both the officers and the civilians at this scene of chaos didn't want us showing the dead and injured Israelis.

They yelled at us to stop. Yaniv, besides being deeply loyal and hardworking, is also very protective of me and our shot; he's happy to get physical with other cameramen in a scrum of people. As we kept shooting, two guys ran up to me and Yaniv and punched us both in the face. I felt a cut on the inside of my lip and spit a small amount of blood.

A screaming match ensued in Hebrew between them and Yaniv. *Stay focused*, I told myself, and I went around the side of the car and continued filming on my phone. I was mad about being punched in the face. Looking back, though, I understand.

For a few hours, we were the only press at the intersection—just me, Yonat, and Yaniv, covering the chaos and carnage. Then NBC News correspondent Raf Sanchez pulled up. Like me, Raf is based in the Middle East. He's a brilliant and dogged reporter with a background in print. We met in 2018 and lived in the same building when he was a reporter in Jerusalem for the *Telegraph*.

Raf and I were among the first American network journalists in the south that day, along with a handful of still photographers, some of whom later got caught in a gun battle between Israeli forces and Hamas fighters. We both had the IDF media briefing ongoing on our phones—a giant conference call with Lieutenant Colonel Richard Hecht giving the information.

"Richard, it's Raf Sanchez from NBC," Raf said. "I don't know if you could hear me earlier. I'm just wondering if you have an estimate of how many Hamas militants have infiltrated, or are we talking in the hundreds? In the dozens?"

"Still don't know, still don't know, Raf," Richard said.

When Richard said he didn't know, I tended to believe him. A Scot from the suburbs of Glasgow, he had quickly become one of the faces of the Israeli military, as international spokesperson for the IDF. Unlike some military spokespeople around the world, I'd always found Richard to be an up-front guy. A few years back, Yonat and I met him for coffee and I told him I needed two things: for him never to lie to us, and an embed in the West Bank or with one of the Israeli units that responds to protests on the Gaza border. As far as I know, he's never purposely lied to me in our private conversations. And days before the war broke out, Richard had arranged for me to be the first foreign journalist in ten years to embed with elite military units during a nighttime raid in the West Bank. The raid went sideways and we ended up in the middle of an hours-long gun battle between Hamas and the Israelis.

He is a man of his word, and I could tell this morning he didn't have many words to provide.

He and the rest of the country were trying to make sense of what was happening. The attack was still unfolding, nearly fifty years to the day of the anniversary of the Yom Kippur War. A war that, until today, had been the worst surprise attack against the Jewish state in Israel's history.

*　　*　　*

The first person I saw die that day was an Israeli soldier or officer with a long beard. He had arrived at the impromptu triage station in critical condition. His friends placed him on the ground and two paramedics tried unsuccessfully to get a pulse. He was hooked up to a defibrillator.

It didn't matter. One of the paramedics took out his phone and called someone while pacing back and forth. I could see the frustration on his face: he wasn't able to save the man. The man's body was covered. They moved on to the next casualty.

Time stood still as I took a few photos and a video from a distance. It's that first moment of death, as surreal as it seems in real time, that makes a war truly immediate. No amount of fire or sound has the same effect. Something in my brain wanted to believe that the guy wasn't actually dead, that he was asleep or just unconscious. But I knew the truth. A lifeless body lay there on the pavement. He was gone.

There was no time to identify him, let alone mourn. The attack was still unfolding. As soldiers and civilians were put into waiting ambulances, it was hard to tell if some of them were alive or dead. Dead Hamas militants were also being brought to the location. In one case, once it was clear that the body was not that of an Israeli, the corpse was dumped unceremoniously onto the median.

I've thought about that first dead Israeli often. I hope to meet his family one day, just to tell them he didn't suffer, that he passed with his fellow soldiers around him, that he wasn't alone.

We watched as mothers arrived in civilian cars, dragging their injured children out of the back, shoving them into waiting ambulances. And as we watched, I realized something. The injured had bullet wounds—not shrapnel wounds. They largely hadn't been hurt by rockets. They'd been hit by live fire.

Despite the reports we'd seen and the sound of gun battles in the distance, the team and I still couldn't believe this was happening. Maybe it was a state of shock or just a desire to believe it wasn't true, but the idea that all of these people were *shot* meant that there were at least dozens of gunmen.

I still didn't consider the prospect of hundreds of gunmen. Let alone thousands.

I also realized that my team's brief delay earlier in meeting up probably saved our lives that day. Had we arrived at the intersection only a few minutes sooner, we wouldn't have stopped; we'd have driven straight to the next intersection, where Hamas had launched the ambush whose casualties now surrounded us. Driving time between the two intersections was forty-five seconds.

We listened to gun battles between Hamas fighters and the Israeli army. Occasionally, army jeeps rushed by. Injured soldiers spilled out of jeeps screaming in pain. Some jeeps took no time to stop at the evacuation points but drove straight to the hospital. We would later discover that hundreds of Palestinian militants were still in Israel. The fight was only beginning.

At 11:36 a.m., I tweeted: Active ground fighting continues along the border. We hear machine gun fire in the distance. Multiple Israeli soldiers being loaded into ambulances next to us. Lots of confusion in the air. Israeli police believe dozens of Palestinian militants are still inside Israel.

In between our live shots and reporting, I checked online for updates. Throughout the day, Hamas began to release images of the attack. It was now clear they'd taken military equipment and were battling the Israelis at military bases along the border. The entirety of this operation—whatever it was—had to have been coordinated far in advance. By early afternoon, amid ongoing confusion over where fighting was taking place, emergency services confirmed that two dozen people were dead.

Almost five hours after the initial infiltration, Netanyahu made his first public statement.

"Citizens of Israel," he said, "we are at war."

3

MOMENTUM

When the prime minister was making his statement that morning, Chen and her family in Kfar Aza, at their emotional breaking point, had been in their bedroom shelter for five hours, still listening to bursts of nearby gunfire by the Hamas fighters who had gotten into the kibbutz and blown off a wall of their home. Chen had left the shelter to use the bathroom and found it demolished by the blast. Yam had to go too—she ended up using a plastic bin in the shelter, apologizing in embarrassment as the family assured her it was okay.

Suddenly screaming, "Al Yahud, Al Yahud!," Hamas fighters breached the shelter door.

Chen would never forget the looks in the eyes of her kids under the bed. She, Yam, and Nadav had their backs to the door, a big teddy bear on top of them, as if that would stop bullets.

Nadav broke off a piece of Yam's bed, turned, and brandished it. The gunmen shot him twice in the chest, and he dropped to the ground and lay still, quiet, legs folded. The gunmen kept screaming, demanding the panicking survivors get dressed and exit the building. Scrambling in terror to comply, to get out of the room, the family had to walk over Nadav.

He was still breathing. The younger daughter, Agam, heard him saying "No." Again and again: "No."

Yam was struggling to get jeans on over her pants. One of the gunmen started yelling in Arabic, but they couldn't understand him: Chen only saw his big green eyes, heard the yelling.

"Maybe he's asking if I have a weapon," Yam said.

At that moment, the gunman noticed her shirt.

Her IDF shirt. It labeled her an active-duty soldier. The gunman froze. So did Yam.

As the militants were trying to herd the group chaotically out of the house, Chen, looking back, saw that Yam seemed to have fainted in the bathroom doorway. That wasn't uncommon; she'd fainted once when giving blood. Chen went and tried to revive Yam by splashing water on her face. Yam opened her eyes, and Chen ran outside to see that her three younger children were okay. The militants hadn't hurt the kids or taken them away yet, and Chen rushed back inside to attend to Yam.

The side of her daughter's head had a big, open, bloody exit wound.

She'd been shot in the face while Chen was outside. Yam was shaking her head and gasping for air as she bled out.

Chen watched in horrified shock, helpless, as Yam's head stopped shaking.

They'd killed her.

Chen ran outside. It was eerily quiet. The Hamas men hustled her and her three surviving kids into a car.

She couldn't think what to tell the kids to do. Run? Hide?

Where is IDF? She found herself looking around for them. Nothing.

The car started, then hit the road. It was clear that they were being driven toward the Gaza border. Riding, Chen told her kids that Yam was no longer with them—she felt it was important to say, so they didn't think their sister was being left behind.

They listened, giving her very piercing, deep looks.

They asked, "Mom, what happened to your lips?" They were white and dry.

Chen held on to a hope. Maybe Nadav had survived. Maybe the IDF had made it there and were saving him.

*   *   *

At the intersection, with the tragedy of the dead and wounded soldiers and civilians unfolding before our eyes, I did the only thing I know how to do: report.

I also remembered something else: *Breathe.*

Those two things might not seem that difficult, but they are. This work requires clarity, patience, and discipline, especially in times of chaos and horror. A former correspondent in Jerusalem for Fox News once gave me good advice: "Be the calm amid the storm."

So I documented what we were seeing. Let the world know about the attack unfolding in Israel. "You can see right now," I reported, my voice slightly shaking. "Soldiers are picking up injured children out of cars and they're loading them in the back of ambulances." "A number of soldiers were also wounded here. But there are wounded civilians who still haven't yet been rescued from the Gaza border."

I knew that being live on Fox would consume most of the day, but before that began, and when I had moments between live shots, I tried to post to X as much as possible. People needed information, and few could provide it that morning.

As we did the reporting, civilians, soldiers, and police officers tried to block our camera, and we had to explain over and over again that we were press, based in Israel, just trying to do our jobs. One man, named Ziv, was particularly aggressive. He thought we were going to broadcast sensitive information.

"We aren't going to put any of this on TV for hours," I explained to him. "I promise, you have my word."

"You are a journalist, I don't believe you," Ziv said, visibly upset.

I wanted to build rapport—and to get him used to Yaniv filming. "Who did you vote for in the elections?" I asked.

"Benny Gantz. He was my commander," Ziv said. "He was my commander for three years."

"Let me show you something." I pulled out a picture of me interviewing Benny Gantz.

His tone immediately changed. He went from wanting to stop us to wanting to help us. As we chatted, Yonat brought Ziv a cigarette while he read a text off his phone.

"One house, they take hostages," Ziv explained, talking about Be'eri: he lives there but had been away that morning in Tel Aviv. He kept talking, reading reports and messages off his phone. Be'eri, Kfar Aza, Nahal Oz, Nirim, Nir Oz . . . the list of kibbutzim went on. They'd all been attacked. And the battles against Israeli security forces were ongoing.

Something new. In the distance, smoke rose from air strikes inside Gaza and along the border. We knew what that meant. Hours into the attack, Israel was already responding against factions in Gaza.

"This is fucked. Holy shit," I said, reading an update from a Hamas WhatsApp group I was in. "Hamas says they've kidnapped thirty-five Israelis."

This was the first confirmation we had of kidnappings by Hamas.

"Even five—it's a number that would make the army go inside Gaza," Yaniv replied.

"This is going to be weeks, right?"

"Weeks? If this is the case, more even. For thirty-five people, they will go into Gaza," he said.

"And control Gaza," he added.

I reached out to a senior Hamas contact I had developed years earlier. "Do you have any statements about the current situation?"

No response.

By now Yoav, our engineer, had arrived and was pitching in. But he was also checking his phone every few minutes. He had a brother, Gil, who lived in Kibbutz Nir Oz. He'd heard from Gil early that morning, then nothing, and now it was becoming apparent that Hamas were inside the kibbutz, slaughtering civilians. Still no calls to Yoav, no replies to texts. At down moments, I saw him sitting by the roadside, checking his phone again and again, pain and uncertainty in his eyes.

He was one of thousands of Israelis who waited in agony to hear from their loved ones. We were getting further news of Israelis under attack. One man ran up to Yaniv and started speaking in Hebrew, which Yaniv translated for me: "The party is three kilometers [about two miles] from here. And they are shooting. And they have nowhere to go. They're stuck in the middle."

The "party" was the Tribe of Nova Music Festival, where concertgoers had come under fire by Hamas gunmen who came in on trucks and motorcycles and with paragliders. Videos were circulating of young Israelis running through fields, chased by Hamas.

These reports were shocking. The victims had nowhere to hide. Hamas was gunning them down for sport. Some young women who couldn't outrun the attackers were raped and executed. On a road next to the festival, concertgoers who hid in a bomb shelter were encircled; Hamas threw grenades into it. Those who survived the blasts were dragged out at gunpoint and put on waiting pickup trucks.

After one of our live reports from the intersection, my dad texted me. Video kept freezing & dropouts. The signal was spotty in the south, and we had some trouble getting our LiveU to connect. But I didn't want to move, for security reasons. There was also the possibility that if we left the hot zone, we might not be able to get back into it.

When I looked up from my phone, I saw a line of army Humvees headed toward the firefights, toward Gaza. I was telling Yonat and Yaniv that we should push New York to take us live right now—it would be a powerful background to show soldiers responding and heading into battle—when one of the drivers yelled. "Trey!"

It was my friend Itay. It took me a second to realize it, but I rushed over and gave him a dap, the sideways handshake, through the window.

"Itay! How are you, bro?" He'd arrived at his base with no plan or direction: as a combat medic and driver, he'd been told simply to head south to a nearby base. He wasn't with his unit—just a soldier who could drive and fight.

"Dude!" he said. "I can't believe it's you! Man, it's a mess, a *balagan*."

"I know. I know. Be safe, okay? Keep your head down."

*   *   *

Meanwhile, in Gaza, Dr. Abdelwahab Abu Warda was treating emergency room patients nonstop.

A thirty-year-old gastroenterologist, Dr. Abu Warda had been awakened suddenly at home that morning, in the large building in Gaza City that he shared with his wife and young daughter and all of their extended family; his home practice was there too. What woke him was the sounds of war.

He found the rest of his family up as well, in confusion. They had no idea what was happening until the doctor got a call, about an hour later, to report to Gaza's largest hospital, al-Shifa, where he'd worked for five years as a general surgeon.

He was to report to the emergency department. It was all hands on deck.

We will be destroyed. That was his first thought.

He'd seen a lot in his five years at Shifa, but nothing could have prepared Dr. Abu Warda for what he confronted on arrival at the emergency room that morning. The flood of patients had one thing in common: they were all military-age men. And most of their wounds were from gunshots, extensive, all over their bodies—not from explosives. Dr. Abu Warda is a specialist in the abdomen, but today his job was just to provide critical care of every kind: stop the bleeding, keep patients alive. As he began, he could tell that these were Hamas fighters and Palestinian civilians who had made a ground attack on Israel.

Gaza has many hospitals, but al-Shifa is the biggest and most central—best able to handle a mass emergency like this. Amid the chaos, Dr. Abu Warda heard someone say that at least one Israeli hostage had been brought in too.

*   *   *

From the intersection, at 2:10 p.m., I texted Nael: I worry this is only just starting.

We were getting a sense that nothing was under control in southern Israel. Heavy rocket barrages continued to hammer the southern and central part of the country. Some reinforcements were arriving at our location, but fierce battles were unfolding at the kibbutzim along the border. Israel had also started a widespread air campaign against Gaza, but given how fluid the situation was, it would take them hours, if not days, to stop the initial wave of attacks.

At 2:19 p.m., Nael texted me back: No worry for Palestinian because they have number of prisoners and Netanyahu will sit at the table for deal.

I understood what he was trying to explain, but I also understood that if Hamas truly had dozens of Israeli hostages or more, they wouldn't just jump into negotiations. This was going to be a major war. Many people were going to die.

By around 3 p.m., we started to hear and see more of the Israeli response to the attack. We heard the deep thumping of an attack helicopter firing toward the border. The buzz of an Israeli drone overhead. I was putting out updates on these developments. But I needed to balance them with reporting live. Our editor in Jerusalem was also cutting together a piece to air in the evening, showing the chaos of the morning.

One of the medics at the intersection gave us a case of water. "That's okay, you guys need it, we're fine," I told them.

"It's okay, we have enough." We took the water, but I wasn't drinking it. Yonat grabbed a bottle.

"Drink," she said, pushing it at me. "You need to stay hydrated. It's going be a long day."

In the edited piece, the first clip shows wounded civilians loaded into an ambulance as smoke from a rocket impact rises in the distance. Then: two soldiers, wounded by gunfire, being loaded into other ambulances. Then: the blurred body of an officer on the ground.

I did a taped piece to camera, to give viewers as much information as possible about what they were seeing. "It's a constant flow of civilians being loaded into ambulances here along the Gaza border. People are using their personal cars to drop off their loved ones who were hit by gunfire or wounded by shrapnel . . . the military also bringing their wounded troops here. Severely wounded soldiers are being evacuated from the front to here.

"There is active fighting continuing in the distance. Machine-gun fire.

"As Israeli police believe dozens of Palestinian militants are still inside Israel."

*   *   *

At 3:13 p.m., I got another text from Nael: Khan Younis hospital: 30 bodies for Palestinians we have.

He was giving me an accounting of the Palestinian deaths he could confirm.

3:15 p.m., me to Nael: Civilians or fighters? Or mixed?

3:16 p.m.: Most of them civilians raid the border.

3:19 p.m.: Woah.

3:20 p.m.: Because thousands of Palestinians raid the border after Hamas attack.

There, Nael was giving us the first evidence that civilians from Gaza had participated in the massacre. Later we'd see videos of the border fence being torn down and people streaming across. Soon Nael was at Shifa hospital in Gaza City, where Dr. Abu Warda was working in the emergency room. "It's very hard condition. Every minute ambulances and vehicles arrived with injured and bodies of Palestinians from east of Gaza."

For me, much of that afternoon was a blur. The heavy rush of adrenaline from the morning was starting to wear off. I could feel myself getting tired. I hadn't felt well the night before; I'd been a little sick, and had slept only five hours before waking to Yonat's urgent call. As someone with attention-deficit hyperactivity disorder (ADHD), I've spent much of my life struggling with focus. The struggle involves some contradictions. When I'm under the pressure of immediate danger, I go hyperfocused: everything is all too clear. When the adrenaline flags, I can drift. After I moved to Israel, I was prescribed Adderall to help with the condition, but I didn't like the crashes, so I stopped taking it. My own adrenaline, coupled with caffeine and the occasional cigarette, usually does the job.

Another contradiction: My tendency to become consumed by work—an understatement—makes me not only productive and successful but also unable to separate from the stories. And yet, when witnessing things that most people will see only in a horror movie, I don't process them in real time. I feel numb. I get into a flow state. It's difficult to describe, but if you ask Yonat or Yaniv or Yoav the one word I repeat over and over, it's *momentum.*

I drew on that now. I kept going, recording more videos for social media in between reports live to camera, known as live hits. I kept two thoughts firmly in mind. One, it was my job to make sure the world knew what was happening in Israel. Few international journalists were in the country, let alone in the south during the attack. Millions of people were relying on my reports to stay updated on the latest information.

Second, I needed to be careful with what I was telling the world. I didn't want Hamas to use my information. I didn't want to add to the distress of already panicked families who were searching for their loved ones.

"Just another update on the situation," I reported. "There are dozens of hostages inside Gaza. We don't know exactly how many, but I would encourage you not to share the videos that are circulating online and on the instant-messaging service Telegram.

"Right now, rocket fire continues, though. It has subsided a bit in the southern part of Israel. There are still ground battles ongoing. We've heard gunfire in the distance. And many wounded soldiers taken to this evacuation point."

It would be critical to share those videos later, so the world knew what happened. But the families of those people needed to be kept in mind. I imagined the parents of those people, how they would feel seeing their kids dragged into a car or, worse, lifeless bodies lying on the ground.

By 4:30 p.m., the Hamas-run Palestinian Ministry of Health said that 198 Palestinians had been killed and more than 1,600 injured. I hoped Nael wouldn't be killed or injured, especially in the initial response, but I knew him, and like every good journalist, he wanted to be where the action was.

Users on X had already started to refer to the day as "Black Saturday," and the term was being picked up by Israeli media, which also used "Black Shabbat." Black because it was objectively the darkest day in Israel's history, the largest surprise attack against the state since its founding. And the fact that it occurred on a Saturday—the one day during the week that Israelis have their guards down—held grave significance for the Jewish people. Sabbath: a day of rest. A day to reflect and spend time with loved ones. A day so important that observant Jews are forbidden to work or travel on that day. Most religious Israelis won't even turn on a light switch after the sun goes down on Friday night.

*   *   *

Given the security sensitivities and confusion, Yonat and I decided to hold much of the information we were getting until families were notified and the situation stabilized. Too often journalists want to be first to report information, despite the consequences, which aren't easy to know in advance. Sometimes taking information to air means a family will find out their loved one is injured or dead. Sometimes the information causes panic or even starts a protest. In this case, Hamas might be able to use information to their advantage. We have to be very careful—especially during breaking news.

I'm also lucky to work at Fox. They don't put extra pressure on us to be first; my bosses often err on the side of caution. We'd rather be right than first, and I knew that day the power that our words might have, in real time, to create chaos, concern, and confusion in Israel and around the world. At this point, nobody knew the dimensions of what was going on, not sources, not soldiers, not us.

We had to just report what was in front of us at the intersection—while trying to stay as safe as possible.

"Get away from the woods!" a soldier yelled at us over the sound of distant gunfire. We didn't know it then—Israeli forces were engaging Hamas nearby, around Zikim Beach. "They're here!" the soldier warned us, meaning Hamas, pointing toward Zikim.

Switching to the other side of the road, we did what we had to do.

Continue to report.

4

THE WORLD WOULD BE WATCHING

From the moment we were racing southward toward Sderot, during the first outbreak of the attack that morning, and throughout the awful day, some members of the Israeli military had been mobilizing to respond, on their own, in an improvised manner. I later learned that, like us, soldiers and officers who were awake and aware tried to piece together the scope of the war thrust upon the people of Israel. And given their responsibility to defend the country, they had an acutely urgent task—personal too.

Some soldiers drove straight to their bases to wait for orders. Others grabbed weapons and tried to rescue friends and family after receiving panicked WhatsApp messages.

Lieutenant Colonel Gilad Pasternak, detachment executive officer of the 828th Infantry Brigade, was at home in bed early that morning in his apartment in Petah Tikva, a city of more than 250,000 people, just six miles to the east of Tel Aviv. Most of his unit was at home too. The Sukkot holiday had given the soldiers a rest from the daily grind and training on base. The seventh of October marked Simchat Torah, the end of annual Torah readings for the Jewish people. For Gilad it was a particularly special holiday. His wife, Hila, had delivered their second child two weeks before.

Hila was already up. Gilad planned to go pray later in the day, then celebrate. When Hila came into the bedroom and told him the rocket alarms were going off, he said, "Honey, it's the wind. Please come back to sleep." But he did get up.

Living in the center of Israel, Gilad and his family were no strangers to rocket fire. Hamas and Islamic Jihad had fired on Tel Aviv many times over the past several years, often hitting suburbs like Petah Tikva. Given the distance from Gaza, residents there have around sixty seconds to rush to their bomb shelters and wait for the all-clear. This normally involves listening for the booms outside as the Iron Dome intercepts the fire. Then waiting up to ten minutes, to make sure no shrapnel will fall from the sky. The experience is psychologically taxing, but if instructions are followed, it is relatively safe.

Gilad and his wife knew the drill. Soon they and their two-year-old son and newborn daughter were in their building's bomb shelter. The rocket fire stopped. The family left the shelter and went back to the apartment, and Gilad went straight to the TV. That's when he saw a video that quickly became infamous.

Hamas fighters. On the back of a pickup truck. Inside the southern Israeli city of Sderot.

Gilad was twenty years in the military; he'd fought Palestinian militant groups on the battlefield. There had always been rumors that a day like this might come.

But a Hamas truck—inside Sderot? Unimaginable.

"Okay," he said to Hila. "This is war."

Unlike me and my team, Gilad knew almost right away, at least in a general sense, what was going on.

At 7:40 a.m., he called his commander and got no answer—the commander, like so many others, was in synagogue. Gilad called again, then twice more, still no answer.

At the same time, Israel formally deployed its first group of troops. More than an hour after the attack began, the government called on all available emergency forces to head south.

Around 9 a.m., Gilad got in his car and started toward the base, Camp Har Tsavua, in the Negev Desert, seventy-five miles southeast of where he lives. As he drove out of town, many people dressed in white were running from synagogue to their homes. It reminded him of a documentary he'd seen on the Yom Kippur War.

On the drive south, with rocket interceptions overhead, one thought raced through his mind: "I need my weapon." He'd left it at the base for the weekend. Getting armed was his first order of business.

He arrived at the base around 11 a.m. and grabbed his gun. At 11:30 his commander gathered all battalion commanders. Gilad is the second in command of the 828th Brigade: he oversees three battalions, consisting of hundreds of soldiers each. Unlike many who responded to the call, Gilad is a full-time soldier, not a reservist. His brigade is meant to fortify all of the squad leaders in the IDF. But during emergencies it is a fully functioning fighting unit with light-armor vehicles.

And this certainly was an emergency. Battalion 450, one of Gilad's, on standby that weekend, was already engaged in fighting Hamas in Kibbutz Kissufim, thirty-five miles from the base and only a mile from the Gaza border where Hamas led an attack on the whole line of kibbutzim. By noon Gilad had received a report of five casualties among his men there; the battalion commander himself was wounded with a bullet to his back.

By afternoon, Gilad's entire unit—about 5,000 men, including reservists—had come to the base. The commanders were informed that more than twenty communities, including Kissufim, where Gilad's Battalion 450 was fighting, were under attack at the same time.

Hamas gunmen were going door-to-door, systematically executing civilians. In some homes, grenades were thrown into living rooms and bedrooms. In others, children were shot in front of their parents, their bodies disfigured. Terrified residents clung to their bomb shelter doors as militants fired on the handles. When they were unsuccessful at breaching the rooms, Hamas burned houses down, reducing the people inside to ash after they suffocated from the smoke. Those not immediately killed were kidnapped and taken hostage into Gaza.

In many towns, residents who made up a security force engaged the militants, killing many. Yet by and large, they were outnumbered, in dire need of help.

Having organized his unit, Gilad sent two armored personnel carriers (APCs), known as Namers, to Kissufim with a commander. This wasn't great: those light-armor carriers are based on the tank chassis of the Israeli Merkava tank: not made to speed down paved roads on long trips, they go up to 50 miles per hour at best. It would take them six hours to get to their destination. Better than nothing.

Over the next five or so hours at base, Gilad and his fellow officers kept trying to understand the scope of what was taking place. They relied on news reports, social media, and information from contacts near the Gaza border. Normally the Gaza division, stationed at the Re'im base, would be coordinating a response to an attack along the border, but Hamas was assaulting that base itself; soldiers there, pinned down, were simply trying to survive.

Hamas had also strategically targeted communication systems along the border at multiple military positions. Using armed consumer drones, they went after even the semiautomatic machine guns that sit atop watchtowers.

With so many units' communications out, Israel's southern command had no clear picture. For eighteen hours after the attacks began, officials would have little idea how large the event really was.

So officers and infantry soldiers had to make decisions that would normally be made by generals: those at the bases nearby were to take what weapons they had and head toward the border. It was all based on initiative—taken by small forces.

Around 5 p.m., Gilad, who wouldn't receive real orders until Monday evening, took his jeep and, accompanied by four men with two other jeeps, left his base and headed out onto Route 232. He was bound for the base near Sufa, well to the south, where Hamas had slaughtered civilians at the kibbutz; Gilad's battalion at the outpost had been overrun by Hamas fighters. His first order of business, though, on the way to Sufa, was to check on Battalion 450, which had suffered casualties at Kissufim. He needed a firsthand assessment of who was still able to fight, who needed to be evacuated. Given the wounded commander, he also had to appoint someone to lead the troops.

As Gilad and his men pulled onto the highway, they saw dozens of dead civilians lying next to and inside cars all over the road. With no commanding officers on the ground, everyone had to deal with whatever was in front of them. Gilad told his soldiers to start pulling over and collecting bodies. The only plan was to respond. Collecting the dead was part of that response. There were so many that they put ten in a single jeep.

After checking in on Kissufim and assessing the situation there, Gilad and his staff of four moved farther south toward Sufa on 232, a drive of less than half an hour, given the empty road.

Suddenly they heard shooting from the trees beside the road to their right. It was aimed first at the car in front of them—then at them.

Gilad and his men pulled over, got out, raised their weapons. Right in front of them was a Hamas militant, shooting. They opened fire, eliminating him. They didn't have time to assess the situation: they needed to keep moving. The last thing they wanted was to be sitting ducks awaiting another ambush.

They got back on the road and headed to Sufa.

*   *   *

Just after 5 p.m., Rear Admiral Daniel Hagari provided an update on the situation in the south. Fighting between Hamas and Israeli forces continued at twenty-two locations—so the ground battles weren't even close to being over, nearly twelve hours after the attack had begun. Thirty-one Israeli battalions were now participating in the fight. Other divisions were on their way.

By sunset, Gilad was back in Kissufim. He'd traveled thirty-five miles from the base at Camp Har Tsavua to Kissufim, then to Sufa, and back to Kissufim. He'd seen bodies lying on the road, exchanged fire with Hamas, and made contact with three of the battalions under his command, organizing their deployment to the Gaza envelope, one with Gilad in Kissufim, and one farther south, in Sufa. The third—Battalion 17, his unit—was now just north of the northern Gaza border, in the Zikim beach area, near where we'd been reporting at the intersection.

Gilad had fought in two previous wars. He'd been wounded in battle and returned to the fight. October 7 was the hardest thing he'd ever faced. So far.

*   *   *

Gilad's efforts were matched elsewhere.

By Saturday evening, the Israeli military had retaken areas along the border, including Kissufim, and started to evacuate civilians from others. As my team and I began to understand it, in the early hours of the attack civilians and police officers, eventually elite police and military units like Yaman, Maglan, Duvdevan, and Shaldag, had indeed responded—but without any clear objectives. Army units had joined the response, and by the evening heavy air strikes were launched against positions inside Gaza. Meanwhile, attack helicopters helped to secure the border.

At the same time, active fighting continued near more than half of the border communities. At least two hostage situations were unfolding. And Hamas militants were still launching new attacks.

Israel had to develop a strategy on the fly because there was no plan in place for an attack like the one that was happening. My contacts in the Israeli military explained that the first order of business was killing or capturing the Hamas fighters still in Israel. The next order of business was to secure the border between Israel and Gaza.

But that first task was a tall one. Eighteen hours after the attack on the south began, Hamas fighters had infiltrated up to eleven miles into Israeli territory. It was impossible at this point to know all the places they were hiding. It wasn't clear how expansive the search for militant infiltrators needed to be. They were still crossing into Israel at locations along the border and attempting to infiltrate by sea.

Furthermore, it wasn't clear if Gaza was the only front Israel needed to protect. As ever, the nation's leadership was considering the possibility of a multifront conflict erupting from attacks by Hezbollah in Lebanon, the Houthis in Yemen, or Hamas militants in the West Bank. The Israeli military would have to establish all of those parameters. Then, like a Greek phalanx, forces would need to link shields, seal the gaps in the borders, and brace their side for further attacks.

For me, in the midst of the confusion and shock of the day, two truths stood out with absolute clarity: the fight was only just beginning, and the world would be watching.

5

THE BATTLE IN SDEROT

As the sun set at the intersection, Israeli soldiers, recently arrived, were loading their weapons and preparing backpacks on the side of the road. I went to snap a few photos. There was an ominous feeling about the coming nightfall. Hamas militants were still in Israel, hiding in the tree lines in the distance. It would be harder to spot them without light. You could tell the soldiers and police at this checkpoint knew it.

At dusk, a few of the police raised their weapons and pointed them down the road toward Gaza. They'd gotten information on the radio that Hamas gunmen might be coming down the road, having ambushed forces closer to the border. If those forces had lost the battle, Hamas would be at our intersection next.

After dark, rocket fire from Gaza got even heavier. During my live reports and social media updates, I saw more fire coming from Gaza at one time than I'd ever seen before. The red ambulance lights illuminated my face as I reported on camera:

"This war is escalating each and every minute." At the field to our right, Israeli troops fired illuminator flares to light up the field and expose Hamas fighters. In the field to our left, an Israeli helicopter came in extremely close to the ground, to avoid taking fire, landed with no lights, and began to take on more injured soldiers for evacuation.

It was now believed that around 200 Israelis were dead and more than 1,000 injured. Even at 200, this was the worst terror attack in Israel's history. Two hundred people meant war.

The rocket fire continued, and again it started to overwhelm Israel's missile defense system. I reported on camera as dozens of rockets flew overhead: "Right now, a massive barrage of rockets coming off the Gaza Strip . . . It's just a constant barrage, one after another. You can hear the explosion there." Given the number, it was clear that the two largest factions, Hamas and Islamic Jihad, were participating. They were believed to have around 15,000 total rockets combined.

While there was no way that Israel, under attack, could identify all the Hamas launching positions in real time, and thereby conduct the most effective counterstrikes, Israel was already going after Hamas sites in Gaza with widespread bombardments. At the intersection where we were, explosions lit up the distant sky.

*   *   *

Around 6 p.m., confused Palestinian civilians, on the receiving end of Israel's initial response, started hearing and feeling heavy bombardments in their neighborhoods of Gaza City. Among them were Dr. Raed Mousa and his wife and four children. They struggled to make sense of what was going on as blasts echoed between tall buildings and flashes of orange light illuminated the sky.

The Mousa family was well-off. Raed, a family man, always eager to do whatever he could to protect his children, was an eye doctor and surgeon for the United Nations Relief and Works Agency for Palestine Refugees (UNRWA); the family had a home in Gaza City and a home in Rafah, Gaza's southernmost city. That morning, he'd been getting coffee and preparing for work when the attack on Israel began, and the family had then waited in their apartment, unsure of what exactly was going on.

This wasn't the first time rockets had been fired by Hamas into Israel, but soon Raed started seeing pictures from southern Israel on his phone. He'd studied in Tel Aviv and lived in Israel for almost four years. He had friendships in the medical community there. Thinking about the Israelis he knew, he felt sheer shock at what he was seeing.

There was nothing to do but keep his family inside all day. He tried to help the kids stay calm and distracted, but he knew the situation was not good. The horrific images coming out of southern Israel reflected a situation that would certainly draw major Israeli retaliation.

And now, in the evening, the bombardments had gotten heavy. Raed had looked into thousands of eyes as an optometrist. Tonight he was looking into the eyes of his children: afraid, vulnerable, totally unaware of what was about to happen.

After two hours, around 8 p.m., someone working at the UN sent him a map showing the areas expected to be bombed that night. He could see that a very large zone would be targeted. Raed had the impression that the map had been made available to international organizations but not to civilians. That seemed awful.

*   *   *

At Shifa Hospital, Dr. Abu Warda had been working all day without stopping.

By sunset, thousands of wounded had come through the doors of the emergency room.

And that was just the first day. The doctor wouldn't be leaving for a long time.

*   *   *

Around 8 p.m., I checked in with my dad by text.

You look close to the road, he said. I flinch when one goes by.

Making up for weeks of boredom today. Just be careful and try to stay safe. I love you. Don't forget to eat! Done for the day on air?

No, going all night, I replied.

Amid the incoming fire and Israeli bombardment, the team and I had decided that it wasn't safe or smart to stay out under fire all night. We needed a base for the rest of the night's reporting. So we headed for Ashdod, a city of 220,000 people in southern Israel, fourteen miles from the Gaza border.

Around midnight, we established our base in the Leonardo Hotel in Ashdod. Tension gripped the city: nobody knew how far north Hamas had made it. We continued to do "live hits" from the hotel balcony, often for Fox News Channel and Fox Business.

My dad texted again: You look beat. But you've only been at it 18 hours+. Maybe a 4-minute nap? Might help. Need to take care of your voice too. You're doing an amazing job.

I knew he was glued to the TV screen and of course worried about my safety. It would be impossible to take his advice and try to sleep—there was too much to do.

After midnight, Palestinians in northern Gaza said they were already receiving text messages to evacuate. That meant Israel had decided on a military operation to dismantle Hamas in Gaza.

It might take months, and a ground campaign probably couldn't start right away. But the air campaign against the strip would be on-going. With the events of the seventh slowly becoming clearer, new questions arose—in fact, the biggest questions:

How exactly would Israel respond? What response was it entitled to? What would it be justified in carrying out?

As a journalist, I had to stick to the facts and avoid opinion or emotion-based analysis. I had prepared for years for this day, hoping it would never come. I'd put in years of extra work to develop sources, which would now become the many faucets of information filling our pool of reporting. Ready to execute on the mission and lead global coverage, tired but determined, like the war correspondents before me, I felt I was built for this moment.

*   *   *

Just after 1 a.m., Yoav came into the hotel room. "Surprise!" he said, carrying four boxes of pizza.

Nearly every business in southern Israel was closed that night—but in classic Yoav fashion, he'd convinced a local pizzeria to stay open and bake us a few pies. He can do everything, from fixing our camera to ordering food to pulling our crew car to safety after getting stuck in the sand. While he's on the conservative end of the political spectrum, he's a company man and doesn't let politics interfere with his work.

I don't eat much pizza. I try to eat as clean as possible. But I hadn't eaten all day, hadn't even had a coffee, and Yoav's delivery felt like when you had a pizza party in elementary school: a treat. Unlike in elementary school, I was so hungry I ate the crust.

After scarfing down two slices, I went back to reporting and kept at it all night. Around 2 a.m., I opened the hotel room window to listen. We'd chosen rooms on the north side of the hotel, to reduce the likelihood of getting hit by a rocket. But even facing north, you could hear the Israeli air strikes clearly.

I stayed up reporting, sometimes on-air, sometimes gathering information for the day ahead. Things were developing so quickly. We needed to stay ahead of the updates. I had thousands of messages from viewers online, and from friends and acquaintances, saying things like stay safe! and great work! I appreciated the outpouring of support—but because of the volume of personal messages, I was having trouble finding message feeds with sources.

I also continued to tweet updates about the unfolding news. I saw that I had tens of thousands of new followers—people desperate for news about what was really happening.

So at 5:35 a.m., I put up photos of me with Hamas militants; with Israeli special forces; with Israeli prime minister Benjamin Netanyahu; and with a former leader of Islamic Jihad. I wrote: Over the past few years, I've embedded with both the Israeli military and Hamas fighters. I've interviewed leaders from Hamas and Islamic Jihad, as well as the Israeli Prime Minister. This previous reporting is critical for you to understand the context of what is unfolding now.

I wanted to establish my voice with the new audience watching my reports—to have them understand that I take no sides in this conflict. I am not pro-Israel or pro-Palestinian. I am pro-truth. I speak with all sides to get a clear picture of what is unfolding, in any news context.

*   *   *

As Sunday the eighth dawned, updates flowed in regarding the Lebanese militant group Hezbollah firing rockets into northern Israel. A second front was heating up. Israel was already responding with at least one drone strike in southern Lebanon.

It had been a full day since the massacre began, and we still wanted to get to Sderot, our intended destination of the day before, and report from there—specifically from its police station. We'd learned from Israeli media that Hamas militants had slaughtered multiple officers there and occupied the station. The building had then been destroyed by Israeli forces.

As my team gathered outside the hotel lobby to prepare to leave, we saw border police officers loading their weapons. We knew the risks of going into Sderot—it still hadn't been cleared. But we really wanted to get the police station story. It would illustrate the nature of the battles that had unfolded throughout the south. We'd also seen photos from inside Sderot of dead Israelis, the horrific aftermath of the attack. We needed to document this, to gather information, to do our work as journalists and explain to the world what had happened.

Given our contacts within the IDF, we figured we had a chance. So again we headed for Sderot.

* * *

Meanwhile, still reeling from the surprise attack, the Israeli security cabinet had formally issued an "approval of the war situation"—a declaration of war.

The cabinet, consisting of twenty ministers and security heads, voted on a declaration of war, which was unanimously accepted. Sunday morning, it was announced to the public in two sentences:

> *Last night, the Security Cabinet approved the war situation and, to this end, the taking of significant military steps, as per Article 40 of Basic Law: The Government.*
>
> *The war that was forced on the State of Israel in a murderous terrorist assault from the Gaza Strip began at 06:00 yesterday (Saturday, 7 October 2023).*

The Israeli declaration of war was the first since the Yom Kippur War in 1973, and to the Israeli public, it made perfect sense. October 7 had seen the largest slaughter of Jews since the Holocaust and a systematic attack on the state of Israel. The attack was sure to draw a massive military response.

Complicating that response was the understanding that scores of people had been kidnapped as hostages and dragged into Gaza. The decision to declare war allowed Israel to rapidly expand its army: 300,000 reservists were called up, and throughout the country, roads outside military bases were turning into parking lots as reservists arrived, in many cases before being contacted by their commanders.

The declaration dovetailed with a wider response. In the U.S., amid concern that the attack by Hamas was the beginning of a larger regional war, President Joe Biden's administration decided to send Israel's other enemies across the Middle East a message that any attack on Israel could trigger an American response. U.S. secretary of defense Lloyd Austin called Israeli defense minister Yoav Gallant to convey the information that a deterrent U.S. deployment was underway. It included additions to the U.S. Air Force squadrons in the Middle East and moving the USS *Gerald Ford* Strike Group to the eastern Mediterranean.

Yet disagreement over appropriate next steps was already roiling Israeli officialdom.

From the first hours of the attack, Defense Minister Gallant, driven by his concern about Hezbollah attacks from the north, had been taking a strong and clear position with Prime Minister Netanyahu and the rest of the cabinet: Israel needed to enter Gaza on the ground, now. But in a series of meetings, the cabinet had been resisting this idea. They worried that in the event of a ground invasion, Israel would take thousands of casualties. Gallant found that absurd. For one thing, he trusted IDF. For another, the cabinet's numbers seemed way off.

"What do we have an army for?" he asked the cabinet. Since October 7, he'd been wearing a black button-down shirt adorned with two pockets, over a black undershirt. "This is the reason militaries exist," he said. He'd fought in Gaza, commanded soldiers against Hamas; a son of Holocaust survivors, he believed that threats to Jews would amplify, not just in Israel but around the world, if Israel projected weakness.

He'd already been out visiting the troops that were still battling Hamas fighters. "Keep working, prepare yourselves," he'd reassured the soldiers. "I will send you to Gaza—be patient."

But even while the heavy bombardments of Gaza had begun on Saturday night, Sunday morning saw no ground maneuvers underway. Israelis, Gazans, and the rest of the world held their breath in anticipation of the impending invasion of the Gaza strip.

* * *

Our drive from the hotel to Sderot on Sunday, if uninterrupted, was about forty minutes. We were all in one car now: Yaniv's company Jeep Grand Wagoneer. I sat in the front passenger seat, Yaniv at the wheel. We found an open gas station and grabbed some tortillas and a pack of lunch meat. That would have to be breakfast, lunch, and dinner.

We'd have to try to enter the city from the north: the army was engaged in battles with Hamas along the border, so the road from the south, exposed to Gaza, was too close to the fighting. We drove south to Ashkelon and turned left on Route 35. Trucks were transporting Merkava tanks; Humvees were filled with soldiers. Yaniv passed them, sped ahead, pulled over, and we got out and taped a report, trucks and tanks going by over my shoulder.

Back on the road, the radio announced the names of soldiers who had been identified as killed in the Hamas attack. We passed prickly pear cacti, known in Israel as *sabra*. I'd been told that it is used to describe Israelis: sharp and hard on the outside, soft and sweet in the middle. My Israeli team in the SUV seemed to fit the description. Listening to the announcement of names of dead soldiers, they kept their composure as we headed toward the front line. But I could tell they felt immense empathy and sadness for what had happened to the Israeli people, their fellow citizens.

At about 2:15 p.m. we turned into Sderot. Normally it has a population of around 30,000. Today, few remained. Less than a mile from the border, this is a city more than accustomed to rocket fire and attacks coming out of Gaza. The homes are built like large bomb shelters. The local emergency medical service station has a menorah built from rockets. When I first went to Sderot, in 2014, a local police officer showed me an area behind the police station where they collect rockets like you might collect pairs of shoes.

We headed for the police station on the suburban modern roads through many roundabouts. The drive was tense now. No one spoke. We knew militants were still in the town, hiding from the army and law enforcement—and everything we saw was deeply shocking. Cars in the middle of the road, blinkers on, windshields pocked with bullet holes. At a bus stop, pools of blood seeped into the sidewalk, blue medical gloves on the ground nearby.

Sderot is far less isolated than the kibbutzim along the Gaza border that had suffered attack. That meant that help, such as it was, had arrived here much faster than in other areas. Still, it was a bloodbath, so if Sderot was any indication, the death toll across Israel would continue to rise.

At the edge of a roundabout, a white pickup truck with a Gazan license plate sat abandoned, the word TOYOTA painted on the back. It was identical to a truck I'd seen in Gaza in 2019 on the way to a Hamas military parade. We stopped and looked inside.

There was a T-shirt, with a logo: a gunman wearing a green headband, standing on the Al-Aqsa Mosque compound, a gold dome behind him; he's holding a rifle and a Quran. That's the logo of the Al-Qassam Brigades, the military wing of Hamas. A Quran, some dates, and bundles of rope. We stopped to film and report at the location.

In a way, that car reminded me of seeing the one that Depression-era robbers Bonnie Parker and Clyde Barrow had used, riddled with bullet holes, on display in a museum in Washington, D.C., years ago. But this wasn't an exhibit. It was evidence of a crime committed only the day before. This vehicle had transported the gunmen who entered Sderot and slaughtered civilians.

Winding through Sderot, we arrived at the burned and demolished police station. Officers had cordoned off the area and were using construction equipment to dig through the piles of debris, twisted and burned metal, piles of rubble. You could see right inside the station: the side of the building was torn off.

*　　*　　*

There, amid the rubble, I started piecing together what had happened in Sderot. In part I learned it from Police Corporal Mali Shoshana, who normally worked out of a station in the southern city of Ashdod but picked up extra shifts here and there at smaller stations in the area. A single mother, she was providing for her family and enjoyed her job.

On October 5, Mali spoke on the phone with an officer from the office of operation, a usual check-in before a freelance shift. She wanted to know what to expect in Sderot—anything she needed to know?

"You know it's Saturday, in Sderot, on a holiday," the officer reminded her.

She laughed. "So we'll be bored to death."

On the morning of the seventh, she arrived at 6:20 a.m.—just before the shift change. But before she could start the daily brief, red alerts interrupted the chatter of the morning changeover.

Sderot was under rocket attack. The officers, used to these attacks, went to the shelter. When the alarms stopped, they left the shelter. When the alarms resumed, they rushed back in.

Like a game, Mali thought. Then they got a surprising call from the army. Four or five pickup trucks had been spotted near Zikim—filled with Hamas militants. The officers thought someone was pranking them. But now the radio buzzed: a van had been stolen and was headed toward Sderot.

Mali ran outside to get her vest from the car. She met another officer arriving from home. As they started speaking, they heard gunfire in the distance.

They ran inside. From the window, they saw a white pickup truck approaching, with five or six Hamas gunmen wearing bandanas.

Mali couldn't believe her eyes. Her first thought was that no one had said the TV show *Fauda* would be shooting in Sderot this morning, but this, she then realized, was real. She ran through the halls, yelling for people to go to the roof with their weapons. Because they'd been between shifts, more than the usual number of officers were in the building.

As she ran, Hamas started firing rocket-propelled grenades at the station.

Mali and six other officers got to a door to the roof, but it was locked. As some climbed through a window, Mali used her gun to break the lock, get onto the roof, and get in position to fight. Presuming they held the advantage of higher position, the officers looked down and prepared to engage, when suddenly, from the other set of stairs, two

Hamas gunmen burst onto the roof, shooting. In the firefight, one of the gunmen was killed right away, the other wounded.

As Mali went toward the wounded gunman, he reached for his weapon, and she shot him in the head, took his gun, and tossed it to her fellow officers. They were already low on ammunition.

Adrenaline pumping, Mali got on the radio. "Friends, we need help!" she said. "We are on the roof of the Sderot station. There are terrorists in the station and on the roof with us."

Minutes later, another wave of militants arrived on the roof—three this time—and another battle ensued. In this round, an officer next to Mali was wounded in his leg and stomach. Another officer ran to him and used her shirt to make a tourniquet.

The police would hold the roof for hours. At one point in that long battle, an officer yelled to Mali: "You have a grenade between your legs!" She looked down, grabbed the grenade, and threw it back where it came from. It exploded next to the Hamas gunmen in the stairwell. She thought she killed two.

Two waves of attackers, appearing out of nowhere, had been killed—and somehow, the police officers on the roof were still alive. Euphoria and hope surged with the adrenaline.

But then came the third wave. Hamas fighters were throwing multiple grenades onto the roof. Two officers were quickly injured. They were getting very low on ammunition.

At this point, Mali was certain she would be killed. Again, she went to the radio. This time she didn't ask for help but sent a message. "Tell my son that I love him," she said.

Then she peered around a corner: two more Hamas gunmen were coming up the stairs. She shot at them both and they fired back, hitting her in the right hand. She yelled in pain, fell back into cover, falling in and out of consciousness.

"I'm hit," she said into her radio.

*   *   *

Outside the station, Master Sergeant Guy Rozenfeld, forty-six, a tactical shooting instructor in the IDF reserves, was arriving with four young soldiers, eager to engage Hamas. Still lacking orders, like others in the Israeli army and reserves, Guy was improvising.

He had awakened that morning in his apartment in Sderot to the sound of rocket sirens on the edge of town, and while he never got up in response to alarms—"Never," Guy told me later—for some reason, that morning he did. He took his fiancée and two children, ages six and twelve, to the bomb shelter and went outside to smoke a cigarette.

That's when he got a shock. He heard shooting.

Not rocket fire. Gunfire.

"I don't think in my worst dreams I thought that the terrorists will be inside my city," Guy recalled. From a phone call with a friend and a video message forwarded on WhatsApp, it became clear what was happening: this was a ground attack on Sderot. The cell phone video, recorded inside the city and now circulating online and worldwide, showed Hamas gunmen in the back of a white pickup truck driving through the streets, firing on a police car driving in the opposite direction.

It was like something out of a movie, and to anyone who closely followed the conflict and security of Israel, it was an impossibility. Like many Israelis that morning, Guy didn't believe what he saw on the video.

It's fake, they do it in Gaza, he texted a friend: no way this could be happening inside Israeli territory. Yet he found himself wrestling with the possibility.

Then his group chats on WhatsApp—one for his building, another for his CrossFit gym—started buzzing with messages. The CrossFit group had about fifty members, with a training scheduled for 9 a.m.

7:26 a.m.: I'm canceling the 9am, because there are missiles, Guy posted in the chat.

Back in the shelter by 7:30, he began to understand that the impossible was actually happening.

7:28 a.m.: There are terrorists in Sderot, they're shooting underneath my house.

7:30 a.m.: Terrorists near [the supermarket] Rami Levy.

Is there army?

No army, nothing.

8:00 a.m.: There's still gun fighting and explosions, don't go out.

People were sending videos and photos.

8:05 a.m.: They are now in Be'eri, a man from Kibbutz Be'eri wrote.

Now the messages flowed in. They are everywhere.

The war started.

8:24 a.m.: Give us the exact places of the terrorists, someone wrote.

[Kibbutz] Kfar Aza, terrorists, someone else wrote.

Guy grabbed his pistol and five magazines and headed for the door. His fiancée tried to stop him. "Where are you going?" she asked.

"I'm going downstairs," Guy replied.

"No. You'll stay here with your kids and me," she replied.

Guy left the apartment, went to the floor below, found a neighbor—a young woman whose fiancé was out fishing on the beach—and brought her upstairs to his apartment. "Say hello to each other," he told her and his fiancée. "I'm leaving."

Jumping in his jeep, he drove toward the Rami Levi, the local supermarket. On the road, he looked left and right and saw only dead bodies. Bus stops filled with dead residents. Cars hit by RPGs. Shattered glass on the road. He found himself in shock.

Then his phone buzzed: a message in the CrossFit group chat. It was from Yotam Haim, a young Israeli from a nearby kibbutz, Kfar Aza. Guy trained with Yotam, a drummer with a sheepdog-like shock of red hair and big tattoos on his arms and side.

Yotam was sending a video with the message: there are terrorists inside my kibbutz. Still, he seemed calm enough in his safe room.

That was at 8:30 a.m.

At 8:51, someone provided the specific location where Hamas militants had been seen in Sderot. Guy decided to head that way.

As Guy traveled, the chat kept going:

My uncle is badly injured. He's underneath the market in Kfar Aza.

Somebody in Kfar Aza, please come help.

My parents are dead.

9:24 a.m.: The Israeli swat team is here, someone wrote.

10:14 a.m.: Don't go near the police station.

*   *   *

Don't go near the police station.

Undeterred, Guy was already on his way there, driving through neighborhood roads with roundabouts every few blocks. On the way, he ran into a group of four young soldiers from the Golani Brigade, one of the five Israeli army infantry brigades. The soldiers were walking on the road; a trained tactical instructor, Guy told them to come with him, and they did.

He knew they had to get close to the location where the person in the WhatsApp group had reported the presence of Hamas—but they also had to avoid driving in front of the police station. If Hamas had taken the station, Guy and his newfound cadre of soldiers would be killed right away. They parked and started moving on foot.

Suddenly they saw three men wearing Israeli military uniforms—but ill fitting. One of them turned. Guy saw a dark beard and a Hamas headband.

"IDF!" one shouted. He'd seen Guy and the soldiers but was trying to trick them. Another raised his Kalashnikov rifle and the firefight began. The soldiers took cover behind a nearby car, Guy behind a wall. With Guy taking the lead, they popped out, fired, killed all three of disguised Hamas gunmen. They moved forward to the police station.

Here they found the fight ongoing. The Hamas militants had entered the city with a detailed plan based on solid information: they knew the important buildings' locations, knew people would be home on Shabbat. The attackers, having come in waves, had stormed the building and taken officers hostage. Guy and his four soldiers entered into a fight with the gunmen firing at them from the windows.

They exchanged fire with no notable progress for about thirty minutes, until Israel's special counter-terrorism police unit, Yamam, arrived and entered into the battle. It would last all day.

* * *

On the CrossFit group chat, at 10:16, Yotam Haim, the drummer, sent his live location:

They're shooting at me, please someone.

10:20 a.m.: They're inside my house.

10:28 a.m.: Someone is shooting inside my house. All my door has bullet holes.

10:36 a.m.: They're burning my house, help. I'm inside the safe room.

Then: nothing.

* * *

With Yamam now engaged in battle with the hostage takers in the station, Guy left the scene and headed in his jeep for the entrance to Sderot. In the end, Israeli forces would bulldoze the station, regaining control and killing the Hamas fighters inside. That's what my team and I would see on Sunday: piles of rubble, the ruins of the building.

Traveling away from the scene, Guy saw bodies littering the street. He stopped every so often to check for a pulse. Maybe he could save someone? But after pulling a few bodies from cars, he realized everyone was dead.

Then he came across two Orthodox Jewish men walking on the sidewalk.

"What are you guys doing?" Guy asked them.

"We're going home."

"What going home? There are terrorists on the road now." Guy tried to usher them into his jeep.

"It's Shabbat, we cannot go into the car."

"Fuck the Shabbat," Guy said. A Toyota Hilux came racing toward them and Guy pulled out his pistol and fired two shots into the engine block. Luckily no one was hurt: they were Israeli soldiers. The entire scene was confusion and shock.

After helping other civilians, Guy got back home around 12:30 p.m. His kids and fiancée were in the safe room with the neighbor from downstairs. He breathed a sigh of relief. They were okay.

His phone rang. It was one of his friends.

"Listen, I have friends in Re'im, in a party," the friend said. He was talking about the Nova Music Festival. "They need someone to pick them up."

"I cannot pick anyone up," Guy said. "They're fighting in my city now." With his family secure, he turned to his next immediate move.

As part of an anti-terror reserve group focused on the border between Israel and Jordan, Guy's official responsibility was clear. He was supposed to be serving in the northwest a few times a year. But on the afternoon of October 7, he knew where he needed to be.

The next day, he arrived at his unit on the border with Jordan and told his commander his plan. "Listen, I want to go to the south. . . . I want to be in Gaza. I don't want to be over here.

"You know, they attacked me in my house," he explained. "I want to go to their house."

*   *   *

Mali had passed out on the police station roof and awakened—it seemed a couple of hours later—to the sound of more gunfire, right there on the roof.

She found herself lying in a pool of blood mixed with water sprung from one of the roof's boilers that had been hit by gunfire. Her body was shaking, but she tried to play dead. A Hamas gunman, having killed one of the last officers, right across from her, was walking around on the roof.

He left. Mali lay still.

When she heard talking on the roof again, she thought about seven hours had passed.

Was the talking by Hamas or Israelis?

She took a chance. She put her arm up.

The battle was over. Crying and shaking, Mali came down from the roof in a crane. As she rode to the hospital in an ambulance, the teenage driver told her not to look around, and she wondered why. How could anything be worse than what she'd just experienced? She did look around and plunged back into horror.

A burning car. Bodies on the road. Destruction everywhere.

At the hospital, one of Mali's friends from another police station came to hug her and started to cry. "We all thought that you were dead," he said. "We heard you on the radio sending your love to your son."

She had a broken finger and shrapnel in her body and head. Yet she was back at work the next day. Eventually she got a tattoo on her right hand: a lotus flower, the symbol of rebirth and resilience.

*   *   *

As my crew and I absorbed the magnitude of what had happened the day before, here at the Sderot police station a bomb disposal unit on the scene picked up a rocket from the street. Yoav went over to ask them if we could film an on-camera report next to it. They agreed, but after that brief report, we noticed the signal was bad.

Interest in the story was extremely high. We needed to keep working, to get TV hits every twenty or thirty minutes. We decided to move to another location.

On the road again, we passed a moving truck that had been hit by an RPG, with a large hole in the back. In the distance, thick plumes of black smoke rose from Gaza—less than a mile away.

We went to the house of a friend of Yoav, hoping to use their Wi-Fi to get a live signal out of Sderot, but they didn't have any power. The family seemed to be in a state of shock. Outside their house lay pieces of rocket shrapnel.

When we finally found a field where we had a signal for live reporting, we saw tanks and military vehicles beginning to stage. Israel was moving equipment to prepare for the invasion of Gaza—a new stage in the unfolding story.

With an armored personnel carrier rolling behind me, I did a video for social media:

"Israeli troops are moving closer to the Gaza border. You can see behind me, through open fields, they are preparing for the possibility of a ground invasion into Gaza. Simply waiting on those orders. Israel is at war. And the rocket fire and incursions into Israel continue."

As we stood in the field, we watched more rockets coming off the Gaza strip toward Israel. Smoke trails streamed through the sky. Loud booms echoed in the distance as Israel in turn launched a fresh round of strikes against northern Gaza. The situation was already changing. We had to stay on top of it.

*   *   *

At this point, a current of organization, response, and attempted control was running through all levels of the Israeli military. Sunday afternoon, Betty Ilovici, Defense Minister Yoav Gallant's senior advisor and right-hand woman, sent out a note to the press. Always on top of developments on the ground, Betty knows better than most press liaisons how to handle the media and is often open to off-the-record conversations to provide clarity.

Two hours after the attack began, she'd sent out an update: Gallant had approved the draft of reserve soldiers and that he announced a "special security situation within 80 kilometers of the Gaza border."

This statement revealed that Gallant had met with the Ministry of Defense director general, the head of Homefront Command, and other senior officials at the Kirya in order to make a situational assessment.

Among the notable pieces of information: they were continuing to
evacuate communities near Gaza. Gallant also instructed them to prepare similar plans for northern Israel, should conflict erupt with the
Hezbollah or Hamas offshoots in southern Lebanon.

The militants of Hamas and Islamic Jihad, and indeed some Palestinian civilians, had put Gaza in the crosshairs. The strip was at the mercy
of an Israel that, while not yet prepared to invade on the ground, was
fully prepared to surround it militarily—and pummel it, killing thousands in the process.

6

"THIS TIME WILL
BE DIFFERENT"

The next morning, the ninth, I began trying to catch up on reports from inside Gaza. There were many concerning developments. I saw reports of entire families wiped out by the Israeli air strikes since the afternoon of the seventh.

Again we left the hotel in Ashdod. We had information of activity around that area, and things had stabilized somewhat, so it seemed reasonable to head back into the action.

This was the first time that we had a moment to reflect on what had happened so far. Only a moment—but the shock was starting to set in. We tried to talk and stay focused, but it was hard. As information continued to trickle in, revealing the true scale of the attack, we were exhausted, shocked, and determined. It was like experiencing stages of grief. We knew that our lives would never be the same.

As we stopped for gas, rocket alerts flashed nonstop on my phone from across the country. Suddenly, sirens started sounding in Ashdod, and we were exposed. There were no shelters near the gas station. With my vest already on, I grabbed my helmet out of the back. I didn't even have time to attach the chinstrap as we rushed to the side of the building and set up.

Fumbling the microphone in my hand, I reported:

"Right now, more rocket fire over southern Israel. Hamas and Islamic Jihad have launched a massive barrage, attacking not just the
parts of this country along the border, but also hitting the central part
of Israel. Targeting Jerusalem and just north of Tel Aviv."

As I spoke, I could hear rockets streaming overhead. Some were
intercepted, but others slammed into buildings nearby. It was a huge
barrage. In the distance, black smoke started to rise from a building.

We hopped into the car. "Let's get *there*," I said to Yaniv, pointing
toward the smoking building. Racing toward the impact zone, we saw
a fire truck and started to follow. As we got closer, it was clear that
multiple buildings in the neighborhood had been hit. At a dead end, we
jumped out of the car and ran across the road to a building on fire. First
responders rushed in, looking for injured people.

Flames spewed from an apartment building as a small secondary
explosion popped. First responders talked among themselves and decided that some of them should go to another impact site nearby. Panicked civilians paced on the sidewalk, their eyes wide as they watched
their neighborhood burning. Later that hour, Hamas announced that it
had launched 120 rockets toward Ashkelon and Ashdod in response to
the "bombing of civilians" by the Israeli Air Force (IAF).

We headed farther south, toward the spot we'd reported from in the
first hours on the seventh. The body of a militant lay rotting on the
median.

*   *   *

With extensive strikes against Gaza ongoing—the IAF was targeting
command centers, rocket-launching positions, and weapons storage—
Israel was trying to determine how it would respond even further to
the attacks of the seventh. The security cabinet also had to consider
what was coming, not just from Gaza but also from southern Lebanon.

On the eighth, Defense Minister Gallant had traveled to the IDF
Gaza division headquarters in Re'im—down the road from the Nova

Music Festival, next to the kibbutzim still under attack in some areas; he also went to meet soldiers in Ofakim.

On Monday, the ninth, Gallant traveled from Tel Aviv to the southern city of Be'er Sheva. There he received an assessment of how to take back Israeli territory, secure the border, and evacuate surrounding communities.

After that assessment, he said something publicly that made the world pause.

"I have ordered a complete siege on the Gaza Strip," Gallant announced. "There will be no electricity, no food, no fuel, everything is closed."

"We are fighting human animals," he added. Israel should "act accordingly."

Israeli officials are known for making over-the-top, highly aggressive, disdainful comments about Gaza, especially amid rounds of violence. But this wasn't simply a round of violence—to Israeli leadership, this was a fight for Israel's survival. Gallant also wasn't one of the figures in the Israeli cabinet who normally made such comments; his words quickly drew backlash from organizations like Human Rights Watch, which called use of the word *animals* to describe the people of Gaza "abhorrent," noting that such collective punishment is what they call a war crime.

It's important to keep in mind that with a population of more than 2 million civilians, the Gaza Strip is one of the most densely populated areas on earth. Despite what some have said with caustic casualness, Gaza is—obviously—filled not only with militants. Most Palestinians in Gaza look to live a free and healthy life. They want to participate in their volleyball league, have ice cream in Gaza City, raise their children, go to work, go to the beach. The similarities between the civilian lives of Gazans and Israelis shouldn't surprise anyone, but they do.

A tragic reality is that those civilians are governed by an organization, Hamas, that practices terrorism, as defined by the American government. Another reality is that, as in Israel, civilian viewpoints lie along a spectrum. Some civilians truly want peace and to be good neighbors to Israel, albeit without a blockade. Others call for the death of Jews and consider it the highest honor to die fighting them. Numerous videos from October 7 showed Gazan civilians cheering in the streets as the attack was unfolding and the bodies of Israelis, both alive and dead, were displayed like trophies.

One video in particular stood out to me. The naked, possibly lifeless body of twenty-three-year-old Shani Louk, a German Israeli taken hostage from the Nova Music Festival, was paraded through the streets of Gaza in the back of a white pickup truck while men holding guns chanted "Allahu Akbar." As the truck drove away, a crowd of Gazans was revealed chanting and cheering.

It wasn't clear if Shani was still alive. You could only imagine what had been done to her before she was taken into Gaza.

A sick scene. And it and others like it were not denounced by loud or known voices in the Palestinian diaspora. Facts like that make life in Gaza, progress in Gaza, and covering Gaza incredibly difficult. Many Israelis want to believe that all Palestinians are bad and many Palestinians want to believe all Israelis are bad. As "the messenger," I often feel I'm being criticized by both sides simultaneously. Those affected by conflict have many emotions, of course, and I find that during interviews or conversations, people will dump those emotions on me. It's almost cathartic for people to speak with a reporter. Yet as a journalist, I'm a trained storyteller, not a trained psychologist. And often I take the trauma and frustrations of others home with me. It can feel like there is no escape. Privately, Palestinian friends have acknowledged to me that the October 7 attack and its immediate aftermath have set the Palestinian cause back decades.

*   *   *

It was only on the ninth and in the days to come that we were able to start putting together a clear story of the attack of the seventh. To that end, on the ninth I got in touch with an old contact, Major Doron Spielman. He and I had met years ago, when he worked as the spokesman for the City of David Foundation in Jerusalem. On the eighth, Doron had texted me that he was "in service"—called up as a reservist in the Israeli army.

Now he was determined to make sure I saw what had taken place in southern Israel. On Monday, the ninth, he sent me a video. Wearing a green vest and blue kippah, he addressed me:

"Trey, hope you're doing well. Have you been to this area? With the cars all along the main strip where the jihadis came in from Gaza and came all the way through here. If you haven't, I'd like to take you here." He was showing me the scene, a road that Hamas had used to enter Sderot and kill civilians.

"Also here, these are all cars that have been left here on the street after a massive firefight. Please tell me if you've been here."

Then he called and sent driving directions. Our calls weren't getting through, so I sent him a voice note that we were coming—but that if we didn't have a signal, we'd have to keep going. We still had to get live shots out every half hour.

When we arrived where Doron had said to meet, half a mile from the Gaza border, I saw his car. Rockets soared overhead. Doron didn't get out, so I called him. He spoke in Hebrew to Yaniv, telling him to follow him through a checkpoint ahead maintained by Israeli soldiers. We did, and when we got out, Doron gave us a tour of the devastation.

The bloodstained cars and children's clothes told their own story. A van on the edge of the road was pocked with bullet holes and spattered with blood. One of the cars had a Palestinian license plate; it had been driven from Gaza on Saturday morning. Bullet shell casings littered the ground.

The body of a Hamas militant lay in the grass, covered by a white cloth. Pulling back the cloth, Doron muttered, "The bastards killed a family on the way to a picnic."

You could see the pain in his eyes. The look reminded me of those soldiers we saw on the morning of the attack. "This time will be different," he said.

I asked him if we could push farther toward Mefalsim, a kibbutz up ahead.

"Are you crazy?" he said to me, half joking. "It's not cleared yet."

Dean Elsdunne, the international police spokesman, pulled up and spoke with Doron. Based in Jerusalem, Dean had arrived in Sderot the day before to coordinate the media arriving in the south. He agreed to let us follow him to the Sderot police station to report on what had happened there on Saturday and into Sunday. It was getting dark, but I figured I could interview Dean live from there at the top of the 12 p.m. show—7 p.m. local time.

Dean's job, explaining ongoing Israeli police events to the world, gave him a unique perspective on the unfolding warfare—and gave him a unique internal struggle. He and I had communicated only once before, back in April, when he was responsible for handing out permits for the Holy Fire ceremony in Jerusalem. But he grew up in the United States and spoke Hebrew as a second language. Five years earlier, he'd been a real estate investment advisor in Miami. We'd both grown up on the U.S. East Coast and shared a culture; we could talk pretty freely.

Dean's October 7, as with most Israelis, had started early. Just after 6:30 a.m., his phone rang. It was the dispatch responsible for informing him when an incident was occurring so that he could get up to speed and alert the international press.

Normally these incidents are small terror attacks. A stabbing in the Old City. Clashes in East Jerusalem. Even a shooting of civilians.

This call was different. "The guy had no idea what the hell was going on," Dean explained to me. "There was mixed chatter on the radio and nothing was making sense."

By 7 a.m., Dean was called in to police headquarters in Jerusalem. He dressed quickly and headed to the command center. On arrival, he went to the control room, where large screens display all the news stations next to a computer system that flashes updates on incident reports coming in. Dean saw all of the Israeli channels broadcasting similar videos. The initial cell phone footage from Sderot. Footage from the Nova party. Hamas gunmen infiltrating Israel.

At a long desk at the back of the room, young women operating a line of computers listened to the police radio and dispatched help as needed. Today they were listening to the police radio of officers under fire asking for more help. But with no help available, some of the officers realized they were going to die. Knowing the lines are recorded, they were calling in to leave final messages for their family members. With bursts of gunfire in the background, they let their spouses and kids know they loved them.

The women monitoring those calls were crying. Dean looked on in despair.

He was organizing incoming information when his phone rang again. It was his old unit. For three years, he'd served in Israel's undercover counterterrorism unit of the border police, whose main job was to go after those suspected of committing or planning attacks. Dean knew the tactics of Hamas, of Islamic Jihad, of lone-wolf terrorists. His old unit was heading south to respond to the attack. Another van would be leaving at 9 a.m.

Dean went to his commanders and told them his plan. "I'm going with my guys and we're going south."

His commanders told him no.

Right at the outset, Dean was facing one of the most difficult moments he would experience in the war. He knew officers were under fire and needed backup, but his role was to tell the world what was happening. He urgently wanted to leave that role and join his fellow officers in combat.

Ultimately, he decided to stay—and get to work. All day on the seventh he pieced together officers' locations, sites of attack, whether the attack was just in the south or across the country. Might the attackers be trying to pull all security forces southward to leave other regions exposed to additional offensive operations?

Then on Sunday morning, the eighth, after a few hours of sleep, Dean drove south to Sderot to connect with the field command center and check on the officers.

There were still bodies in cars, gunfire in the distance, militants in Israeli territory. He knew Sderot itself wasn't fully cleared of attackers; it wouldn't be for weeks. The police would be putting up a drone at nighttime, with thermal capabilities, to find militants and Gazans hiding among houses and in bushes. Driving through what seemed an apocalypse, feeling only a kind of blankness, he arrived at Sderot and went straight to the command center at the city's entrance.

Now, having followed Dean to the Sderot police station, standing by the ruined building and the piles of debris, I urged Dean to bring the scene to life.

"Dean, first of all, I'm sorry about what happened to your fellow officers. Can you tell us what took place here and what was it like for Israeli police in the hours after these militants invaded?"

"Trey, I don't even think there are words to describe what took place right behind us at the Sderot police station. You see the rubble, you see this big building, but behind on the other side of your camera is a residential neighborhood . . . terrorists decided to infiltrate our country, hold our civilians hostage. What we saw at the station itself was officers fighting for these civilians, fighting for their lives."

After the live interview wrapped, I continued to report, talking this time with anchor and former press secretary for President Donald Trump, Kayleigh McEnany.

"What you're reporting now," she said, "is that the Qatari government is actually on the phone, trying to secure the release of women and children."

Before I had the opportunity to respond, a heavy rocket barrage began. I looked to the sky and spoke over Kayleigh.

"Pan up here, Yaniv!" I said, pointing up. "I'm going to interrupt you here," I told Kayleigh. "We've got Iron Dome interceptors coming off." The rocket alert sirens blared. "Everybody get down, pull it off the sticks!" I said, industry-speak for "Take the camera off the tripod!"

"Stay with us here. Stay with us here. Everyone get down. Just everyone go flat, we don't have time," I said. "Go up, point up here," I called to Yaniv.

Dean used his body to shield mine. He looked to the sky, his eyes filled not with fear but with focus.

"You're going to see some interceptions taking place," I reported as the sky flashed with light. "There are going to be some loud explosions, don't be alarmed."

Years ago, Greg Headen gave me advice for these situations. He told me to describe the safety protocols we take as they happen, live. That helps the viewer understand the gravity of the situation and the risks in real time, while conveying a sense of control and calm. After a few booms, Yaniv panned down. "Everyone is laying flat on the ground here, we've got to take cover," I said. "This is what communities along the border are dealing with. It is constant, constant fire."

When that barrage was over, I was continuing to report live when a man came up and wanted to say something. I began interviewing him and immediately regretted it. He went on a long rant about the slaughter of Israelis—a rant filled with profanities, not okay for live TV. I understood his emotions and explained that to the viewers afterward.

I didn't realize it at first, but in the distance, rescue workers were pulling bodies from the debris of the police station. I kept the feed up and transitioned the report live to show that process.

So we were live on TV when I saw the first body being pulled from the rubble.

Remember what you're talking about, I reminded myself. *These are human beings. That is somebody's father, somebody's brother. A friend or a coworker.*

It was a dark and hazy night. I was exhausted, but the constant waves of rockets and mortars kept me going. We stayed live as the covered corpses were pulled from the rubble and loaded in body bags onto a pickup. I had to make many decisions in real time. How graphic can these images be? How do I explain what we are seeing yet not numb the viewer so that they turn off the TV? This was the reality of war.

Maybe it was the bodies being piled in a pickup truck behind me, or the realization of what we were witnessing, or losing track of how many times we'd come under rocket and mortar fire that day. For the first time since the war began, I cracked.

Only for a moment. My voice shaking, as I spoke live on TV, I had to pause to say, "Sorry. It's difficult." A rare time when I broke the fourth wall of my reporting. I was overwhelmed. As I held back tears, I recalled an Israeli media report on family members bringing strands of hair to authorities to help identify the bodies of their children—I'm still not sure why that came back to me after all the horrific things we saw firsthand. I was tired. I was trying to balance all the editorial decisions I needed to make.

I thought back to a conversation I had over the phone while in Ukraine with a mentor and boss of mine, Kim Rosenberg. She said to always think about the tone you use when talking about the dead. A brilliant producer, now an executive, she knew that field correspondents could easily become numb to the atrocities they saw.

And on that day, I did feel mostly numb. That pickup truck was stacked high with bodies. Only the feet were hanging out of the body bags.

"Everyone down, flat, cover your head!"

An even heavier rocket barrage was coming in while we were live on-air. Rockets whizzed close to the ground overhead. We felt explosions as some of the rockets hit the ground nearby.

Dean, meanwhile, had left Sderot. After watching bodies being pulled out of the police station, he'd decided to visit his friend Akiva in Maglan, in a military unit at Kibbutz Sa'ad that included a soldier named Daniel. Later, Dean told me that the whole roadway to Sa'ad was infested with gunmen. "Like, they didn't even want to set up checkpoints there," he said, "because they didn't want the checkpoints to get ambushed by the terrorists that were inside of the bushes."

The danger of that situation was soon made dramatically clear when, using a drone, the unit spotted a militant, and as Dean's friend's and Daniel's team headed out in a convoy of Humvees, Dean said goodbye to the guys and went in the other direction.

The second Humvee in the convoy had an issue with a tire and had to pull over. Minutes later, gunmen ambushed the team, killing Daniel.

*　　*　　*

By now, everyone on my team was exhausted. Reporting live, I dived for cover so many times that my forearms and elbows were covered in scrapes and bruises. The chyron on the screen read:

FOX CREW TAKES COVER AS EXPLOSIONS ROCK ISRAEL

I was also making sure to gather updates from Gaza so I could report on the situation there. There are two sides to every story, and this was no different. The Israeli response was already starting to kill many terrified Gazan civilians.

"This is truly a nightmare, and the people inside Gaza are experiencing hell on earth," I reported. Everyone was living in hell. We'd need to be cool and collected amid the flames.

Late that night, back at the hotel, with the confirmed Israeli death toll now above 900 people, I lay for a moment in bed and tried to figure out what our schedule should look like in the coming days. The burnout was so bad that earlier in the day Yonat and I had gotten in a fight about logistics. When we were talking with Doron next to the dead militant, I asked her to call New York about one of our live shots. She didn't do it because she was working on something else. I said that if she didn't want to be here, she could work from home. She snapped back.

Later, we apologized to each other. We hadn't slept. Everyone was stressed. Fights happen when a team is operating in these conditions.

It's important to be able to make up and move forward. We had to continue—momentum takes cooperation.

As I closed my eyes for a moment, the sounds of rocket alerts and explosions banged in my head. This is a common occurrence, a weird sensation, a symptom of post-traumatic stress disorder (PTSD), where you actually hear and see—not imagine, but hear, full volume, and see, in full color—the things you've heard and seen earlier. Sometimes there's an in-your-face trigger, bringing on a hallucination. Sometimes it's just a repetition of the day.

I've had to learn how to handle that and the other mental health stresses endemic to war reporting. For me the problems started in Ukraine, where I'd arrived before the Russian invasion, a twenty-eight-year-old thrilled to have another opportunity to lead Fox's foreign coverage. I was also eager to work again with the cameraman Pierre Zakrzewski; we'd done extensive reporting together in Afghanistan, Pakistan, and Qatar. Hours after I landed, we were on the road to Kherson and the border of Crimea, diving right into the story, as Ukraine braced for an anticipated Russian attack. Soon we would be under artillery fire from the Russian-backed separatists in the Donbas region of eastern Ukraine, running for cover live on Fox News.

When the Russian invasion actually began, we reported from Kyiv, heading each day to the outskirts of the population center. We'd been warned that the city might fall into the hands of the Russians in a matter of days. That didn't matter. We were witnessing history firsthand and showing the world the realities of war.

That all changed when Pierre was killed, alongside our local Ukrainian producer, Oleksandra "Sasha" Kuvshynova; my Fox colleague Benjamin Hall was gravely injured in the same attack. After Pierre's funeral, I went home to America. But I just sat there, itching to go back to the war zone, so days later I was back in Ukraine, reporting from the mass graves in Bucha and attending Sasha's funeral.

After more than 180 days in Ukraine, I was burned out and suffering. Some days I would wake up depressed, feeling that the work we do is irrelevant: I could show the world the atrocities of war—but would the world ever stop *committing* atrocities? Was it even worth it, especially given the risk of such work?

Other nights, I'd wake up in a cold sweat, panting, after a nightmare: a Ukrainian battlefield transported to my yard in Pennsylvania, Russian troops hiding in the tree line. The nightmares became so common that I dreaded going to bed.

I've been told that I'm seen as a tough, manly, stoic reporter who runs toward battle with no fear. I like to think that some of that is true—but the realities of this job are much more somber. Viewers, followers, and notoriety are irrelevant when you wake up panicked from a dream where you're being tortured and thrown into a mass grave, or where your childhood home is under attack and you have nowhere to hide.

I've seen so many of the great war correspondents ruin their lives with drugs and alcohol. I have empathy for them. I've also determined not to fall down that rabbit hole.

Instead, I've turned to a healthy diet, consistent exercise, and meditation, or simply doing breathing exercises I've learned from YouTube. I like to meditate near the beach. Something about the Mediterranean Sea reminds me of the mind: sometimes it's rough, but eventually it turns placid again. Cold exposure is a more recent addition: a plunge into literally near-freezing water, then training the mind to stay in there, to become comfortable in discomfort. After an ice bath near my apartment in Tel Aviv, I would sometimes walk home, have a double espresso, and watch motivational videos.

Tonight, though, I couldn't sleep.

For the first time since the massacre on Saturday, I scrolled through reporting on our work to see what kind of coverage we were getting. In an opinion piece in *Poynter*, a well-respected journalism publication: *As a significant moment unfolds in Israel, the media reaches deep*. I received a shout-out from the author for "superb work." When you're seeing the things we saw, hearing the things we heard, people at home believing in you and appreciating you help, and it's not about your professional ego.

It's about feeling like you're useful in a time when everything around you is falling apart. It's a piece of hope, as trivial as that may seem.

*   *   *

Even while we'd been live-reporting under heavy fire that evening, Prime Minister Netanyahu was making one of his first public addresses since the massacre, speaking to the Israeli people and the world.

He began his remarks in front of four Israeli flags and wore a blue tie to match the flags.

"Israel is at war." Netanyahu gripped the edges of the podium, looking straight into the camera. The speech sought to lay the groundwork for what was to come.

"Hamas will understand that by attacking us, they have made a mistake of historic proportions. We will exact a price that will be remembered by them and Israel's other enemies for decades to come."

The prime minister went on to compare Hamas to ISIS, noting that they executed civilians. He thanked President Biden, then other world leaders, and finally the U.S. Congress for their support.

This was calculated.

Netanyahu understood that Israel's response would draw world condemnation. He also understood that the United States would be supplying many of the weapons, bombs, and financial support that Israel needed to defeat Hamas and maintain a defensive posture against other regional threats.

For the United States and the Biden administration, the attack by Hamas was deeply personal. The U.S.-Israel relationship aside, American citizens were directly affected by the actions of Hamas. Thirty-two American citizens were killed on October 7, 2023. More than twenty of them were serving in the Israeli military and had dual citizenship, but they were no less American, especially in the eyes of the U.S. government. In addition, Americans were taken hostage by Hamas and were being held inside Gaza.

7

HAMAS IS HERE

As new information and harrowing firsthand testimonies of the events of October 7 continued to pour in, our ability to understand and report on what happened that day began to sharpen.

Among the most intense were the personal accounts and chilling video and audio files from the Tribe of Nova Music Festival.

We had already been made generally aware—in real time on the seventh—of the horrific attack on the concert. Trying to get to Sderot that first morning, one of the first videos I'd seen on X showed Hamas militants using paragliders to infiltrate southern Israel in that vicinity. Other cell phone videos showed young Israelis running through fields and hiding in the woods. At the triage intersection, a man had run up and told us, "The party is three kilometers from here. And they are shooting. . . . They're stuck in the middle."

The next day, photos of missing young Israelis started popping up in group chats. People searching for their loved ones weren't sure if they'd been taken into Gaza, slaughtered at the party, or escaped. This was also the festival that Master Sergeant Guy Rozenfeld, not realizing the desperation unfolding here, had been asked to pick people up from.

As evidence was pieced together, it became clear that the thousands of concertgoers were arguably more exposed than anyone else that morning. Drone video footage of the aftermath and social media posts made during the attack in real time revealed how chaotic those moments were: people trying to drive away before getting out and simply running for their lives. Police officers trying to fight off Hamas but overwhelmed by the sheer number of militants. There was a video of Noa Argamani, a twenty-five-year-old festivalgoer who was taken into Gaza on the back of a motorcycle. She shrieked in terror, her face contorted with fear, arms reaching out, one of so many young Israelis dragged into Hamas captivity.

By the morning of the tenth, as the team and I were determining priorities for coverage, we knew we needed to find out more about the attack at the festival, interview the survivors, see the aftermath, and report the awful reality of what had happened.

*   *   *

The official invitation from the Tribe of Nova described the "Supernova" party as "a truly exceptional and unprecedented event that will take place for the very first time in Israel." According to the event page, it was a festival celebrating unity and love; the invite, clad in drawings of mushrooms, went on to explain, "The word 'Supernova' refers to the explosion of a massive star, causing an immense burst of light in galactic terms."

At the thirteen-hour rave, music was meant to blast through the night. And for those who got tired of dancing, they could meditate or do art, with no shortage of drugs like MDMA, weed, or booze. Israel's trance community is relatively small, so the party would also be a gathering of a close community of music and dance enthusiasts.

The event had been months in the making. Attendees followed updates on a Facebook page. The exact location wasn't known even to ticket buyers—for security reasons—so on the page, the place was described only as "between mesmerizing trees and open spaces, under bright stars and blue skies, lies a virgin plot of land that is about to become the private culture and music temple of the Nuba tribe, the

Ashram community and the Universo Parallo festival" (translated from Hebrew). It was explained that there would be three main stages: the Nova stage, the Mushroom stage, and the Chanti stage. The first two were for music performers only, among them a group of more than twenty DJs/producers who would spin up a variety of trance music. The Chanti stage—in Sanskrit, "peace"—would include artists and meditation workshops.

The day before the event, further instructions and rules were posted to Facebook. Among them: no firearms or sharp objects. The instructions also encouraged those arriving at the event to come in a shared vehicle, for environmental reasons.

A map released only hours before the event revealed the layout. In front of the main entrance, a large blue-and-pink tent would cover the dance area of the Nova stage. To the left, near the Mushroom stage, an art area and a food court. To the right, a wooded camping area and the Chanti stage. The party was scheduled to start at 10 p.m. on October 6 and last until 11 a.m. on October 7.

*   *   *

In June, Yasmin Porat, a forty-four-year-old mother of three living in northern Israel, bought tickets to the Nova Festival for herself and her boyfriend, Tal Katz, thirty-seven, who lived in Tel Aviv. The couple had been dating for two and a half years, and Tal bonded effortlessly with her kids. Yasmin found joy spending time with Tal, and they shared a love of electronic music. The couple had made friends at parties just like the Nova Festival, and had even attended a festival marking Rosh Hashanah. That had made them even more excited for the October 6 event. They talked about it all the time.

On the evening of October 6, Yasmin met Tal in Tel Aviv. Only at the last moment did they get a text message revealing the event location: a big outdoor space in the Negev Desert, about an hour and a half away. Not yet fully oriented, they put on Waze, left Tel Aviv around eleven o'clock, and started driving south. They didn't bring a tent; their friends would have one. For most of the drive, they talked excitedly about a night they'd been looking forward to for months.

As they drew near, Yasmin recognized the area. Events had been held here before—the space was near Kibbutz Re'im, about three miles from the Gaza border. "My sister lives eight minutes from the party!" Yasmin told Tal. She sent a message to her sister Inbal to say they were nearby and would stop for coffee on Saturday morning.

They arrived at the edge of the festival grounds, parked, and met up with their friends at the tent. There were about three thousand people in attendance, Yasmin thought, and the fast-paced psychedelic trance beats, coupled with the drugs and alcohol, created a euphoric ambience. They joined the dancing.

By dawn, Yasmin and Tal had gotten separated, but that wasn't uncommon. She did her own thing and he did his. The sun was rising, and Yasmin, alone now, felt a little tired.

A set by a DJ she liked was scheduled to start at 7 a.m. It was a good time to head to the tent. She wanted to bring her phone and wallet to Tal's car: they'd be safer there, less likely to be stolen or go missing amid the fun. Then rest, refresh, have a bite to eat in the car. She'd been partying for hours and needed a break. She scanned the crowd for Tal, spotted him in the distance, then went up and hugged him.

"Will you come to the car with me?" she asked. They stopped at the tent to grab her phone and walked down a dirt path to the car.

*   *   *

Aharon Sabag, a festivalgoer born and raised in Jerusalem, was also looking forward to the 7 a.m. set. He had once been ultra-Orthodox but had left that community at fourteen. At eighteen, Aharon enlisted in the Givati Brigade in the "Zabar" regiment and did his service there. Now, having studied electrical engineering, he worked as a solar technician and loved rave and dance parties.

Aharon and his fiancée, Yuval, arrived at the party late. Or early, depending on how you look at it. At 4:30 on the morning of October 7 they rolled up to the dark parking area. In the distance they could hear the bass thud and see the flashing lights marking the festival space. Aharon had been to a festival at this very location for a celebration of Purim, the joyful spring holiday commemorating the salvation of the Jewish people from destruction by a Persian ruler, as told in the book of Esther.

At about 6:30 a.m., after a solid hour on the dance floor, Aharon walked toward the tent, sipping a cup of wine with his friend Daniel. They'd met through a mutual friend Aharon had served with in the army; Daniel too loved the dance parties and the music. Looking out over the crowd, he saw many familiar faces. Those still awake—Yasmin and Tal too—were the serious ravers, those who really wanted to hear the sunrise set.

Music blared through large speakers. The festivalgoers continued to dance and party.

*   *   *

After twenty minutes of rest in the car, Yasmin asked Tal, "Are you ready to hit the dance floor?"

But seconds after they stepped out, they saw the rockets. An Israeli music producer, Artifex, was playing his set; some festivalgoers didn't hear the first explosions over the sound of the bass. But the fire seemed so unusually heavy to Yasmin and Tal that they feared the music would be stopped.

Not far away, Aharon and Yuval were by his tent talking to a friend who was shocked by the explosions suddenly popping around the horizon. "What is this? Fireworks?" the friend asked.

Aharon looked up. "It's not fireworks," he said. "It's rockets." The group lay on the ground next to their tent, hands covering their heads. That was standard procedure. Aharon wasn't worried. Still, it was becoming clear that the rocket fire was intense. Within minutes, a police officer was saying over the loudspeaker that the party was over.

Someone else on the speaker said "red alert" in Hebrew. Aharon and others started evacuating to their cars.

Yasmin and Tal, already by their car, knew there would be a lot of traffic. They should leave right away, Yasmin told Tal. But now the fire seemed so heavy that it was best to stay put, Tal thought.

He took some convincing, but soon he and Yasmin were heading out of the Nova Festival, among the first cars to leave. They took a left and headed north. It was terrifying: rockets were everywhere. Tal wanted to stop and get into a shelter on the side of the road, but Yasmin told him to keep going.

He insisted. They pulled over.

*   *   *

At the festival, with a lot of cars pulling out, some people were still striking their tents and heading toward the cars when police ran up to the tents and told everyone to leave immediately. There was a lot of laughing. "Hamas closed the party," Aharon joked.

Near the cars, a man ran up behind him. "They shot my girlfriend!"

"Are you crazy?" Aharon asked. "Maybe you had too many drugs."

Suddenly, instead of laughing, there was a lot of panic: people were yelling that Hamas gunmen were on the festival grounds.

As Aharon and his fiancée started running for the car, Aharon told Daniel to come with them, but Daniel said he needed to wait for the friends he came with. Aharon tried to convince him but at this point he knew they should move. Still, when another friend told him that terrorists had infiltrated Israel, he brushed it off.

That couldn't be true. This was a rocket attack. Nothing more, nothing less.

At the entrance, he saw that traffic and confusion consumed the area. There was only one main road leaving the grounds, Route 232. With people running to the cars and drivers trying to flee, a traffic jam formed, making it impossible to move.

Then bursts of gunfire cracked the air.

Some left their vehicles and started running. The traffic had already hit gridlock. Police trying to make sense of the situation had guns raised. From the north, a car sped toward the crowd and stopped. A man got out with his hands raised. "Don't shoot me," he yelled in Hebrew. "I'm Jewish!"

To Aharon, it started to make sense. Maybe there really had been an infiltration? He ran back to his friend. "Let's go, get in the car," he said. "We have to get out of here."

All three got in the car, but there was nowhere to drive. Traffic had them stuck.

They decided to get out and make a run for it. As they ran, the gunfire seemed to be getting closer, and Aharon pulled out his phone. Maybe go to Be'eri? Maybe another kibbutz? Deciding to just keep running east, they sprinted with dozens of other festivalgoers through a field.

Suddenly, in a hail of bullets, people began dropping around them. The Hamas gunmen were catching up.

The fire got so heavy that they couldn't go on. Aharon and Yuval lay facedown next to a row of lemon trees.

As Aharon shifted his body on top of Yuval, a guy next to them was shaking uncontrollably. The man grabbed a lemon from the ground and put it in his mouth to stop his teeth from chattering.

When the shooting stopped for a moment, Aharon yelled, "We can't stop!" They got up and kept running east. Some in the group Aharon knew; others he didn't.

Eventually a group of ten reached a dairy farm. They drank water. They rested for a moment.

*   *   *

At the roadside bomb shelter, Yasmin and Tal figured the rocket fire would be over in ten minutes. Standing at the edge of the shelter with others who had pulled off the road, she lit a cigarette.

As she took her first puff, they heard gunfire.

Someone said, "There are terrorists here!" Tal didn't hear it. "There are terrorists here!" Yasmin said. "Get in the car!"

They jumped back in and drove until they hit heavy traffic. In the distance Yasmin saw two gunmen firing their weapons. Tal made a U-turn. The couple knew Kibbutz Be'eri was nearby. They could try to shelter there.

*　　*　　*

Aharon's friend Daniel had gone up the main road with another group from the party. As the rocket fire continued, they went into a bomb shelter on the side of the road. Hamas fighters ambushed the shelter and threw grenades inside. Daniel was killed in one of the blasts.

*　　*　　*

At the dairy farm, Aharon's group was exhausted after staying up all night partying. Some had lost their shoes, others pieces of clothing. But Aharon had a bad feeling that they weren't safe yet. He insisted they keep moving.

Most stayed.

As Aharon and his fiancée ran, his phone rang. It was his commander from reserve duty.

"You need to come to the army now!"

"I know I need to come because I'm being attacked, I know!"

Aharon told his commander he'd call him later. At the end of a road, a car was approaching. By sheer chance, Aharon recognized the driver: a guy he knew through mutual friends—also named Yuval.

"What the fuck are you doing here?" Yuval asked. Aharon and his fiancée jumped in the car and he drove them to Patish, a moshav—cooperative agricultural town—in the desert.

They would wait there for five hours. Within a day, Aharon would go to the reserves and prepare for the war ahead.

Everyone who had stayed behind at the dairy farm was killed.

*   *   *

By October 8, the Tribe of Nova Facebook page had posted this message:

Tribe and Nova Production shocked and pained. We support and participate in the grief of the families of the missing and murdered. We are doing everything we can to assist the security forces, we are in continuous contact with them and we are located in the area with scans and searches in order to locate the missing. Additionally. We pass on to the relevant authorities any piece of information that comes to us about additional missing people. We are attaching here a file in which you can upload the details of the missing persons and people who are still looking for them in order to pass them on to the patrol forces and the army. We urge you to upload there any additional information about the family members and friends who have not yet made contact. We are full of hope and pray that good news will come to us and to you soon. In moments like these, it is important that we be strong and united, full of faith, support each other and be there for everyone who needs it. Hugs to all, the Nova tribe.

*   *   *

Five days after the attack, my team and I followed the IDF in a convoy of cars toward the site of the festival. The Israeli army had agreed to take a group of journalists to see the aftermath. For this operation, the team was joined by Sean, our security member, who had arrived on the night of the tenth. Sean has deep military experience and serves multiple critical purposes on our team. He served in the Australian army. He did multiple tours in Afghanistan, then lived there for years as a contractor. He's a trained medic, so if something happens, he can provide immediate medical care. As an expert in military situations, he gives guidance when needed.

His consistently calm demeanor has helped me to stay calm during embeds. I look at Sean's face to gauge how things are really going.

The road to the festival grounds was filled with debris and the burned remains of cars. In some of the fields you could see where people had tried to drive off road before getting ambushed.

When we got to the site, I saw Israeli soldiers against a backdrop of golden sky. It was 5:30 p.m.—before sunset. That was a relief, because I knew Hamas could still be hiding in the area, and daylight felt safer. From a military perspective, though, daylight was actually more dangerous: Hamas and Israel had equal visibility during the day; only at night could IDF deploy night vision and other thermal technology.

The soldiers at the site were armed and seemed in surprisingly good spirits.

The festival parking lot was filled with charred and abandoned cars with colorful bags and clothes between them—things someone would bring to a festival. Next to one of the cars, we saw a Hamas motorcycle on its side. Some of the vehicles had bullet holes in them, others were burned. Many had backpacks in them, with makeup and sunglasses strewn around.

Up a steep hill, we arrived at the festival gate. The site was frozen in time. Under one structure, paintings lay on the ground, half-finished. Four long tables made up a square bar area. In the center of the bar, red Coca-Cola coolers sat with green-and-silver Heineken buckets on top. Nearby, we could see the debris-filled campsite and tents where so many had spent the night. The festival had been turned into a killing field.

"We're here at the site of the music festival that was targeted by Hamas militants on Saturday morning," I said into my phone, making a short video to post.

"Complete scenes of devastation. Two hundred and sixty people were gunned down here." That was a low early estimate—later it became clear that the number was over 360. "Everything frozen in time. People were listening to music, they were having a joyous weekend when they were gunned down."

* * *

Men in green army fatigues, blue cloths covering their boots, bent over a charred patch of earth. Some wore gas masks. They were digging through the black dirt and scooping remains of festivalgoers into garbage bags.

Videos later showed various instances of bodies being found at the festival site. In one of them, an officer arrives at the scene on the seventh with his pistol raised. "Police! IDF! Wounded?" he yells.

"I have casualties here. One, two, three, four, five casualties."

"Anyone here?"

"Everyone is dead. The entire bar is full of bodies."

"Is anyone here? Give me a sign of life."

That video wasn't released until weeks later. It showed just how many bodies were found in the area we were viewing this Thursday morning. Next to the digging soldiers, I saw a burned van lying on its side. In the distance, you could hear the thud of outgoing artillery: the war raging on.

"No pictures here!" one of the soldiers yelled in my direction.

I understood. But it's our job to document even the most horrific scenes. I pulled out my iPhone, pressed record, and zoomed in as far as I could. While the soldier spoke with someone, I documented the scene with the phone by my side. Even if we didn't plan to run that video on TV during a report, I would have it as a reminder of what we were seeing. I couldn't stop thinking about what their last moments must have been like, these people, just a few of the 360 killed at the festival.

As my team and I continued to comb the festival grounds, a shot rang out. I knew right away what it was. The others didn't seem fazed, but I saw soldiers running and told the team, "We need to go, run!"

As we ran, another shot rang out. We hit the ground. "Lay flat!" I yelled.

We turned on the camera and started recording. I explained what was happening: in a small way, we were reliving the horror those young Israelis had experienced. We got up, ran a few hundred feet, and made it to the edge of the festival grounds, where dozens of soldiers were screaming at us, "Get back! Go!"

Between them, I could see a man on the ground, hands above his head. They blindfolded him and stripped him to his underwear. The group of journalists, eager for the latest story, tried to film over and through the fence as the Israeli soldiers escorted the Palestinian man away.

The army told us that this was someone who entered on October 7. He was armed with a knife. The shots we'd heard were an Israeli soldier firing at him.

On the way out of the festival grounds, we interviewed Rear Admiral Daniel Hagari, the top spokesman for the Israeli military. It was almost dark, so we would need to finish up our reporting, but Hagari's voice was an important one to include. You could see the pain in his eyes as he described how Israel would take the fight to Hamas.

"Those people have blood on their hands. We will reach each and every one of them. Not just [Hamas leader Yahya] Sinwar. We're taking now the cameras from all the cars and we will see the faces of everyone that was part of this massacre. We will reach them, he will be dead. There is no other way.

"We're going to bring all the warriors of Israel to pass through this festival. That was supposed to be love and music. We're going to pass through here. They're going to see the massacre. They will know what they're fighting for."

"The last time this kind of thing happened, it was seventy-five years ago," Hagari said. "We remember it. We understand it."

*   *   *

Aharon already understood it. Having run with his fiancée, he knew that his friends and the other festivalgoers who had lagged and fallen behind were among those whose remains were being bagged. Within a day of the attack, he was with his fellow reservists. By Thursday the twelfth, when I was interviewing Hagari, Aharon was preparing for what had become an expanding war.

With the Israeli response ramping up against Gaza, a top Hamas official and longtime source of mine was sending me daily updates from inside the strip. The next day, Friday, I asked him to send videos of himself talking, so I could use the information on-air.

I was also told by a diplomatic source in Jerusalem that despite Israeli warnings of upcoming air strikes, Hamas was keeping people in Gaza from leaving their homes. And Nael, my long-standing Gaza source and friend, was keeping me updated on the movement of civilians there. Palestinians who had a place to go were already heading south, some driving, others walking.

A crisis was developing on the other side of the border. I had a responsibility and desire to cover every angle.

8

KIBBUTZ BE'ERI'S
HOUSES OF HORROR

On the morning of October 11, U.S. Secretary of State Antony Blinken arrived in Israel for scheduled meetings. While the trip had practical aspects, Blinken was largely sent as a display of U.S. solidarity with the Israeli people.

The big questions were now looming: "Will Israel invade Gaza?" "If so, when?" Hamas claimed they had dozens of hostages, but hundreds were still missing. The international attention and pressure surrounding the story was growing, and many were already starting to criticize Israel's response.

With the Israeli air campaign in full force, my team and I needed to simultaneously gather information about the attack on the seventh, understand the scope of the attacks at the Nova Music Festival and in the kibbutzim, cover the war that was unfolding, and cover the rising death toll inside Gaza.

To get information out of the kibbutzim was especially difficult. We could get to Sderot. We could get to areas where rockets were landing in southern Israel. We could get reports from people inside Gaza and updates from the military. But we couldn't get into the communities along the Gaza border: the army had declared the area a closed military zone.

I knew that reporting from that zone would be the most important thing. Having covered wars for a decade, I know that even in the most horrific circumstances, people can forget why wars start. It's part of our role as journalists to write that first draft of history, to give our audience immediate context yet also cement the truth in the history books with evidence of crimes that have been committed.

I wished I could also have been in Gaza, reporting on what was happening to Palestinians there, and the aftermath of the Israeli response. But I could only be in one place at a time. So far, I was still reporting only from southern Israel.

Early on the eleventh, I quoted a post on X with the simple comment. "Read this post. It's important." It was a statement from a Palestinian woman:

"I am a Palestinian who doesn't celebrate Hamas actions. It's personal, it's my Jewish friends hurt. I am terrified for my family & friends in Gaza & West Bank. This US vs. THEM paradigm is wrong. This isn't Arabs vs. Jews. Many of us on the same side of justice & peace."

A story like this involves very high emotion. I had to make sure that our coverage wasn't demonizing Palestinians. Some Palestinians entered Israel to slaughter Israelis, some entered to loot, some to look around. Others never entered but cheered when hostages were brought back to Gaza. Others, albeit quietly, condemned the actions of Hamas as setting the Palestinian cause back decades. It was my role to understand the nuance on both sides of the conflict and take it into consideration, even as I reported from the scenes of murders committed on the seventh.

*   *   *

I had fallen deeply asleep the night before, after a failed attempt to get to a kibbutz near the border with an intelligence contact. Having passed out without bothering to take off my clothes, I woke up on the morning of the eleventh, quickly washed my face, and took the elevator downstairs. Just before 10 a.m., we headed back toward the border.

En route, I got a text message from my friend Hamdah Salhut that detoured us to Sderot. Then an i24 journalist, now an Al Jazeera correspondent, Hamdah, a Palestinian American, was alerting me to bodies being pulled from rubble in the city. There's Hamas bodies here, she wrote. Still at the police station. She sent a photo and said, They are preparing to move them.

The security situation in Sderot was still uncertain. Further infiltration attempts had been reported along the border. This time we approached the police station from the other side, but I couldn't even make out where we were: they'd begun to completely tear the building down and remove the debris. With dust filling the air, we walked around to the other side.

The Israeli volunteer civilian rescue unit ZAKA, in full white disposable body suits with blue gloves, was using a yellow JCB backhoe to drag the bodies of Hamas militants out of the wreckage of the station. The bloated body of a fighter lay facedown, a red rope tied around the waist. Next to that one, two other corpses were transferred into white body bags.

In the background, another backhoe, this one with a jackhammer attached, blasted away at the pile of twisted metal and concrete.

I met up with Hamdah, giving her a hug. "This is crazy," she said. Her eyes were sad. Hamdah is one of the strongest and hardest-working people I know—but I could tell she was affected by the war erupting all around us.

We headed to an artillery position nearby, in a field, and reported from there throughout the morning. At this point in the war, our hits were usually multiple times an hour on Fox News Channel and Fox Business. Israeli units in the field were firing constant barrages, raining shells into the eastern side of Gaza. A variety of shells sat next to each cannon. The crack of outgoing missiles raised dust around each position before the next order was given.

Occasionally, rockets were fired from northern Gaza. This was a true exchange of fire.

During one live report on *Mornings with Maria*, I held the mic in one hand and my ear with the other. Back in May I'd been standing too close to an Iron Dome battery when it launched an interceptor. That, along with not using enough ear protection during the Tulkarem raid in September, had damaged the hearing in my right ear. I'd been to the doctor in Jerusalem and was told it could be temporary.

Now I reported: "The military is telling us today that more than three thousand targets have been hit since Saturday morning. I'm going to step out of the way here and just show you what it looks like as this shelling is taking place." We panned to soldiers in the distance, marching in a straight line, training for their mission ahead. The chyron read, "Israel Prepares for Ground Invasion of Gaza."

"Fields have been turned into bases, dirt roads have been turned into arteries for the army to deliver supplies and to deliver weapons to their fighters because it is not a question of if Israel will go into Gaza, but rather a question of when," I reported.

Before our hits for *Fox & Friends*, we ran into Lieutenant Colonel Richard Hecht, the international spokesman for the military, and his team on the side of the road. Hecht and I had a good relationship, and I figured this could be a good chance to interview him live.

"Where do things stand now in terms of preparation? It appears the Israelis are staging to enter Gaza."

"So before talking about Gaza," Richard replied, "again I'm here, you're here, to see what happened here. We're around and with the communities. Yesterday I entered Kfar Aza with journalists to show the world what happened there and it was an ISIS, even worse than ISIS carnage. Bodies, decapitated people. Horrific.

"And we are now preparing ourselves," he said. "We're now striking Gaza also from the air and all future options are on the table. We are focusing mainly on compounds in Gaza and it's a very, very severe strike right now in order to take out their capabilities."

The crack of outgoing artillery.

"In Kfar Aza," I said, "we understand there were mutilated bodies. Decapitated women and children. Is that accurate?" I had seen the reports but was skeptical—I needed to continue investigating the claims.

"Yes. We spoke to soldiers. It wasn't me speaking as a spokesperson. We went in there, there were Israeli reserve paratroopers. And they told the stories. They told the stories. And again, I'm still recovering from that day. I even get emotional thinking about it."

After the interview I talked with Keren Hajioff, a longtime contact, friend of my friend Ariel, who was now in reserve duty. Keren is the former spokesperson for Prime Minister Naftali Bennett. "You're coming, right?" she said.

She was talking about Kibbutz Be'eri.

*   *   *

Established in 1946 in the northwest of the Negev Desert, Be'eri was known for its art gallery. And the small farming community of just over 1,000 people looked like a painting itself. Rolling hills lead to luscious fields. A small printing factory employed many of its residents, and like many kibbutzim along the Gaza border the community had good relationships with Palestinians and was home to many peace activists. Its proximity to Gaza, only three miles from the border, nevertheless left it vulnerable to frequent mortar and rocket attacks.

Families in Be'eri knew the drill. Mortars or rockets came a few times a year. If there were sirens, you entered your bomb shelter, known in Israel as a *mamad*, and waited for the all-clear. By 2023, the red-alert-sirens iPhone app, serving as yet another warning of incoming fire, was as common as the calculator app. The attacks were never much of a problem.

On the night of October 6, residents had gathered in the dining hall to celebrate seventy-seven years since the founding of the kibbutz. It was Shabbat, so the wine flowed, as neighbors gathered for a small party. It was also the last day of the weeklong Sukkot holiday. The crisp October evening turned into a chilly night. As in most communities in the Negev Desert, the lack of light pollution allowed residents a clear glimpse of the stars on their walk home. It was quiet. It was peaceful.

Early Saturday morning, everything changed.

Loud blasts pierced the air of Kibbutz Be'eri as Qassam rockets were intercepted overhead in that initial 6:29 a.m. barrage. The blare of rocket sirens echoed through the streets. "Zeva Adom, Zeva Adom": Red Alert. That was an alarm clock for Be'eri residents. They woke up and hurried into their safe rooms.

*   *   *

Meanwhile, in flight from the Nova Music Festival, Yasmin and Tal had seen the militants at the bomb shelter, fled, run into a traffic jam, and pulled a U-turn; now they were arriving at Be'eri. The community was known to Yasmin as one of the richer kibbutzim in Israel, a protected and safe place. With rockets flying, they drove up to the yellow sliding gate behind another car, which opened the gate.

A few hundred feet inside, they encountered the Be'eri security team, in the process of responding to the rocket alarm. "Hello, we are from the party," Yasmin told them. "There was a terrorist at the *migunit* [outdoor bomb shelter]. Please help us!"

They were told to get out of the car and get into one of the Be'eri *miguniot*.

They did, but back at the entrance to the kibbutz, what would become an hours-long nightmare for Be'eri—and for Yasmin and Tal—was now underway.

CCTV video shows the beginning of the attack on the kibbutz:

At 6:55 a.m., two Hamas fighters approach the yellow sliding gate at the entrance of Be'eri, Kalashnikovs in hand.

The first militant, dressed in camouflage, tries to slip under the gate.

Unable to make it through, he gets up, goes to the empty guard
post, smashes the window with the butt of his gun, and climbs inside.
Seconds later, a bluish-gray Mazda approaches the gate.
The Hamas gunmen ambush the car as the gate slowly opens.

That's how Be'eri was breached. Minutes later, militants began to flow in on motorbikes, two to a bike and carrying weapons, including RPGs.

Yasmin and Tal had spent ten minutes in the shelter when they heard the whole security team outside yelling, running. "Go out from here!" one man yelled at them. "There are terrorists all over the kibbutz!"

Yasmin thought this must be the two gunmen they'd seen on the road—assuming that those relatively lone gunmen must have made it to Be'eri—and she and Tal left the shelter, made a run straight to their car, jumped in, and drove. But now the gate was closed. Tal made a U-turn and drove uphill toward a parking area.

They jumped out again. They started going house to house, knocking on doors, seeking shelter.

At the first two doors there was no answer. At the third, an elderly man opened the door in his underwear, his wife behind him.

"I'm from the north of Israel," Yasmin said. "Please help us!"

The man invited them in and made them coffee. He was Adi Dagan, his wife was Hadas. They must be tired after staying up all night at the party, he told the couple. Yasmin and Tal told them what had happened there. Now the elderly couple started receiving WhatsApp messages: the kibbutz security team was responding to the attack—but were outgunned.

Many of the WhatsApp messages I saw that morning, as I was driving south, were coming from Be'eri. Ella Ben Ami, living on the western side of Be'eri, called in to Israel's Channel 12. The *Times of Israel* translated the call:

"I need help. My father was taken hostage. I saw a picture on Telegram. A picture of him in Gaza. He was taken there. He texted me that they're breaking in and taking them. And I couldn't do anything." The messages and reports were turning into desperate pleas for help.

At about 7:30 Hadas said they should move from the living room to the bomb shelter. To Yasmin, Tal now seemed very anxious, and Hadas spoke to him, trying to help him to calm down. They watched the updates on their phones, shocked by videos coming out of the Nova party. Their WhatsApp chats from the trance-dance communities were buzzing with people asking for help or searching for loved ones.

Yasmin messaged Inbal, her sister. Inbal told Yasmin the army was surely on the way and to wait in the shelter. Together, the older and younger couples stayed put.

At noon, the electricity went off.

At 1 p.m., Yasmin left the shelter to go to the bathroom. She heard shooting and shouting in Arabic outside and assumed the army had arrived. But no.

At 1:50 p.m., Hadas was looking at her phone. Adi, there are terrorists in Pessi's house. That was their neighbor. Now both Yasmin and Tal were shaking from fear. "You need to be quiet," Hadas told them. Tal and Yasmin climbed into the closet of the shelter.

Like Jews in the Holocaust, Yasmin thought.

Five minutes later, an explosion went off—inside the house. "Allahu Akbar!" someone shouted, also in the house. Two minutes later, a knock on the safe-room door. "Open the door," someone said in Hebrew.

"Adi, come out," said one of the militants. "I won't kill you, because you are old." He must have picked up mail or bills that had been lying on a table and gotten the name. Adi, Hadas, Yasmin, and Tal stayed still and silent. Gunshots were fired into the door. Then more knocking.

After thirty minutes of this commotion, it stopped. Yasmin thought of her kids, two girls and a boy: thirteen, eleven, and nine. She sent them a message on WhatsApp saying she loved them.

The shelter door exploded.

"I can't hear!" Adi yelled. The blast had deafened him. Three Hamas fighters opened the closet door, held Yasmin and Tal at gunpoint, and walked them out of the room, hands up.

"Please don't kill me," Yasmin pleaded. "I have three children."

One of the gunmen gave her pants and a towel from the floor: she was wearing skimpy attire from the festival; they wanted her to cover up. Ten men were now in the house, some with green headbands. They tied Tal's hands behind his back. Yasmin was shaking.

One of the men spoke softly and smiled. "Please relax," he said. "Nobody is going to kill you. They're just going to take you to Gaza."

"But I don't want to go to Gaza," Yasmin replied.

"We're going to Gaza, and they will return us tomorrow." Yasmin didn't yet know that this man was Suhaib Abu Amr, twenty-two, an Arab-Israeli bus driver from East Jerusalem. He'd been working at the Nova Festival; apprehended there by Hamas, he'd been forced to call his family to prove he was Arab, and they didn't kill him then. Instead they took him and forced him to translate. It was that or be killed.

Yasmin, Tal, Adi, and Hadas were taken to a house where forty militants had gathered on an outdoor porch, now with a total of fifteen hostages, including Suhaib Abu Amr, the Arab Israeli. The captives sat there and waited with no idea what was next. After twenty minutes, Suhaib asked Yasmin, on behalf of their captors, if she had friends in the army or police. She replied she had many. Hamas wanted her to call them.

Like the Israelis being held captive, the fighters had expected the Israeli army to have responded by now. It had been hours. How could they not already be here, inside the community? Hamas, like everyone else that day, didn't comprehend that the Israeli military response was not what might have been expected. They were hoping to negotiate a path out of Be'eri, using Yasmin's connections, threatening to kill all the hostages if they weren't given safe passage back to Gaza.

But her phone had been left at Adi and Hadas's house. Through Suhaib, Yasmin told the Hamas commander, Hasan, that if they could go back to the safe room and find her telephone, she would make the calls.

Suhaib and three Hamas fighters took Yasmin back to the house. Everything there was broken, rubble. They would have to dig to find the phone. She felt herself in shock.

"What kind of telephone is it?" one Hamas fighter asked.

"Samsung 22."

"Samsung 22!" he yelled. She and the fighters dug for five minutes. No luck. On the walk back to the porch, another Hamas commander approached, very large and intimidating. He looked at Yasmin very seriously.

"Listen to me," he said in Hebrew. "I'm a Muslim. Muslims don't kill women. So please calm down. Nobody's going to kill you.'"

Back at the house with the fighters and hostages, the commander, Hasan, had taken a phone from one of the hostages and now called 100—the 911 of Israel—and told Yasmin to say there were fifty hostages, not fifteen. She made the call. When he said he wanted to speak with the police, she asked the dispatcher to get someone who spoke Arabic on the phone.

Hasan took the phone and told the police that if they didn't help get Hamas and the hostages to Gaza, they'd kill everyone.

The militants seemed very nervous. *They think the army is all over*, Yasmin realized: they assumed Be'eri was already surrounded, that they would need special passage to get the hostages to Gaza.

And yet it wasn't until about 4:30 p.m. that Yasmin saw a jeep.

Then another. The army had arrived.

And suddenly everyone was shooting. Yasmin ran into the house and hid behind the sofa in the living room. Hasan was hiding in the kitchen with another militant and a hostage. He wasn't firing, but other militants were firing from the windows. The firefight seemed endless. Hostage children were shouting, "Please help us!" At about the forty-five-minute mark, a bullet grazed Yasmin's leg. She could see her pants running with blood.

Hasan was yelling in Arabic on the phone. Yasmin started to cry.

About ten minutes later, the fighting ongoing, Hasan smiled at her and signaled to come over to him. He wanted to use her as a human shield so he could surrender without being killed. He put his hands on her and they started to leave the room, the other Hamas gunmen still exchanging fire with the army and police. As they moved toward the door of the house to go outside, Yasmin yelled "Stop shooting!" in Hebrew.

The gunfire continued. It was only by chance that she wasn't hit. As she and Hasan continued to the door, she saw Hadas and Adi. She saw Tal, lying facedown with his hands over his head. "Are you okay?" she asked. He looked up, nodded his head yes. She and Hasan walked on, toward the army and the police outside, Yasmin continuing to shout "Don't shoot!"

Outside, as they neared the police line, Yasmin in front of Hasan, the police and soldiers ordered him to take off his clothes. She felt a push on her back. Hasan knew he was captured; he was letting Yasmin go.

She ran to the officers and soldiers. It was 5:30 p.m. She was safe.

A tank arrived. Yasmin told the soldiers not to shoot into the house—more hostages were inside. Soldiers assured her that the tank was only there to break walls. Gunfire was still coming from the house, but only sporadically: Hamas didn't have unlimited bullets and seemed to be preserving them. Around 8:30 p.m., sitting in a jeep, Yasmin heard that injured hostages were being brought out. She got out of the jeep and saw Hadas, looking terrible.

A soldier decided the two of them should go to the hospital in an ambulance. As they got in, Hadas said, "Adi is killed, he's dead. All the blood that you see is his blood. I'm not injured."

She'd been taken from the edge of the house amid rubble and debris. No one else was taken with her, she said.

Yasmin asked about Tal. Hadas didn't know.

* * *

A couple of days later, Yasmin learned from neighbors and family that Tal was dead. Her boyfriend of two and a half years, he was thirty-seven.

In the beginning, Yasmin assumed her story was the only one like it. For days, she didn't understand the scope of October 7.

"I'm in shock until now," she told me later. "I don't understand he's not here."

Everyone else who had been in the house was dead too. Later, Hadas told Yasmin that an IDF tank had fired into the house and had likely killed the majority of the hostages not already dead from small-arms fire. She told the press the same thing. In April 2024, an IDF investigation would clear the Israeli tank commander of any wrongdoing.

On the Wednesday after the attack, Yasmin spoke at Tal's funeral and said it was the Israelis who had killed him. Some who attended Tal's funeral, his friends and family, asked Yasmin how she could say such a thing: how could she blame Israel for the attack on October 7? "I told them, I am saying the truth!" she told me.

As someone who had survived the attack, she tried to explain to the people who questioned her that it was more complicated than they knew. "I think in another aspect that these soldiers and all the commanders did a lot of mistakes. You know everybody wants Hamas to be the bad guy, but in our case there was a lot of mistake of our army that caused the reason Tal and the others are not here today."

Anyone who has experienced any sort of grief knows that it isn't a linear emotion. Yasmin was still in shock that the attack had taken place at all—and that the love of her life was gone. She went through many emotions during the traditional stages of grief. "I'm very angry about Bibi [Netanyahu] and all them," she said.

"Everybody needs to go to jail. The blood is on their hands."

Weeks later, Hadas did an interview on Israeli television Channel 12. The conversation was translated by Anadolu Agency, a Turkish state-run news agency, and posted to their website:

"A suddenly horrific boom . . . I couldn't move my legs. I was not hugging Adi anymore. At that moment, I told him once more that I love him so much. It was clear to me that there was a tank outside. And then came the second boom."

Hadas went on to describe the two Israeli tank shells hitting the building, then explained how she tried to save her husband. "I turned my head to see what exactly happened to me, and then I saw a hole in Adi's main artery. And I pressed my thumb on the artery to block the flow of blood, what else could I do? Then I realized that he wasn't moving and there was no need to press my thumb on his artery since I was already in a pool of blood."

Israel was responsible for the deaths of some of its own citizens.

The vast majority of people who died that day were murdered by Hamas.

Both these things are true.

*   *   *

On Wednesday, October 11, we got our chance to see Be'eri before it was "cleaned," meaning the bodies had been removed. This was the one place the army was allowing a small group of journalists to enter, just for a couple of hours—a major opportunity. I'd been feeling immense pressure to report from a scene of massacre before it was cleaned. It's one thing to tell people that civilians were massacred in their homes and yards; it's another thing to show them. I'm constantly asking myself, *How do I make people care?* The question stays on my mind so much that it can distract me. I make people care the only way I know how: by explaining who these people are and were. Tell their stories in a way that makes people think of their own families: the photos on the fridge, the food on the table, the children's toys.

The army still wasn't in control of the entire Gaza border, but we needed to dive into this reporting, take a moment out of the chaos, slow down, do the thing we do best: telling the story. There were still many unanswered questions and a lack of understanding of just how bad the Be'eri massacre—and the others—really were. As I prepared to go into Be'eri, I knew that the humanizing details would be painful to focus on. It would take an emotional toll. But that made my task all the more important.

The plan was to meet at a gas station turned staging area before heading into Be'eri with an IDF escort. When we got there, we saw five Humvees full of soldiers locked and loaded, the first with an Israeli flag waving from the antenna. It reminded us all that this was technically a military embed: they were still fighting.

I knew Be'eri was going to be bad, and the army also warned us about what we were going to see. But there was very little that could have prepared me.

Looking back, I'm glad we went. Despite our having shown the world the images, live, people still send me messages claiming that what we saw was fake or staged. But this was the real, unvarnished truth: the worst of humanity on display.

The first thing you noticed was the smell. The road to Be'eri was lined with burnt cars and corpses. Following the army, we turned into the normally placid kibbutz. In the distance, we could see what looked like a mound of dirt. As we got closer I realized it was bodies of Palestinian militants thrown into a pile. I snapped a few photos on my still camera.

On the other side of the road, Israeli soldiers waved from their APCs. Three days after the attack, they'd been able to secure the area. In the parking lot, a dead militant lay on his back, legs bowed.

After the smell and the bodies, the next thing I noticed was the huge number of soldiers. With large backpacks and a variety of weapons in hand, lines of soldiers marched past us. Be'eri had quickly become a staging area for the army—searching for Hamas militants still in Israel and ensuring the border was secured. At the bottom of the hill, the commander on scene briefed us.

"How would you describe what we're seeing here?" I asked.

"At six thirty in the morning, all this peaceful community was in bed. Some of them wake up to a holiday. A vacation. Hundreds of terrorists suddenly came from some directions. Many, four, five, six directions. With machine guns, shoulder missiles. People locked themselves in the protection rooms that they have here. And the terrorists go from room to room, from family to family, killed mothers with their son, killed their son in front of their parents and took their parents. In this building, they collected fourteen people and held them hostage."

"What did you see when you came in here?" I asked.

"Scenes that I never saw. And never think that I'd see. People that someone cut their head, people that had their hands locked and someone killed them. Children in the same room and someone come and killed them all . . . This is a massacre, it's a pogrom. It's not something I've ever seen."

*   *   *

I'll never forget the first house we got to see. Streaks of blood stained the patio next to large knives. On the patio table were extra magazines filled with bullets. Walking inside, you could see magnets and photos on the fridge, food still on the table, like any average home around the world. Someone shined a light into the kitchen: the entire floor was filled with pools of partially dried blood.

That would be the first of dozens of horrors we'd encounter in the kibbutzim near the Gaza border. These were the sites of a massacre, an execution of civilians. I was overwhelmed in that first house. The smell and sights hit me and the team hard. Military restrictions prohibited the live shots that could compromise the locations of Israeli forces, so we shot the pieces to camera that we needed and then went on, a walkway leading us to a backyard next to a destroyed house.

And then I nearly tripped. Bodies littered the area, covered partially by white body bags, the feet of Be'eri's residents sticking out. One wore a pair of running shoes, the same Nikes that I have. Some were militants, others residents. It was hard to tell who was who. I held my breath, trying not to take in the smell.

It was too much for Yonat. She started to gag and was escorted away by our security team member, Sean. He gave her a mask and we continued. For all of us, I think this was one of the hardest moments of the war, and for me, it didn't feel real: I got so detached from the trauma that it felt like a horror movie, that we were just actors. *You have a job to do*, I kept repeating to myself. *You have a job to do, you have a job to do*. And *Stay focused on the mission*.

By the time we planned to leave Be'eri, it was dark, and on the walk out, we saw Lieutenant Colonel Hecht again. Yonat and I told him we needed to get one live shot out from here: it was essential that the world see inside that house.

Despite the restrictions, Richard gave us the nod. "I don't know anything about it, okay?" he said.

We ran back through the dark toward the house to get the shot. On the way, we saw Doron Spielman, the Israeli army reservist and who had shown us the edge of Sderot over the weekend, "Where are you going?" he asked.

I started to explain we had approval. "I'm not letting my favorite correspondent go back there alone in the dark," Doron interrupted.

He had a point. The area wasn't cleared of militants. Two days later, more Palestinians would be found hiding near Be'eri. "I've only got two magazines. This isn't smart," he said.

"I know, I know, but we need to show the world what happened here," I said.

On the walk down the hill I called the Fox control room and said I needed to speak with the executive producer. "Look, it's going to be graphic," I said. "I will give a warning beforehand, but we need to show this to the audience."

The woman on the other end agreed and I rushed off the line. We had to get this done quickly.

The Faulkner Focus was on, with Harris Faulkner anchoring, and as the show's team tossed to me—went live to my report—the viewers could hear me giving the pronunciation of Kibbutz Be'eri to the producer: the signal was so spotty that I didn't realize I was live at first. I said "IFB," meaning my earpiece, and pointed to it: I couldn't hear anything.

"Guys, I need to warn our viewers, what I'm about to show you is the aftermath of the massacre against Israelis on Saturday morning. We are in Kibbutz Be'eri that sits just over the border from Gaza."

We entered the house of horrors.

As we made our way inside, the signal dropped out. But Yoav caught it on the LiveU and waved for us to step out of the house and finish the report. Despite a spotty signal and a quick report, we got the shot off— live on Fox News.

Harris Faulkner said it perfectly: "This is going to be hell."

We wrapped our coverage, and Doron made eye contact with me, turning his head sideways. "Now let's get the fuck out of here," he said.

9

AN INFORMATION WAR

Throughout the week following the October 7 attack, Defense Minister Gallant remained frustrated by the cabinet majority's uneasiness about launching a ground war. The majority seemed to think that sticking with air bombardment and negotiating with Hamas for prisoner exchange would get the hostages released. To Gallant, that was totally unrealistic. In meeting after meeting, he argued that he knew Hamas: they would fight until they died. Hamas had named its campaign after Islam's third-holiest site, the Al-Aqsa Mosque. The aspirations were clear to Israel's defense minister.

"They want Jerusalem," he told the cabinet.

Not that he couldn't understand the trepidation. The government had just experienced the worst intelligence failure in Israel's history, leaving the country and many top officials in a state of shock. Some in the cabinet believed that in the event of a ground invasion, Hamas would start killing the hostages or put them on rooftops as human shields.

The concerns were real enough. But given Gallant's strong sense of the stark realities of Hamas's goals, they didn't play for him.

"You need to take the enemy out of balance," he urged the cabinet. "Then they will not know what to do. . . . Only power, they don't understand anything else. . . . Create the pressure. Hit them, kill them."

"We will fulfill our mission," he told the cabinet at one point, "even if I have to go by myself to Gaza."

Regarding Hezbollah, however, he was getting somewhere. He'd focused on the threat out of Lebanon from the beginning, and by the tenth, he'd evolved a plan that had the prime minister's and the cabinet's support. A special committee assigned to quicky evaluate the likely extent of Hezbollah's involvement in the fight had determined that the organization intended to launch not a large attack against Israel but a set of small, sporadic ones along the border. Such an operation would threaten hundreds of thousands of Israelis. Also, Iran was using Hezbollah as another front against Israel, further destabilizing the region.

So on the night of Tuesday, October 10, after much evaluation and discussion, Gallant reportedly arrived at a determination: Israel would attack Hezbollah. The next day an opportunity arose, which Gallant, for security reasons, would later decline to discuss in detail on the record.

That morning, Wednesday the eleventh, the cabinet sat together, and Chief of Staff Halevi came to the same conclusion: Israel would go to war with Hezbollah. The decision might change conditions in the region forever. In any case, it would be a difficult struggle. But an attack now would keep Hezbollah from carrying out a long war of attrition.

The attack was planned for that night. The Israelis would catch Hezbollah by surprise and hit them with heavy air and artillery strikes. With an opportune window for action closing, the fighter jets were in the air, the targets chosen, the clock ticking, tensions high.

Then, an hour before the first bomb was to drop, the mission was called off. Prime Minister Netanyahu had spoken with President Biden and overruled the cabinet and Gallant at the last minute.

*   *   *

A week into the war, the world was glued to the story of the attack. Not only was the southern front with Gaza still active, with incoming rocket fire targeting large Israeli cities, but the northern front remained hot as

well, with Hezbollah launching daily attacks. So just as in previous conflicts between Israel and Gaza, the team and I settled into a routine for
covering the daily breaking-news developments.

We'd wake up early and drive toward Gaza, some days heading to
Sderot, others to Ashkelon. When sirens sounded, we'd take cover,
and then, like first responders, race to the site of the rocket impacts to
report to camera. Sometimes we arrived at the same time as firefighters
and saw chaos still in progress. Shrapnel marks on buildings. Blood on
the ground.

We were exhausted. We got only a few hours of sleep each night. We
were eating once a day, at best. But we had to keep going.

Thankfully, we couldn't have asked for more supportive bosses. Everything we needed was a phone call away: an armored vehicle, food
delivery, schedule changes to accommodate our work. I heard from
Fox executives, including the CEO Suzanne Scott, and the president,
Jay Wallace. They all had the same message: great job and let us know
what you need.

What they couldn't provide was rest. Nor were we asking for rest.
We were leading the global coverage on this story and wanted to maintain momentum.

We had one moment of calm in the endless storm. On October 14, we
arrived at Yonat's parents' house, in Moshav Nir Moshe, a small community that had narrowly missed a massacre on the seventh. Hamas
gunmen had been stopped just one field away.

I followed Yonat, hanging back a little, as she approached the door
to the house and then knocked three times. Her father answered. Yonat
and her parents hadn't seen each other since the attack. She and her
father embraced. Then her mother came to hug her.

Her mother invited us inside, and we sat for coffee: my first real
espresso since the war started, plus a fruit crumble cake, which tasted
like one of the greatest foods I'd ever eaten. It was the feeling you get
as a kid when you have a snack after a long day of swimming. It satisfied
the soul.

*   *   *

Unlike Israelis, Palestinian civilians have no bomb shelters, and inside Gaza, hundreds of targets a day—sometimes close to a thousand—were now being hit, leaving panicked civilians with no place to hide. The siege that Minister Gallant had called for was blocking food, electricity, and water from entering the enclave.

On Friday, October 13, the Israeli military added to the pressure. They announced that every person in northern Gaza had twenty-four hours to leave and get below Wadi Gaza, a riverbed south of Gaza City.

The United Nations demanded that this order be rescinded. It was unreasonable, the UN said, to expect 1.1 million people to move in that time frame.

The Israelis didn't budge. Evacuation orders were delivered by phone call, text alert, and sporadic leaflet drops—small pieces of paper dropped from planes, with evacuation instructions in Arabic, sometimes a map. The orders seemed to give hard evidence that an Israeli ground offensive was looming.

In the first week of the evacuation, a quarter of Gaza's population fled their homes, as Israel continued to strike.

The eye surgeon Dr. Raed Mousa and his family, having gotten through that first awful night of bombardment in their Gaza City neighborhood, had continued to stay inside, at first in the apartment, then in a corridor on the first floor, where Raed hoped they'd get better protection from the bombing. One night a strike hit within a hundred feet of the building. Since there was no electricity, he also got a generator up and running.

And now came the evacuation order.

Raed had learned that UN vehicles were scheduled to be on the move between 9 and 11 a.m., so he chose to leave then: bombardment of the roads might be lighter. Taking two cars, their own and one belonging to UNRWA, the family brought only paperwork and passports. Raed figured they might be home in a few weeks. Driving through the empty streets and hearing the bombing nearby, they headed south for their home in Rafah.

All parties were just wasting their time, Raed thought. No one was going to allow militants to destroy Israel; no one was going to allow Israel to kill all the Palestinian people. He and his family were being forced to drive south—but the war, he predicted, would end by negotiation.

It always ended that way. Why more killing?

*   *   *

Most Gazans didn't have the means to make a journey like the Mousas'. Where were they going to stay? What would they eat? Thousands were seeking shelter in UN schools and hospitals in Gaza City, the best hope for safety against an ongoing onslaught. Others were scared to leave their homes at all.

My own emotions were high. I'd been in the south of Israel on the seventh, witnessed the massacre, seen the horrific aftermath at other sites. But I knew I needed to maintain the objectivity to let the world know what was happening to the Palestinian people. A week after the seventh, I posted a copy of my live report on X:

> There is a developing humanitarian crisis in Gaza. Israel has warned all civilians to head south ahead of a pending ground operation.

I gave a breakdown of the current situation inside Gaza—again, to be a voice for the voiceless.

> It's critical that some solution come to the surface here because we're talking about more than 2 million people in Gaza. The vast majority are not militants. And there are many people caught

in the crossfire of this developing war. We've seen the images from inside Gaza. We're talking about many women and children. Hundreds of them that have been killed since this war started with a massacre on Saturday morning here in southern Israel. And there is a continued effort by the international community to put pressure on the Egyptians and the Israelis to allow the passage of Palestinian civilians, verifiable civilians, into northern Egypt. And this is something that will continue to be part of the discussion as this conflict develops.

I reiterated this point the next day, the fifteenth. Regarding the siege of Gaza, Israel's energy minister, Israel Katz, announced that he had ordered the strip's water supply cut off. While Israel doesn't control all the water going into Gaza, both the concept and rhetoric were dangerous. I posted: It's critical that Palestinian civilians have access to food and water in Gaza. War crimes must not be met with war crimes.

From the beginning of my coverage in the Middle East, and especially since the war began, I have stressed that two things can be true at once. The killing of innocent Israelis on October 7 was horrific, and a horrible slaughter will have consequences. Also, innocent Palestinian lives must be protected, international law followed.

That same Sunday, the fifteenth, I discussed that issue with Fox's Howard Kurtz, regarding our coverage over the past week. Though exhausted, I tried to keep a firm and serious face. I often feel like I have a character to play on TV. It's hard—really hard—to see what we see. To have the pressure coming from all sides, people from the pro-Israel crowd and the pro-Palestine crowd attacking me for the same report. They post hateful comments, send death threats, mass-report my social media videos. It takes thick skin, which I normally have. But on little sleep and waning adrenaline, the backlash was weighing on me.

Howard, maybe sensing this, asked, "What kind of toll is it taking on you personally?"

The fact is that war hardens you, makes it difficult to connect with people outside of work, sometimes makes you feel numb. The PTSD and nightmares—that's what you want to escape from but can't. I told Howard that we were seeing the worst of humanity on display. And I meant it. In war, an aspect of human beings emerges where it's all about survival and winning at all costs. The people who pay the highest price for this mentality are innocent bystanders.

*   *   *

Ten days after the attack, on the seventeenth, I was relieved to have an assignment that would provide a break from the death and destruction: we would be covering a wedding on a military base. Finding some light amid dark stories can be useful. For the first time in ten days, I saw people smile. For a brief moment, I saw joy again, as I took still photos of young, smiling soldiers.

The feeling didn't last. I was plunged back into the depths of the war, but the break, even for a few minutes, helped keep me in touch with the humanity of the story: that even in war, there is love, and in love, there is hope. I've been to Israeli and Palestinian weddings, Israeli and Palestinian dinners. I've had Israeli and Palestinian lovers. No matter how someone grew up, or what religion they practice, the embrace of a loved one is always just as strong. Maybe it's my late mother speaking through me: I hold on to the idea that love will prevail, that there is some good amid the bad.

Yet even as the vows were said, we heard the roar of an Israeli drone overhead: the constant sound track of southern Israel and Gaza during the war.

After we wrapped up at the military base, we headed to the entrance of Be'eri, where the army was staging for an entry into Gaza. The area was filled with soldiers running drills and waiting for orders to enter the strip. On top of an Israeli Merkava tank sat Jamil Faris, a young Druze reservist from the Golani Brigade. He looked calm as he prepared the tank.

"I have to protect my people, the people I love," he said. "And I know that this Hamas can endanger them after what they did here. After what they did to citizens, innocent citizens that did nothing to them." Recently married, expecting his first child, Jamil felt this was a personal war. Like so many other soldiers, he worried about what would come next for the country and believed in taking the fight to Hamas to secure the border and bring calm to southern Israel before returning to his family.

"I really want to be with my wife, but I also want her to be safe, and my child, who will be born, to be safe as well. So I know that we need to be here."

We were making our way around the staging area, speaking with soldiers, when rocket sirens sounded and everyone ran for cover, lying between the tanks and armored personnel carriers. Two Iron Dome interceptor rounds soared through the air in the distance.

As always, I started to report on camera. "Get down, get down, get down!" I yelled to the crew as I looked to the sky.

"A rocket was fired just over this position," I reported. "You can hear those interceptions taking place overhead. Soldiers who were out working on these tanks and APCs just ran for cover in different positions. They've got to make sure that the shrapnel coming down from these rockets doesn't hit anyone on the ground."

But even that attack couldn't have prepared us for what happened later in the day. We were sitting in the parking lot of the hospital in Be'er Sheva when my phone lit up with a message from someone I know in Jerusalem telling me that I should report this: Hamas was outside the buildings under Israeli evacuation orders, not allowing residents to leave. The source said the information had come from the UN, off the record.

This was the beginning of something big. An information war—part and parcel of the military conflict.

I pushed my source to let me get this statement on background from a "diplomatic source." They agreed. Then I checked with Nael, who remained one of my principal sources on the ground in Gaza. He confirmed that Hamas was keeping residents from leaving.

I also reached out to a longtime source, a senior Hamas official: Dr. Basem Naim. I'm looking for comment about information we received, I texted him. An international official in Gaza told me Hamas is preventing people from leaving their homes in some areas after Israel tells them to leave. Is this true?

Not at all, Dr. Naim responded. This is practically technically impossible.

He then sent me a voice note: "But what is more important [is] that all Palestinians are not ready to repeat the story of a second Nakba"—literally "catastrophe," meaning the displacement of Palestinians in 1948. "We are aware of the consequences of being forcefully expelled, forceful expulsion from your homes. How can 1.1 million Palestinians move from the North to the South? How can they move when Israelis attacking the Gaza City and the northern part of Gaza Strip at 24 hours all the time?"

I replied by voice note, "Thank you, Dr. Naim, for the message. Please keep me posted. We want to include Hamas officials and comments in our reporting and update on the situation in Gaza." I also asked him if I could use the response on TV, and he ended up sending me two video statements.

"Regarding the first question, Trey," he said on video, "this is absolutely wrong. This is not our decision. This is not our policies. And it is also technically and logistically impossible. How can you prevent 1.1 million Palestinians from leaving their houses or homes from side to side if they want to do it? This is impossible. But what is more important? How can these people move from side to side with their elderly, children, women, handicapped, sick people?"

I would later talk to other Palestinian civilians and see additional reports confirming that Dr. Naim was at best unaware of, and at worst lying about, the fact that Hamas was actively preventing some people in Gaza from fleeing, which would quickly become one of the major fronts in the information war. A "roof knock" is a relatively small bombing, with a limited explosive charge, used to warn residents that a building is about to be targeted. According to Israel, Hamas prevented people from leaving their homes after roof-knock strikes were conducted and evacuation orders were given. Drone video later released by the Israeli military showed Hamas also blocking one of the main evacuation arteries southward. Later in the month, the Israelis also released a call between an intelligence officer and a Gazan civilian to show what was being done to block civilians.

"This is an IDF officer speaking," the officer says. "In order to ensure your personal safety, I am asking you to urgently go toward Khan Younis."

"Where?" asks the Gazan.

"In the direction of Khan Younis, urgently. . . . I don't want you to put yourself at risk, which is why I'm telling you to go toward Khan Younis."

"All the roads are blocked."

"Your current location is unsafe. . . . Where is the road blocked? . . . Who blocked the roads? . . . Hamas?"

"Yes."

"Where did they block the road?"

"On Salah al-Din route."

"How did they block the road?"

"They are simply sending everyone back home. . . . They are shooting at people."

But Hamas's preventing evacuation wasn't the only such issue. Dr. Naim's second video message to me on the seventeenth opened yet another front in the information war. This one was regarding the reporting immediately after the October 7 massacre.

"A lot of it was distributed in the Western media, was based on Israeli allegations and Israeli propaganda," Naim said. "Until now, they are not able to show one proof of so-called the beheaded children or killing of civilians. We know that this is a war zone and a lot of civilians were in the middle of the confrontations. But what I am sure of that the chief commander of Al Qassam brigade has sent clear instructions to the soldiers, to the fighters, not to kill men or women or children or any civilians. And we a lot of videos to see how these fighters were dealing with, the civilians, men and women and children in a very high moral values."

The challenge for us in assessing the validity of claims and counter-claims was that both Hamas and Israel were using imprecise language when accounting for atrocities. Given the chaos on October 7 itself, it's understandable that precision was a difficult standard to hold Israel to that morning. Still, time gaps in Israeli reporting allowed for blanket negations like Dr. Naim's, exploiting marginal error for universal denial. That would continue to be a problem: when claims were made regarding what was happening inside Gaza, it sometimes took the Israelis days to respond to our requests for further information; sometimes they didn't respond at all.

The Israelis also lacked a succinct and clear message: low-ranking soldiers were not consistently prevented from speaking publicly without authority or concrete evidence. On the Tuesday following the massacre, for example, a group of Western and local journalists under military escort visited the site of a massacre at Kfar Aza. There a correspondent from the Israel-based outlet i24 reported that a soldier had told her that forty beheaded babies had been found there. The number seemed difficult to believe—but given the atrocities uncovered in the previous seventy-two hours, nothing seemed impossible. It turns out that the number was greatly exaggerated. Yet Israeli first responders did find some mutilated babies and children.

Such was the nature of the information war now well underway. With a growing number of victims mounting on both sides, each would find justification for nearly any action.

*   *   *

It was on October 17, while getting food in the city of Ashdod, that we saw—along with the rest of the world—initial reports of what quickly became one of the biggest flashpoints in the information war.

"Palestinian media says Israel bombed a hospital in Gaza City!" I told my team.

Instantly we began investigating so we could report. This was the al-Ahil hospital. Numbers started to float around: hundreds dead, some Palestinian media claimed. My first thought was *Why*?

The entire world had already seen the atrocities that took place on the seventh: if anyone had an advantage in the information environment at that moment, it was Israel. Why would Israel target a hospital, ruining the advantage with scattershot vengeance, either accidental or intentional? That would be disastrous.

To try to ascertain what had happened, the team and I reached out to multiple people in the Israeli military. I also connected with a top Hamas official from Gaza City, who told us that the bombing had taken place but that he couldn't provide any concrete evidence. He sent many videos from social media that proved an explosion had occurred; none proved that it was the result of a strike.

We started our reporting with that—calling it an explosion, not a strike, which was what we could confirm at the time. I was also skeptical of the high death toll.

Then the Israelis responded to our queries. Via phone and over text, they told us they were investigating and would update soon. We relayed all of this information to our audience in real time.

I wanted more evidence. A longtime source of mine, a Palestinian civilian, went to the site of the explosion and sent me a seven-minute video that I reviewed. There was no large impact crater; the shrapnel marks looked similar to something other than a strike, more like what I've seen when rockets misfire in Gaza City. My source and I exchanged voice notes as I asked questions about the scene. He also sent me videos of bodies taken to al-Shifa hospital. I saw dozens, not hundreds.

I adjusted my language in our reports to ensure I had the most accurate information. Even as my source claimed the number was 1,000 dead, I could not confirm it, so we never reported it. His video also showed significant damage to a parking lot—not a main hospital building, so in our reports, I referred to the explosion happening in a "court-yard" or "parking lot," not the main building.

To get more information throughout that night and into the next day, I spoke with many people in Gaza, Israel, and the United States. I reached out to a U.S. intelligence source, asking, "What are you hear-ing in the intel community about the hospital explosion?"

Over a text on the encrypted iPhone app, Signal, he provided clarity on what U.S. officials were hearing.

I can verify if those videos and the soundtracks that accompany them are authentic. This morning I'm seeing blast photos that lead me to believe it's more likely a Hamas rocket, engine failed and landed on a fuel tank. The hole is just too small and the 2nd/3rd order effects of shockwave aren't even close to jdam effects [Joint Direct Attack Munition (JDAM) turns unguided bombs into precision-guided muni-tions] . . . I've gotta believe the launch rocket failure is most likely . . . but both sides are launching pretty impressive propaganda campaigns to prove the other wrong.

Same thought process, I replied. Had a guy at the scene this morn-ing. The blast photos and videos don't look like an Israeli strike.

Small hole right? I probably know the exact rocket.

Very small for the casualty claims, I said.

Finally I was able to obtain video of the initial rocket barrage, fired by factions inside Gaza. The video was taken by an Israeli soldier on the border and still has not been made public. The soldier confirmed he'd taken the video and provided me with metadata supporting his claim. I cross-referenced the time stamp to live Israeli media video from the time of the explosion.

Based on all the information I could get, I reported that the evidence suggested the hospital explosion in Gaza was the result of a rocket mis-fire launched from Gaza intended for Israel. That night, I also posted on X: Also can't independently confirm the number of dead/injured. Reports indicate hundreds killed. Trying to confirm details. This will take time.

We got it right. Many didn't—and the misinformation and weak reporting led to eruptions of protests across the Arab world, adding gas-
oline to an already raging fire.

The problem, however, is that getting a story right—clarifying
whether it was a rocket misfire or a strike at the hospital in Gaza—
doesn't imply that the loss of life wasn't significant, that innocent
people weren't killed or hurt. It doesn't imply some larger judgment
regarding what actions Israel or Gaza is entitled to pursue. Those are
questions that we must answer collectively, in the much more complicated contexts of politics, diplomacy, national and personal agency,
and moral and ethical consideration. Such consideration becomes all
the more challenging if we're not committed to getting the underlying
facts right—and correcting them in the rare cases when we get them
wrong.

10

THE ARMY ISN'T COMING

KIBBUTZ NIR OZ

The next day, Wednesday, October 18, a friend and U.S. intelligence source sent me a text message:

Separately on a personal note - do you and fox have an exit plan if this gets really bad? Not strategy - well defined plan with locations and points and contingencies. If not, please get one. Nothing imminent that I know of right now, but all the alarm bells are going off. Obviously we'll come get you if we can, but best you have a well thought out playbook before you have to make that call. If fox has you guys covered - awesome. Disregard all the above.

Fox has me covered with our security team. . . . I appreciate you thinking of us, I replied.

The reality was that Fox did have us covered, but I appreciated the concern. I spoke to this friend often on the phone in the early days of the war, and there was real concern about movement across the region: embassies allowing nonessential staff to leave, the Lebanese carrier Middle East Airlines moving most of its planes to Europe. These were signals that the situation could quickly unravel. Those with money and power were getting out of the way.

Coordination to get American citizens, some expats, and some tourists out of Israel continued. Still, U.S. passport holders in Gaza felt abandoned by their government, which was dragging its feet, not exerting enough pressure on the Egyptians to keep the border open.

*   *   *

Nearly two weeks after the attack, the stage seemed pretty well set for a large military maneuver. Thousands of Israeli troops and tanks were ready to invade Gaza at a moment's notice. Every day questions were raised about when Israel's ground operation into Gaza would begin, and yet while some limited raids were being executed, nothing at the scale of the massive preparation was underway.

Hamas was also continuing its rocket fire into southern and central Israel. Iran activated its proxies across the Middle East. It wasn't only Israel under attack now, but U.S. bases across the region as well.

On October 20, the first two hostages were released from Gaza. Yonat and I broke the story for the world, based on reporting from sources not only in Israel but also in Qatar, where I spent weeks in 2021 and made a point of developing deep sources—my best sources, along with those in Israel.

Both of the released hostages were Americans—giving hope that the other 240-plus hostages could be home soon.

That hope was crushed as negotiations fell apart and the war raged on. Hostages' families clung to any information, any development. With the heavy Israeli response, and the death toll among civilians in Gaza rising, a parallel information war started to develop.

All the while, as officials worked to identify the remains of loved ones, Israel continued to uncover atrocities from the October 7 massacre. Eventually the Israelis enlisted the help of archaeologists. They sifted through burned buildings. They tried to find any pieces of any civilians not incinerated.

*   *   *

One of the places where the search for bodies continued through the second week after the attack was Kibbutz Nir Oz, about a mile from the Gaza border. What had taken place there on October 7 was particularly personal for our team.

Yoav had a brother, Gil, who lived in Nir Oz, and on the day of the massacre, Yoav sat on the side of the road, checking his phone every few minutes, waiting and hoping to hear from him. As the hours passed, it became apparent that Palestinian militants were inside the kibbutz slaughtering civilians. Still no calls, no texts. You could see the pain and uncertainty in Yoav's eyes. He was one of thousands of Israelis who waited in agony to hear from their loved ones.

The October 7 numbers for Nir Oz tell an especially horrific story. Far more remote than places like Sderot and Kfar Aza, this kibbutz is a small community that acts as a large family—just 400 residents, on 140 acres where everyone knew everyone. Its name translates to "Meadow of Strength."

Just as elsewhere, on the morning of the attack, Nir Oz residents alerted each other to distant gunfire over WhatsApp. Israel's *Yediot* newspaper later reviewed, translated, and compiled more than six hundred messages from the kibbutz group chat that morning, all of which paint a terrifying picture. Eighty residents were kidnapped, twenty killed: 25 percent of the entire kibbutz. Nir Oz residents, young and old, made up one-third of the 240 hostages initially held in Gaza, from nine-month-old Kfir Bibas to eighty-five-year-old Yocheved Lifshitz.

Why was Nir Oz hit so hard? Simple: the community had both proximity to the Gaza border and distance from help.

Among those we interviewed after the attack was Lior Peri, whose father, Chaim Peri, 79, was being held captive inside Gaza. Chaim Peri is a peace activist. He spent his free time driving Palestinian children to Israeli hospitals and made art to protest the blockade of Gaza. Hamas kidnapped him and dragged the elderly man into the tunnels beneath the strip. His being held hostage in the tunnels, and at facilities above them, is one of the best illustrations of just how indiscriminate Hamas was on October 7. These tunnels vary in size and length. In the years after Hamas took control of the strip, tunnels crossing under the border with Egypt were used for smuggling everything from weapons to Kentucky Fried Chicken to a grand piano. Some are large enough for trucks to drive through; others required a single-file line of hunched-over people. The initial passages were dug by hand; most are now built of concrete. Hamas has created underground rooms, headquarters, rocket storage facilities. Some areas underneath Gaza even have running water and ventilation, allowing Hamas leadership, along with the group's fighting forces, to hide from Israeli air strikes.

The *Washington Post,* citing Israeli intelligence officials, estimates that Hamas has constructed over 1,300 tunnels, more than three hundred miles in total length. Some once crossed into Israeli territory, allowing Hamas and Islamic Jihad to ambush Israelis. In recent years Israel has constructed an advanced above- and belowground border fence to prevent Hamas from digging into Israel. But a number of October 7 hostages, like Chaim Peri, have been held in the Gaza tunnels.

Because Nir Oz is so close to the Gaza border, it took Israeli troops more time to secure the area; we couldn't see it for days. When we finally got the call from the IDF that we'd be among the first journalists to enter on the nineteenth, I saw Yoav's face light up. His brother had made it to safety late in the day on October 7, having come very close to death; Palestinian militants had stormed his home in Nir Oz, just as they had with nearly all the others. Since then, Yoav had been waiting for a chance to go to the house and gather what charred belongings might be left. Some of his family's heirlooms, including five paintings, were thought to have been in the safe room during the attack.

We arrived in Nir Oz on the nineteenth, twelve days after the massacre. As we pulled into the kibbutz in a convoy of journalists, Yoav quipped that Hamas had even tried to destroy "the weed farm," a cannabis grow site at the edge of Nir Oz. That's Yoav's sense of humor. Whenever he leaves on his motorcycle and I say "See you tomorrow," he responds, "Maybe."

I had actually been hesitant to go to Nir Oz with the military, knowing how many journalists would be there. Anderson Cooper came with his CNN team; many other international journalists were there as well. Also, after nearly two weeks of covering the conflict and the aftermath of the massacre, I was mentally exhausted. Still, I felt a deep responsibility to document everything that I could. The adrenaline was still rushing through me. And I knew Lieutenant Colonel Hecht would be there. I always appreciated an opportunity to get an update from him in person.

The Israeli military asked that everyone take their tour of the kibbutz in orderly fashion. We were first introduced to a man who had been there during the attack, but with the swarm of press, Richard Hecht was trying to repeat everything the man said so others could hear. No way were we going to wait in line to report.

I called to Yaniv, "Yalla." Let's go. "Let's go ahead."

We snuck away to the neighboring house and started to report from there. The smell of burned bodies was still in the air. An Israeli soldier saw us inside the home and followed. "Be careful where you step," he said.

He pointed out that many people were still missing. At the time, that list included twelve-year-old Noya Dan and her grandmother. Noya, an autistic child widely covered after the author J. K. Rowling found out she was a Harry Potter fan, had become a beloved figure for the grieving Israeli people. After looking at her grandmother's burned home, I hoped they'd been kidnapped. If they'd been inside, they would have burned alive.

The first house we entered that wasn't burned looked similar to the first house we had entered in Be'eri. Everything was frozen in time. On the floor leading back to the safe room was a long streak of blood. The safe-room door was riddled with bullet holes. Inside you could see where people had been shot. My mind raced. What were their last moments like? What would that amount of fear have felt like?

We did a few pieces to camera, and I tried to capture those questions in my reporting, but again I knew we needed to go live, from here—even if the hits were for the morning show. If Americans were eating breakfast, they'd have to stop. They needed to know the truth. I ended up interviewing Yoav himself, live on-air, from Nir Oz.

*   *   *

Later I would hear the story of the attack from Yoav's brother Gil Shamir, who awoke on October 7 with his wife of forty years, Michal, to sirens sounding in Nir Oz. Both of them naked, without phones, Gil even without his glasses, they ran into their bomb shelter. "We thought it was going to be like the usual time," Gil told me. "Five minutes, go back to bed."

But the rocket fire didn't stop. And so close were they to the border that instead of impact and explosions, the couple could hear rockets outgoing from Gaza.

As the fire continued, they checked the safe-room computer for updates. Using WhatsApp, the pair sent messages to family members, first to Maya, their daughter in Tel Aviv. Because they didn't hear the impacts, they figured the rockets were headed toward the center and wanted to make sure she took the sirens seriously.

After twenty-five minutes there was a pause in the noise. Gil figured he'd be able to go get their cell phones so they could call loved ones, try to make sense of what was happening. He opened the door and heard people outside talking and shouting, in Arabic. He was used to hearing Arabic in Nir Oz—many Israeli Arabs and some Palestinian laborers from Gaza worked in the small community—but not on Saturday morning. Not on Shabbat.

He rushed back into the shelter and shut the door. Still, if Gazans were in the kibbutz, then surely the army would know they were there, Gil thought. He figured the army would arrive in ten or fifteen minutes.

Fifteen minutes went by. More shouting outside. Then shooting.

After thirty minutes, the electricity in the house was cut, and Gil and Michal lost all connection to the outside world.

In those first moments of darkness, Gil had a sinking realization: the army wasn't coming.

The power flickered back on, once, when Gil's generator kicked in. It was just enough time to get a few messages to family members: his brother, Yoav; his son, Rotem, who lived in another part of Nir Oz; Sigi, the wife of a nephew.

At 8 a.m., just after Yoav received a text from his brother, Hamas entered the house and started shooting. Gripping the handle of the bomb shelter door, they tried to open it. When they couldn't, they fired their Kalashnikovs into the door. They hit the lock, and miraculously, that jammed it, preventing entry. Still, Gil was sure he and the others were going to die.

While Hamas was inside his home, with the power momentarily on, their landline phone started ringing. It was Gil's other brother, Boaz. "Not now, they're in the house," Gil whispered and hung up, worried that Hamas might have heard the ringing.

Then, at 8:30 a.m., with the militants still inside, Gil and Michal heard their cell phone alarms sounding, on the other side of the house. They also heard screams outside.

The Hamas group left the house. Gil breathed a sigh of relief, but then a group came back. Gil and Michal couldn't see anything, only hear. They tried to make sense of what was happening. Maybe the army had arrived and the group was retreating? They certainly had no idea that multiple teams of gunmen were in Nir Oz, with Gazan civilians joining them. This time they could hear kids as the team began to loot the house and break things.

One noise stood out: a drilling sound. Gil would later understand that it was Hamas trying to drill into the gas line, to burn the house.

A third group entered: calm, no shouting, just one man giving orders. That concerned Gil the most.

He heard them start to throw books on the floor from a nearby shelf.

Then he felt the heat. The Hamas militants had lit their home on fire.

Trapped in their safe room, Gil and Michal did what they could: put something at the base of the door to try to prevent the smoke from entering, and stay low, since smoke rises. That worked.

Until it didn't. The room began to fill with heavy black smoke. The paint started melting off the door. Worried about chemicals in the melting paint, Gil reached up and cracked the glass window to let in some fresh air, keeping the iron cover latched on the outside. Every so often, the pair would come up for air and then go back down.

Militants were still outside the home. Gil kept thinking of their son, Rotem, on the other side of Nir Oz. Was he alive or dead? Did Hamas take him? The horrible possibilities.

Hours had passed when they heard an Apache helicopter over the kibbutz. *At last, someone is coming, the army is coming,* they thought. But that helicopter was shooting at the border fence to stop new infiltrations.

Eventually the army did arrive. Starting from the southern part of Nir Oz, they worked their way north, clearing buildings and booby traps along the way. Gil and Michal waited until they were sure they heard Hebrew outside. Then they fully opened the window.

They saw a military vehicle next to a burnt tractor—but they weren't convinced. When they'd first entered the shelter and had internet, they'd seen videos from Sderot: Hamas wearing Israeli uniforms. What if the people outside their house were militants? It wasn't until they saw a woman in a civilian car that they thought it was safe.

Without his glasses, Gil couldn't make out the figures in the distance. Then Michal saw her nephew walking down the street. Gil called to nearby soldiers, who didn't hear him.

It was 5:30 p.m., eleven hours since they'd first entered the safe room, when Gil went outside in the only clothes he could find in the shelter: a pair of Michal's underwear. "I needed to draw their attention." Gil laughed as he recalled the moment. "I did."

The soldiers came with a blanket to cover Michal. Then their neighbor's granddaughter saw them, and she brought them clothes from a house that wasn't burned.

At the house next to theirs, the husband, Rami Katzir, was murdered, the wife, Hanna, taken hostage. In the next house lived Bracha Levinson, seventy-four. Hamas murdered her and put her video on Facebook. In another house, they killed the husband, then went into the safe room and killed the wife. Next to that one, a woman in a red dress was taken hostage on a motorcycle.

Gil saw a nurse he knew from Nir Oz and asked that he call his son Rotem to tell him they were okay—he just had a feeling that Rotem was okay. He also asked him to have Rotem call the rest of the family.

Rotem was okay—but barely. Hamas fighters had entered his home while he sheltered with his dog. The door wouldn't lock, so Rotem had to hold the door with his hands. A gunman shot through the door and hit the dog, yet both Rotem and the dog survived. They, Gil, and Michal were reunited at the fortified Nir Oz security building, where the army was putting the rescued civilians.

"I don't remember how many people were inside," Gil told me later. "Some of them were wounded, some with oxygen masks." There the family also saw their nephew's wife, Michal's mother, and many others they knew. But not their nephew—he'd been taken into Gaza.

As I heard stories from more people like Gil, it became clear how many people in Nir Oz were affected. The community security members who survived went with the army to clear specific streets and areas and kept coming back with only partial families. People were missing and dead. "We had two taken," Gil said of his niece and nephew. "Never heard from them again." In the group of seven where he works as a handyman, two were killed, two taken hostage.

"People were in shock. But we didn't know what happened. People were still trying to figure out who survived."

The group of rescuees, separated into families and older people, remained in that building for twenty-four hours. Then a bus took most of them to a government-sponsored hotel in Eilat. Gil and Michal got off at a stop before the bus headed south and went to Tel Aviv to reconnect with loved ones there before joining their community in the south. After a week, they went to Eilat, saw family and friends, and received psychological care.

"I think people started crying only when we got to Eilat. No time for crying. The first weeks, it was like, just let us go through this day. . . . Basically you're inside a big, never-ending shiva," Gil said, referring to the period of mourning and prayer after the death of a Jewish family member.

The adult children of Nir Oz, those who had left the kibbutz as they got older and weren't there on the seventh, came back to volunteer in Eilat—and to help clean up the community. At the end of December, Gil went back to his house.

"It was on fire," he joked. "Like Lag b'Omer," the Jewish holiday of bonfires. His sense of humor is like his brother Yoav's.

Even for those who lived through it, life goes on. But the violence and horror of that day will not be forgotten. The sixty-nine-year-old kibbutz of Nir Oz will now rebuild in Kiryat Gat, far northeast of the Gaza border, in order to stay together. Most members, however, won't return.

* * *

While reporting from Nir Oz that day, we interviewed Richard Hecht live on TV. We wanted to discuss what the army had found here and provide a sense of how the traumas of October 7 would determine the Israeli response.

In the distance Israeli air strikes pummeled Gaza as Richard spoke.

"This is a beautiful kibbutz community," he said of Nir Oz. "And to me I think the most petrifying thing is the silence. We are now reading the manuals that the Nukhba Hamas-ISIL forces had."

Richard was telling the truth here. Hamas had brought manuals on how to communicate with Israelis. How to take hostages. How to live-stream abductions. NBC News reviewed the documents, released by the IDF, translated them, and provided a breakdown of what they contained. Hamas divided the subject into eight different topics: "Gathering," "Isolation and Control Within the Area and Around It," "Safety/Security," "Supplies," "Camouflage and Hiding," "Communication," "Live Broadcast," and "Negotiations."

"You walk into that burned house," Hecht went on, "and the beautiful garden around it and you see that they worked on their doctrine. They took a tire, probably burnt the house and suffocated the people in these safe rooms to death. It's just petrifying, Trey."

The attack was highly systematic. The militants followed the instructions and used tactics that would make rescue and response more difficult. That there was no advance warning only added to the terror inflicted on the civilian population of Israel.

"We have a duty," Richard said, "as a liberal, democratic country, to act based on the conduct of international law. We'll make sure revenge isn't part of our course of action.

"We're angry, but we're going to take care of Hamas professionally, in due course."

*   *   *

After we wrapped up our day in Nir Oz, we had no plans to try to cover anything else that day. But while we were reporting, we heard that New York governor Kathy Hochul was making a visit that same day to Kibbutz Kfar Aza, about twenty-five minutes north by car. We were burned out on the constant death and destruction, but I knew this would be a good opportunity to get an American politician on the record about the massacre. Plus, we had an invite to follow a longtime contact, Major Liad Diamond, who was planning to drive from Nir Oz to Kfar Aza.

As we stood in the parking lot of Nir Oz later that afternoon, waiting to leave, we saw a funeral procession coming into the kibbutz. It was a somber reminder of the people killed just twelve days before. We were asked not to film, so we didn't.

Our team drove north to Kfar Aza in tandem with Major Diamond. On the way, I received the latest information on October 7. The IDF had found Captagon, a synthetic amphetamine, on the bodies of Hamas fighters. This was a significant update: ISIS uses the same drug; its presence on the attackers explained in part how they were able to kill for so long.

New images also showed an American plane landing with fresh armored vehicles for the Israelis, who had lost so many in the early days of the war. New video from the music festival site also surfaced.

We arrived in Kfar Aza shortly before sunset, golden rays of light piercing the community. I had reported from here many times before October 7; now, in the distance, air strikes and outgoing artillery echoed. As with all areas cleared by the army, you could see the letter *C* with a date marked in spray paint on the outside walls of houses. Others had marked the number of bodies that were recovered from inside. Overhead was the constant buzz of an Israeli drone.

I don't normally like going on media tours without any direct reporting: usually a tour becomes a scrum of reporters trying to get the same shot; I like to do my own reporting. But in this case, I needed the access and the tour was our only option. I called the Fox foreign desk a couple of times, trying to pitch a live interview with the governor; there was little interest. *Was another big news event happening that day?* I wondered.

Governor Hochul traveled with her own security, in addition to the soldiers who were on-site; one of her men wore a camo plate carrier and gray New Balance sneakers. He looked noticeably out of place— but he held a semiautomatic gun with a collapsible butt.

The main house the governor planned to visit had been the home of the Kutzes, a family of five who had spent years living in Boston. I wanted to get inside, to document what happened, do a few taped pieces to camera and put together a report. This was a family our viewers could relate to: they had lived in the U.S. for years and were sports fans; they looked more like stereotypical Americans than some Israelis do. Amid the gaggle of reporters, we waited outside while the governor and a delegation went in, came out, and moved on to another house. Then Yaniv snuck in with the team, just to film b-roll, which are sections of video that can run on TV while I speak over them. Yonat pointed out to a police officer on the sidewalk that he was standing in a pool of dried blood; he quickly moved. In the yard there were blue and orange medical gloves.

We were following the delegation toward the next house when I whispered to Yonat that we needed to go back. I wanted to see the Kutz house for myself—to do the work that we were here to do.

We'd heard what happened to this family, but nothing could have prepared us for what we saw. Walking into the house, I thought for a moment we'd gone back to the wrong one.

Everything looked normal. Photos on the fridge. Laundry in a basket still folded. A red suitcase in the hallway. Then Yaniv said, "It's here. Over here."

Walking through the bedroom doorway, you faced an open closet. At its base, black soot spread in a blast pattern. Turning to the bed, we saw a pink mattress pad on the floor, a white mattress still on the bed, and a balled-up gray blanket, everything in a pool of dried blood. The bed. The floor. The walls.

The five family members were found in that bed, with the father, Aviv, embracing his loved ones.

The smell got to Yaniv and me. I felt like I was going to vomit. "Oh my God," I muttered. "Let's wait, *achi* [bro]," Yaniv said. We took a moment outside next to the laundry room, where a New England Patriots cap was sitting on a shelf. I did breathing exercises from the meditation videos and from what I've learned online. I repeated the mantras: *You have a job to do . . . Stay focused on the mission.* We went back into the room and did a few taped reports before getting off a spotty live shot.

When we stepped back out onto the patio, I was numb. I interviewed the governor before we left, but my mind remained with that house. How could they have done this to a peaceful family?

On the drive back I couldn't let go of the Kutzes. They reminded me of my family, and I thought about how my dad would have acted in the same situation. He would have been afraid—yet given his life to try to protect us. As a distraction, I scrolled through headlines. Defense Minister Gallant had met with troops in southern Israel and said, "You now see Gaza from afar, soon you will see it from the inside. The order will come."

It was a matter of days. Israel would take the war to Hamas on the ground.

*   *   *

That night we stopped by the Tamara hotel in Ashkelon, where I got to see Jeremy Diamond, one of my best friends, dating back to my D.C. days. Jeremy and I are like brothers. Although he manages the work/ life balance far better than I do, we both love journalism and come from a background of covering politics. He'd just been scheduled to move to Israel a week after the massacre to take over the empty CNN correspondent position in Jerusalem. I was thrilled that I'd have a close friend living in my neck of the woods. I'm also confident enough about what I bring to the table that I don't have to see Jeremy, or any other journalist, as competition.

"They tried to keep me from ya, but they couldn't," he joked as he walked out of the hotel door.

"There he is," I replied. Jeremy was with his cameraman Matthias Somm, another friend of mine. The job can get lonely, and the industry is very competitive: to see someone I considered a brother gave me a moment of peace, a reminder of what my life was like before war took so much of my mental space and time.

Earlier that day, Hezbollah in Lebanon had launched twenty rockets into northern Israel. A U.S. Navy warship intercepted multiple Houthi projectiles off the coast of Yemen. In the information war, my TikTok account was getting mass-reported for violations, and I was losing access to more than 800,000 followers and didn't have time to fix the issue, so I reached out to my agent and Fox for help. On the morning of the twentieth, on my way to get coffee, I saw a car with a Ukraine sticker on the back, reminding me of another war I'd spent much time covering. Meanwhile, the IDF was announcing the evacuation of residents of the northern Israeli city of Kiryat Shmona.

You have a job to do. Stay focused on the mission.

11

"WE'LL MEET ON THE BEACH IN GAZA"

As the weeks unfolded following the attack and massacres, my reporting shifted focus. Israel was now on the offensive. The number of air strikes against Gaza was unparalleled. In a country of almost 10 million people, over 3 percent of the population was called upon to fight. While the air force and artillery units worked around the clock bombing and shelling targets throughout Gaza, with the death toll there rising, Israeli ground forces were now massed on the border.

In the south, at the Urim junction—we often met the army there, before heading into the affected communities—a large barbecue area was set up for the soldiers, and the gas station at the corner had been turned into a makeshift meeting point. Occasionally we'd even be able to get a hamburger or Coke there—luxuries, after so many days in the field eating anything we could find. We had many informal conversations to get a sense of what the situation was like on the ground and how the soldiers were feeling.

Most of them had been yanked from their normal lives in high tech or other jobs in central Israel. Ron Garashee of the Givati Brigade was one. He had a one-and-a-half-year-old at home, but "It's our job, it's our duty," he said. "I've got a family, waiting for me."

I snapped a photo of Ron and told him I'd like to keep in touch.

"We'll meet on the beach in Gaza," he told me.

Ron wasn't joking. He understood the plan for the eventual ground operation. Israeli forces would fight their way to the Mediterranean Sea, cut Gaza in half, and battle Hamas in urban settings.

The soldiers didn't look afraid. But in smaller conversations, they admitted they were.

"They have nothing to lose," one told me, standing next to a grill. He meant Hamas and other fighters from smaller factions in Gaza. "But we're ready."

Those reserve troops were indeed ready and, during the initial call-up, in eager spirits. They'd seen the massacre. It was fresh in their minds. Their adrenaline was pumping.

But as the days went on, and reserve forces conducted drill after drill, with no movement into Gaza, many began to question if they were effectively being "iced," to use a term from American football. They were ready to go. Was there any plan? It seemed they were just waiting around.

There was, of course, a plan. It was just well above their pay grade. Minister Gallant had been making headway with the cabinet.

*   *   *

Meanwhile, I had started to struggle, in silence, with what we'd seen in the first few days. We're taught in journalism school how to report—not how to clean someone else's blood off the bottom of your boots, as I had to do again and again. The toll of the reporting, the mounting pressure of an expanding war, were building, and moments jumped up on me without warning—indications, given my experience with PTSD, that once the adrenaline wore off, I might have to face some of the demons we walked among.

One of those moments came almost two weeks after the attack on October 7, as we pulled up at the barbecue among the soldiers, when I saw smoke from the grill in the distance. As I got out of the car and walked over, the smell hit me: burned meat, like the smell of a burned body. It made me want to vomit. Growing up, I spent a lot of time in Memphis, Tennessee, where my mother's side of the family lives, and the smell of barbecue, the charcoal and the smoking meat, had always been nostalgic, comfortable: a safe place, friends and family. Now that burning smell reminds me of the kibbutzim, of the burned Israeli bodies. Other smells too now transport my mind. I flash to Be'eri, and to the music festival grounds. By now I can distinguish between the smell of blood and the smell of a decaying corpse.

Another time, almost a week after the attack, I was walking to the elevator of the Leonardo Hotel, where I ended up spending the first two and a half months of the war, and next to the elevator were small metal trash cans, with a granite pattern on the outside. Someone had spilled a coffee next to the can. I stopped, momentarily paralyzed.

The stain on the floor looked just like the blood in the kitchen in one of the houses in Be'eri. I wanted to take a deep breath but couldn't. My mind was trying to process what it knew wasn't real: blood on the floor of our hotel. Yet the stain was real. I stepped into the elevator. The door closed. The elevator didn't move. I'd forgotten to press a button. I stood there, feeling like crying.

Another moment came in Tel Aviv, when I had a rare day off and was walking to meet my friend Paul Ronzheimer, a German journalist for *Bild* magazine, when I passed a garage dump. Another smell: rotting garbage, bringing back floods of decomposing bodies. The dead militant behind a shelter at the entrance of Sderot. The dead militant who lay rotting on the median north of Yad Mordechai. The bodies at the police station.

There were days when we'd get back to the hotel and smell like death ourselves. It sticks to your clothes. It stays in your nose.

There's a stigma in the industry around talking about mental health; it's particularly strong among men who want to appear macho and tough and yet, of course, suffer inside. Enough of that. I've tried to normalize the mental health challenges that inevitably arise when you're operating in a war zone.

I did speak to my dad about my PTSD and occasionally mentioned it to Yonat. But the fact remained that I was embarrassed about the lack of control I had over my brain. I also worried that if I told my bosses, who are incredibly supportive and provide us with many mental health resources, they might urge me to take a break.

I didn't want to take a break. I had a job to do.

*   *   *

I chose my life as a war correspondent, and for all the challenges that come with it, including PTSD, I love it, am trained for it, have learned over time how to cope. Soldiers, too, get training and all too often get experience. For some of us, the horrors of war, while never routine, can become manageable.

But in every war, there are those who, with no preparation, get thrust all the way into some of war's most distressing, even mind-bending effects.

Unlike most reservists, Rabbi Bentzi Mann, thirty-four, had good reason to believe he would never be called up for duty. He didn't even have a unit. As part of the IDF rabbinical team, he only had to show up for training once a month; every year before the Jewish holiday of Passover, Bentzi was in charge of cleaning and blessing IDF kitchens to make them kosher for Passover. That was his role as a reservist, he told me.

But on the morning of October 8, at home in Rehovot with his wife and kids, trying to process the shock of the attack of the day before, he got a message via WhatsApp from an unknown number with instructions to report to Shura base. It was less than fifteen minutes away. He'd never been there before.

On arrival, he was given a uniform and joined a group of other reservists for briefing by a team of military therapists—the resilience team. Their mission, the reservists were told, was to move and identify the bodies that had arrived, and would continue to arrive, at the base.

Me and my grandmother Mary Margaret Yingst, world traveler, on Easter Island.

Fascinated by Egypt, I got to go at age sixteen—and the trip sparked my interest in becoming a foreign correspondent.

Unless otherwise noted, all photos are courtesy of the author.

Inside the Gaza Strip,
2019.
(Fox News)

Interviewing Khaled
al-Batsh, leader of
Palestinian Islamic
Jihad, in 2019.
(Fox News)

With journalists Walid
Abdel Rahman and
Nael Ghaboun in Gaza
City in 2019.
(Fox News)

Gaza, 2019. Reporting on a Hamas military parade in Khan Younis.
(Fox News)

With members of Hamas's Al-Qassam Brigades in 2019.
(Fox News)

Interviewing Israeli defense minister Yoav Gallant for *Black Saturday*. *(Courtesy of Shachar Yurman)*

Interviewing Prime Minister Benjamin Netanyahu in July 2023. *(Fox News)*

Interviewing Jamil Faris near the Gaza border. *(Fox News)*

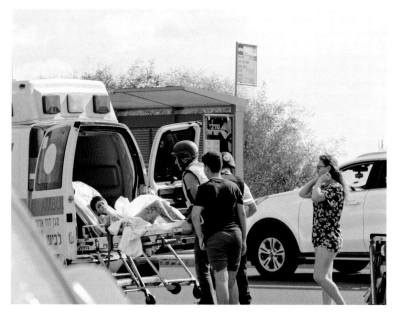

Israel, near the Gaza border, October 7, 2023. A young victim of the attack is loaded into an ambulance.

Smoke rises from rocket impacts in southern Israel on the morning of October 7.

Me, my cameraman Yaniv Turgeman, and a Hamas pickup truck in Sderot.
(Fox News)

The body of a Hamas militant lies on the median on October 9, near the intersection where we were reporting from on October 7.

A pickup truck stacked with bodies in Sderot.

Israeli soldiers heading for training in Kibbutz Be'eri.

Israeli soldiers after retaking Kibbutz Be'eri.

Body-bagged Kibbutz Be'eri residents after the massacre.

The sun sets on the Nova Music Festival massacre.

Paramedics outside al-Shifa hospital in Gaza in 2019.

Reporting from the fence of Kibbutz Nir Oz—breached on October 7.
(Fox News)

Working on
Black Saturday in
the crew car on the
Gaza border.
*(Courtesy of
Matthias Somm)*

Lieutenant Colonel
Gilad Pasternak entering
Gaza in an APC.

On an embed with the Israeli military in Juhor ad Dik, in the Gaza Strip.
(Fox News)

Like brothers: Jeremy Diamond and me in an Israeli APC
in Juhor ad Dik on November 4. *(Fox News)*

Me with my team (*from my left*): cameraman Yaniv Turgeman, bureau chief Dragan Petrovic, engineer Yoav Shamir, producer Yonat Friling, and security member Sean Nolan. (*Fox News*)

A demolished building on the al-Rashid road in Gaza City—with Israeli soldiers' graffiti. (*Fox News*)

Israeli troops driving
through the dusty paths of
Gaza during the war.

Weapons recovered from the
al-Shifa hospital complex.

The Gaza Strip after an
Israeli airstrike.

Palestinian civilians shelter at Gaza City's al-Shifa hospital in November 2023.

What is left of Gaza City, November 2023.

Crowded in the back of an APC with ABC's Matt Gutman and his cameraman Kuba Kaminski on November 22, on our way to al-Shifa hospital during the daytime.
(Courtesy of Kuba Kaminski)

In the tunnels beneath the city of Khan Younis. Hamas maintains more than three hundred miles of these tunnels in Gaza.
(Fox News)

Left to right: Fox News CEO Suzanne Scott, me, Fox News president Jay Wallace, and Fox producer Yonat Friling in protective vests in Kibbutz Kfar Aza.
(Fox News)

Reporting in Khan Younis, Gaza, with NBC's Raf Sanchez.
(Fox News)

Bentzi had never seen a dead body before. "They told us to be strong," he told me later. He wears circular Harry Potter glasses and a yarmulke and speaks in a high-pitched voice, with an American accent: though he was raised in Israel, both of his parents are American. "It's not easy," he said.

Bentzi was instructed to move bodies of dead Israeli civilians from shipping containers to a building where they would be examined for identification and cause of death. Some of the bodies were only body parts, others were whole bodies pocked with bullet wounds. Young and old. Children and adults. In the first few days, the bodies had been transported in bags sometimes only taped shut. When he moved them off shelves in refrigerated containers, body fluids and blood dripped on him.

It was also the heads. The faces. And clothes, shoes, tattoos—all different.

Bentzi kept trying not to mentally connect those things to individuals, but one day, helping out in a room where soldiers organize personal belongings, he saw a yarmulke stained with blood. He couldn't help thinking about whose it was.

Tuesday night he broke down. He remembered having cried as a kid while watching the movie *Free Willy*. "How am I not crying now?" he asked himself—and that's when he lost it. His country and his people had been attacked, massacred, raped, tortured.

During the first week, he had to help move the body of a family friend—a fallen soldier he'd grown up with—and the soldier's brother asked him to join them at the religious room, where families are invited to visit the body for closure. They hugged and cried. When the family sang an Israeli lullaby that had been sung to the dead soldier when he was little, Bentzi sang and mourned with them.

The first time he went home, the smell stayed on him. He showered. It lingered. He couldn't escape. Ten days after first arriving at the base, he was able to see his kids, and they played hide-and-seek, but when his son covered himself in a white sheet to hide on a bed, Bentzi burst into tears. He was seeing the small bodies of children at the base.

When the flood of bodies got heavy, Israel used chocolate milk trucks to transport the dead—dozens of bodies in a single truck—and now, "when I see them in the street," Bentzi told me, "I freeze for a second. These chocolate milk trucks, refrigerated trucks. I know what was inside of them."

If you ask Bentzi what kept him going, he'll tell you that he thinks it's a deep religious understanding. These are holy bodies and souls. Jewish burial customs include both purification of the body and blessing of the soul, and those who do that work are seen as charity workers: giving while knowing the dead can provide nothing in return.

"These are soldiers who sacrificed their lives protecting us," Bentzi says. "The least we could do was the work that we did." When in the aftermath of the October 7 massacre, people started calling the gates of Shura base "the gates to hell," Bentzi objected.

"These are not the gates to hell," he told me. "These are the gates to heaven."

*   *   *

With forces massed and arrayed on the precipice of Gaza, we were almost a month into the war, and Israel was still processing what had taken place on October 7 and the days that followed, still sifting through debris, looking for human remains, accounting for missing people. These tedious tasks took place both in the kibbutzim and in the Shura base in central Israel. The initial number killed was around 1,400 people, with 250 held in Gaza; those numbers were more accurately reduced to 1,200 killed and 240 held in Gaza. Still massive, in comparison to Israel's population. It's like if 50,000 Americans were killed in a single day. Identifying the dead would help to bring closure to the families and get a more accurate death toll.

As the numbers rose, we began to match more faces to names and names to families, from the family of Chaim Peri, the elderly peace activist from Nir Oz taken hostage into the tunnels, to the family of

Yagev Buchshtav and Rimon Kirsht, a couple kidnapped in their home in Nirim. Different stories with a similar thread—civilians at home resting, peaceful people dragged into Gaza against their will. Few had any information regarding their loved ones—though Rimon was an exception. She appeared in a Hamas hostage video.

By now I'd spent time in half a dozen kibbutzim, and I often avoided telling the families what I'd seen there. Each location had its own unique horrors.

We also started to learn more about the massacre—how it took place. The Israelis were now saying that Hamas militants breached the Israel-Gaza border at more than two dozen locations. They targeted remote machine-gun positions, cut at least one surveillance balloon, and took out major communications towers, disrupting communications by soldiers and civilians in the area. Much of this information came from videos taken by Hamas fighters that morning—videos that, along with manuals and plans, had been found on the bodies of the dead militants.

*   *   *

Fox is the top-rated cable news network in the United States, so I knew millions of people were watching my reports. I had also amassed a large following online. X was still a huge hub for news updates, and from the first minutes of the attack, I'd been posting daily. In October alone, my posts garnered 186 million impressions and gained around 230,000 new followers. That added to the more than 800,000 people who already followed my videos on TikTok. While these numbers might not mean much to someone who doesn't use social media, I see them as critical to reaching and educating a younger audience that is increasingly interested in the news.

The larger my following became, the more hate I got from both sides. Internet commenters from the pro-Israel and pro-Palestine sides would call the same report biased.

A social media video, for example, where I discussed the number of targets Israel hit in Gaza was attacked by both sides.

"Why do you call Hamas militants and not terrorists?" one pro-Israel commentor asked, without looking up the definition of either word.

"You are supporting genocide against Palestinians," a pro-Palestine commentor opined, seemingly unaware of my report, posted on the same social media page the day before, saying that the humanitarian situation in Gaza is catastrophic and that it's critical to distinguish civilians from Hamas.

For advice on how to handle the blowback, I reached out to my best friend, Fin Gomez, an executive at CBS News. Fin knows the industry like the back of his hand and is one of the most respected journalists of the current generation. A former White House producer for Fox, now political director at CBS, he has believed in me for years—before I believed in myself—and has always kept me on track mentally and professionally.

We discussed my coverage, and he gave me good advice: stay focused on the basics of storytelling, keep doing the news. The rest will fall into place.

It was a complicated reporting environment, because as much as the world is heated and divided on questions about Israel and Palestine, in the past year Israeli society itself had been more divided than ever. Weekly anti-government demonstrations shut down highways. Clashes with police led to injuries among protesters. The firing and rehiring of Defense Minister Gallant nearly pushed the country into civil war. To say Israeli society disagreed about the country's direction would be an understatement—and the vital point is that Israeli society is not a monolithic identity. Before the October attacks, Israel was consumed by internal clashes over proposed judicial reforms, which many felt threatened the future of democracy in the country and in the Middle East.

Those tensions were, needless to say, eased—temporarily, not permanently—as the horrific events of October 7 brought much of the country together in tragedy. The security cabinet represented a coalition across deep political divides. Five days after the October 7 massacre, the opposition's National Unity party, led by former defense minister and former chief of staff Benny Gantz, joined with Prime Minister Benjamin Netanyahu's far-right coalition. The Israeli war cabinet, a small subset of the security cabinet, consists of Netanyahu, Defense Minister Gallant, and Gantz, along with observers Gadi Eizenkot and Ron Dermer. Eventually Aryeh Deri, a founder of the Shas party, would be added.

Stark online controversies focused heavily on the legitimacy of the security cabinet's military policy. At first, the cabinet had focused on defense: ensuring that the border with Gaza was secure and that the infiltration attempts were over (they weren't). The second priority was to ensure that no Hamas or Islamic Jihad militants were hiding in southern Israel. And that was only on the southern front. Simultaneously, Israel had begun to deploy thousands of troops to northern Israel to fend off the threat from Hezbollah.

Only when the Israelis had gotten their footing did they expand the massive air offensive against Gaza that my team and I had been witnessing and reporting on. The war would come in many phases, defense officials had told us. The large air campaign to reduce Hamas capabilities in Gaza would sooner or later be followed by a ground operation—though when this would happen remained mysterious. Then would follow a period during which Israel maintained partial security control over the strip.

Hence Israel's striking thousands of targets: Hamas command centers, weapon manufacturing facilities, and observation posts, the traditional targets; but also bunker-buster bombs to hit the tunnel network beneath Gaza, as the Israeli navy and artillery units shelled Gaza from either side. Israel was still only using 30 percent of its airpower against Gaza, anticipating that a much larger regional war might be around the corner. Weeks into the war, despite the Israeli bombardments, Hamas retained its ability to fire on major Israeli population centers, including Tel Aviv.

The Israeli government and military also faced immediate questions from the United States, its key ally, which provided weapons and funding to continue the conflict. The biggest question: "What does the day after victory look like?" The Israelis had two goals for entering Gaza: first, destroy Hamas leadership; second, try to rescue the 240 hostages being held inside. But who would control Gaza and its more than 2 million residents after Hamas was defeated (assuming it could be)?

The Israelis don't want to occupy Gaza for the long term. The Egyptians don't want anything to do with control of Gaza. The Palestinian Authority is largely unpopular among the Palestinian people and doesn't solve the ideological issue Israel faces: having a neighbor, Hamas, that wants to kill you.

As I'm writing this—and likely when you're reading it—the question remains open.

12

THE GROUND INVASION BEGINS

Toward the end of October, an estimated 500 to 600 Americans were still trapped in Gaza. The fact that the U.S. State Department wasn't able to get them out was remarkable—especially given its security relationship and funding to Israel and Egypt.

Nael sent me the number of an American woman from Utah named Sireen Beseiso, a single mother stuck in Gaza with her ten-year-old son, Aden. I was glad I could incorporate her story into our reporting. It gave viewers some perspective, both on general conditions in Gaza and on the plight of U.S. citizens who couldn't get out.

On the morning of October 7, Sireen and Aden had been in her family's apartment in Gaza City, where they'd been staying for more than a year. Sireen had enrolled Aden in an American school. While she'd grown up in Gaza, she'd never imagined a day like this would come. She tried to stay calm and soothe her mother and son. Her father seemed more pragmatic. "It's okay, they are going to bomb for a few days," he said. "It will be over soon."

He was wrong, of course, and the first few days were some of the most difficult. The Israeli air campaign ramped up. The house was shaking. Every window broke. There was nowhere to hide. Sireen considered evacuating to the south but feared moving around in Gaza.

She and her family also had nowhere to stay and didn't want to go to a stranger's home.

Hoping for a way out, as a U.S. passport holder, along with her son, Sireen called and emailed the U.S. embassy in Jerusalem for guidance. They told her to wait for updates. Friends in Utah called their senators' offices and the State Department asking for assistance.

She was getting desperate when, on Tuesday, October 10, the State Department told her the border was open and she could cross. The family took a taxi to Rafah. They registered their names and paid the Egyptian officials a fee to confirm their exit paperwork.

Inside the crossing house, Sireen handed over her American passport and filled out paperwork with her sister and cousin, who also have American citizenship. Her son was waiting with his grandparents outside in the taxi. Sireen wanted her parents and son to come into the crossing house, but the border guard insisted they had to wait for their names to be approved—Israeli approval, the guard said.

Waiting, Sireen had a bad feeling.

Then she heard the roar of an Israeli jet overhead. "They are going to bomb!" she told a woman working in the crossing house.

"It's okay, even if they bomb."

"No, it's not okay!" Sireen shot back. "My son is outside with my parents."

"It's okay, then we will all die," the woman said.

A blast rocked the ground. Sireen started screaming and yelling. Her sister was crying. The border guards closed the door to the crossing house and urged people to move to the Egyptian side, but Sireen wasn't going to leave her son and her parents, and she was holding their passports. She went out on the Gaza side and found her family unharmed but shaken by the bombing.

The border closed. The family could do nothing but take the long trip back to northern Gaza.

When the UN building next to her parents' apartment building began to evacuate, Sireen got even more worried. Their own building kept shaking nonstop, and if UN officials were leaving, things must be getting very dangerous. Then, on the thirteenth, a friend called and told them they should head south: the Israelis were calling for a full evacuation of northern Gaza.

Sireen watched people fleeing the neighborhood and didn't know where to go. The next day, a UN driver told Sireen's family that he'd gotten a call from the Israeli military, warning him the area would soon be targeted. They had only until 5 p.m.—a few hours away.

Sireen's nearly ninety-year-old grandmother, like many elderly people in Gaza, said she simply would not leave. She'd been evacuated from Palestine in 1948 with her parents and had never gotten home. She wasn't going to go through that again. It took a lot of coaxing, but she eventually changed her mind, and the family left the apartment.

At first they sheltered in the home of a friend in Deir al-Ballah. After three days there, they got news from the U.S. State Department: they would have an opportunity to leave Gaza. To make that happen, they moved on to Khan Younis, where they lived in a stranger's home. There was no running water. Cockroaches skittered across the floor. At night they were cold and terrified. The only thing that put Sireen at ease was the fact that the owner of the house was affiliated with the Palestinian Authority (PA), since the PA and Hamas are not allies, and a house with links to Hamas might be more likely to be targeted.

Still, not knowing their affiliations, she worried when random people came in and out of the house. There was nothing to do but wait for the State Department to get her family out of Gaza and into the United States.

*   *   *

As the Israeli air campaign continued, we juggled following developments inside the strip and following developments in southern Israel. On the night of October 22, the Israelis claimed they hit 320 different targets in Gaza, still focused on mortar and anti-tank units along the border. Ahead of an expected ground offensive, they wanted to clear pathways into Gaza and leave as little resistance as possible.

Israel was also increasing strikes against the Lebanese militant group Hezbollah, killing eight of their members over a twenty-four-hour period. In the West Bank, Israel continued to go after wanted Palestinians and Hamas members. These arrests served two purposes: prevent more attacks, and give the Israelis leverage for the prisoner exchanges they knew would have to take place. By the twenty-third, 800 Palestinians had been arrested across the West Bank, 500 of them affiliated with or members of Hamas.

For my reports each day, I gathered information and the latest numbers from sources ranging from the army itself to the *Times of Israel* live blog. On the twenty-third, we aired our report on the horrific aftermath we'd encountered in Kibbutz Nir Oz. We highlighted the horror by showing the blood-filled hallways of homes and charred remains of life. We spoke with Lior Peri, the son of Israeli hostage Chaim Peri, the peace activist who had made art to protest the Israeli blockade of Gaza and driven Gazan children to Israeli hospitals for medical treatment.

"If you could just speak to him, what would you say?" I asked Lior.

"'Hold on, we're coming. We're doing our best.'"

Lior's half brother had been killed during the massacre in Nir Oz, and he was determined to do everything possible to bring his seventy-nine-year-old father home. "We didn't take the time to be sad, yet," Lior said. "We didn't take time to mourn, yet. We feel, I feel, and our small family feels that we have a mission."

We ended our report with an update about another resident of Nir Oz, nine-year-old Ohad, who was marking his birthday in Gaza after being kidnapped by Hamas. Ohad's and Lior's separate stories from the same community would have drastically different endings.

After the report aired, we drove toward Gaza to meet a representative from the 360 national rescue unit. Unit 360, as it's known, is one of two main volunteer medical teams tasked with identifying the bodies of those killed in Israel. Today they'd been traveling between bomb shelters along the Gaza border, collecting body parts and bloodstained clothing. It was a morbid task, but an important one for a variety of reasons, including closure for families, fulfillment of religious laws, and minimizing health hazards.

When we arrived, three men were standing next to a white jeep outside a public bomb shelter. At their feet were body bags, one half-filled. The shelter, like most in southern Israel, had a large mural on the outside, a way for the small concrete structures to look more appealing in the landscape. This one had a blue-and-brown bird painted on it to the left of the entrance. I immediately recognized the location and felt goose bumps on my arms.

A dashcam video had been released earlier in the month, time-stamped 7:56 a.m. on the seventh, showing Hamas militants kicking a man sitting outside this same shelter, filled with concertgoers from the festival. One of the militants then throws a grenade inside. A man runs out of the shelter and is gunned down by Hamas. More video and subsequent reporting would illuminate the heroic story of Aner Elyakim Shapiro, an off-duty staff sergeant in the army, throwing seven grenades back out of the shelter before being killed by the eighth. Miraculously, a reported seven people survived from that attack on the shelter, while others were killed or taken hostage.

Before our live report and interview with Moshe Melayev of Unit 360, I looked at the many grenade pins and levers lying in the gravel outside the shelter. Picking up one of the pins, I thought about what it must have been like for the people inside. If they didn't die right away, they would have suffered horribly. They also must have experienced indescribable fear. Blue medical gloves and red police tape littered the ground.

I was in a bit of a daze trying to imagine what had happened here. The crack of the outgoing artillery snapped me out of it. During our live shot, I knew I would need to be careful with some of the descriptions and images. It was 8 a.m. on the East Coast; I needed to consider what the audience would be waking up to. Nevertheless I felt it was critical to document the facts and inform people on just how gruesome this massacre was.

I stood in front of the shelter. Lawrence Jones of *Fox & Friends* "tossed" to me. "This is where so many innocent civilians were hiding," I reported. Inside, the walls were filled with blast marks. The smell of death was still strong. The floors were still stained with blood and body fluid.

In the interview with Moshe, we learned new details, not just about what had happened here, but also about what took place on the seventh. His descriptions were delivered to our audience live.

"We came here Saturday night, this bomb shelter specifically was between twenty and thirty bodies." As he spoke, it occurred to me that I should have given our viewers a graphic-description warning. Too late. I asked Moshe how he would respond to some people around the world saying that October 7 didn't happen the way it had been reported.

Moshe: "I've been in the Shura camp, where they're gathering all of the bodies. All the victims in Ramle. That was actually when I first saw dead bodies from this event. The first body I took out from the truck, she was maybe a five- or six-years-old girl with long hair and that was the moment I understand something big is going on here and it's not what we're used to see . . . It was shock for me."

Trey: "As a first responder to this, what was done to these people of southern Israel?"

Moshe: "I don't want to get people scared from what I'm saying, but I saw beheaded bodies, I saw body parts. There is one of my friends who was in Kfar Aza. He told me that he find in one house, a husband and wife and two children. They killed the husband first. They took his eyes out. I saw the body by myself. They took the eyes out. They cut the breasts of the woman. They cut the leg of the girl. That's the family that I saw with my own eyes."

That evening we went to Kibbutz Shuva, where my friend Mikey was based for reserve duty. He was also among the first responders in a rescue unit in those initial days. Yoav made us both coffee. We sat, smoking a cigarette.

* * *

On Monday, October 23, Yonat got a call from a source who said he had a video that would give the world the first insight into the mind of someone who carried out the attack on October 7. We were warned that what the attacker described was extremely disturbing.

As we waited for the link, we debated if we could show this material on-air. Fox had strict guidelines about showing videos of the massacre and hearing from those who had committed it—not to control what we reported but to ensure that the company wasn't advancing Hamas propaganda. The link came: two videos of an interrogation carried out by Israeli intelligence.

A man from Gaza City sits in a white cloth jumpsuit across from an Israeli intelligence officer who isn't shown. The man was captured, we learn, outside Alumim, just south of Nahal Oz.

The man acknowledges that in Islam, it is forbidden to kill women, children, and the elderly, but he says commanders told them they could do whatever they felt like doing—and that they shouldn't plan on coming back. As the video goes on, the descriptions become more graphic. They were told to step on the heads of victims and to behead them.

"We burned, slaughtered, and beheaded people," the man says. "We became animals—things that humans do not do."

"What type of things?" the interrogator asks.

"He described them," I later reported on TV. "And we can't describe them to you, because they are too graphic to explain on television."

That decision was the result of a long phone call with Greg Headen, the Fox vice president of news coverage, whom I'd spoken to first thing on October 7, along with the director of the Fox News foreign desk. Headen had me explain all the information we had obtained and asked a lot of questions about the source, the video, and its authenticity. I felt his deep desire, as always, to get fresh information out to our audience, but to also be respectful of the victims.

And respectful of the audience. Often when we're immersed in a story, it's easy to forget that what I might find a simple fact or piece of information could be a brutal and disturbing piece of evidence of a crime for viewers. These decisions were not taken lightly by Fox and its leadership. We would ultimately decide not to show the interrogation itself but describe the graphic details and leave out some of the most disturbing parts.

I went on reporting: "They were given a coordinated and specific plan to come into Israel and put all beliefs aside, with one goal in mind: to inflict as much terror on the civilian population here as possible."

Some of what the video revealed was so gruesome that I struggle to find the words to explain it here. Hamas raped women before shooting them in the head, then continued to rape their dead bodies. Using a Telegram group, they sent videos as they were killing civilians in their homes. It pains me to recall what we saw and what we learned. I try to forget a lot of it during the day, but I still see it in vivid nightmares.

*   *   *

Until now, I've largely recounted what occurred on the seventh and the days after. But as the weeks went on, and all signs pointed to an imminent ground operation, the biggest question remained, growing in importance: *How would Israel respond?*

This has been and always will be the hardest part of the story to cover. The October 7 massacre was the largest slaughter of Jews since the Holocaust. It seared a collective trauma into the minds of Israelis that will last for generations; hostages were still being held by Hamas. Yet the level of Israel's response will be the subject of debate for decades to come too.

Before the deployment of any ground campaign, thousands of Palestinians were already dead from the immediate response: the air campaign, which, according to many objective observers, was not proportionate. In a ground campaign, the death toll would rise drastically: thousands of innocent men, women, and children would die along with Hamas militants as long as the 240-plus hostages were held—and it was likely that some of the hostages would die as well.

Many analysts believe that the Israeli war on Gaza will only further radicalize a new generation of Palestinians. As with the Iraq War (2003–11), younger people growing up amid death and suffering will make it their mission to retaliate against Israel for destroying their lives.

How can I report on such events in a way that makes people care and have empathy for both sides? How can I make Palestinians understand that Israelis are not all bad people, wishing death and suffering against Gazans? How can I make Israelis understand that not all Palestinians agree with or support the actions of Hamas and that Palestinians are human too?

It's a challenging quagmire because, as I've been told throughout my reporting, many Israelis would like to see Gaza "turned into a parking lot," and many Palestinians would murder Jews if given the chance and tools. Many on both sides are not so extreme, of course—but when confronted with those who are, I'm constantly thinking, *Don't shoot the messenger*.

Israeli officials told me this wasn't about revenge. But soldiers on the ground often had a different view. Maybe it was age, maybe experience. Either way, this was war, and war is ugly.

*   *   *

"Hey, Trey, can you talk?"

"Yeah, what's up?" It was Thursday afternoon, October 26, when I got a call from Betty Ilovici, the senior advisor and press liaison for Israeli defense minister Gallant. She wanted to set up a briefing.

"We'll do this meeting tomorrow, but I need your thoughts. How can we make this useful to you? Only six people are coming."

"We need information," I said. "Evidence and facts on the record that we can use. Ideally we can get him on camera, but at a minimum, we need him on the record."

So the next day, the twenty-seventh, started with an early-morning meeting in Tel Aviv with Minister Gallant. I waited outside his office with CNN's Jake Tapper, ABC's Ian Pannell, and a few other Israel-based journalists, talking about the war and the stories we were working on. Jake and Ian are heavy hitters, and I sensed that they had developed respect for my leading international coverage from Afghanistan, Ukraine, and now Israel. Ian in particular had always been nice to me when I saw him in the field—he's one of the kindest reporters I've come across.

Then, placing our cell phones in a cubby at the door, we went into the office to meet with Gallant. No recording devices were allowed in, since we'd be talking about sensitive information relating to the war.

"We'll start off the record," Betty said.

Given that he was in the middle of a war that was rapidly expanding to new fronts, Gallant was surprisingly energetic. Weather-beaten face intensely concentrated, he was wearing the black button-down shirt and undershirt he'd worn since October 7. He opened by showing us a video compilation of the October 7 massacre. Some of the clips I had seen, others I hadn't; some were incredibly graphic and taken in places I had been.

A Thai worker nearly getting his head chopped off with a shovel. A dead festivalgoer outside a bomb shelter. The burned bodies of families.

After speaking for a while about the situation as we all scribbled notes, Gallant took questions, and I pressed him on when the ground operation would start. I watched his eyes closely. I tried to read his body language.

"You'll hear it one minute after Hamas," he said. "We are close."

As for the overall timing of the war, Gallant was laying the groundwork for a long conflict. "It's not a question of weeks, but a question of months."

But it was his discussion of the possibility that the war would un-ravel into a wider regional conflict that interested me most. "We are not looking for bigger wars," he said. "But we are preparing ourselves."

The lasting takeaway was Gallant's explanation that the war with Gaza would occur in phases. Phase One, he made clear, was almost complete.

He gave me no sense of how close we were that day to Phase Two.

*   *   *

After the meeting with Gallant, the team and I headed back south, pass-ing a large "Never Again" billboard on the Ayalon highway. It brought to mind the striking parallels between the Holocaust and what many were calling Black Saturday. For most Jews, October 7 was seen as an attack against the very existence of the Jewish people and their state.

In the late afternoon, in Sderot overlooking Gaza, we set an iPhone on top of a pile of bricks and watched Rear Admiral Daniel Hagari's press conference. Hagari revealed a computer-generated graphic claiming to show a command-and-control center underneath Gaza's al-Shifa hospital. Just given how intricately the tunnel network was de-scribed, the video looked hard to believe.

"Today I will be revealing intelligence proving that Hamas uses hos-pitals as terror infrastructures," Hagari said. "I repeat that Hamas uses hospitals as terror infrastructures." He stressed that the video was only an illustration. "We will not show here, the true material."

After the briefing, I talked with Dudi, who was serving as our cam-eraman at the time, about the video, whether he thought it was legit enough to report.

"Look," he said, "they are going to try to convince the world what is there. Let's wait and see."

I agreed. We'd have to wait for more information and couldn't simply take the claims of the Israeli army at face value. Sometimes the Israelis lie to throw the enemy off; sometimes they lie because their actions are controversial. They had lied to us in the past and were capable of doing it again, or at the very least exaggerating the truth.

That night, we stood on a hill overlooking the Beit Hanoun neighborhood of Gaza, on the Israel-Gaza border in Sderot. The location became known simply as "the hill," since most correspondents ended up using it as the war ramped up. It provided a clear line of sight into Gaza: during the day, you could see dark smoke rising at the location of air strikes; fighter jets roared overhead, attack helicopters shot in the distance.

As the sun set along the border, the scene in the distance was familiar: black smoke rising from the Gaza skyline, in contrast with the orange sky. Air strikes pummeling the area in front of us. A few lines of fires burning on a far-off ridge.

After the sun went down, Israeli air strikes lit up the pitch-black sky and flares rained down to mark fresh targets for the Israelis. We knew the Israelis were also conducting raids into Gaza on a near-nightly basis, testing Hamas defenses, gathering intelligence, in some cases recovering bodies of Israelis near the fence.

For many weeks, a kindergarten building at the edge of the hill had remained open, a decision made by the local municipality to give journalists gathered on the hill a place to find protection from incoming fire. Like most buildings in Sderot, it was a giant bomb shelter; it provided us cover many times while under heavy fire. It also had a bathroom, a rare luxury for us, after spending the first several weeks finding a place to go in the woods. Fox had also gotten us an armored van, in case we needed to take cover, and assigned us a personal security detail.

Tonight, however, the air strikes were so big that you could feel the shock waves and the ground quaked. We reported it: this was unlike any of the targeting missions of the preceding weeks. Israel was launching a campaign against Gaza that correspondents later compared to the 2003 American bombing of Baghdad, when the term *shock and awe* came into common parlance.

Our shift was supposed to end shortly. I called New York.

"I'd like to stay up for lives," I told the foreign desk director, meaning live reporting. I hadn't taken a day off since the attack on October 7 and wouldn't for a few more weeks. We were in the middle of a story that seemed, tonight, to be changing before our eyes. I had to keep going.

*   *   *

Defense Minister Gallant was at HaKirya that night, Friday, October 27. He'd slept there nearly every night since the war began, but he wouldn't sleep that night. He'd spent weeks trying to persuade the cabinet that an immediate ground invasion was the best, only realistic option: bring the fight to Hamas, put pressure on the organization, try to free the hostages. They'd been holding massed troops along the border, but at last they'd come around. It was time.

Tonight Gallant would help command ground forces in their most dangerous mission of the war so far: entering the lion's den. Before initiating the operation, he spoke by phone with U.S. secretary of defense Lloyd Austin. "He was with us," Gallant told me later. Now, in the pit, he watched the large screens on which he would monitor his troops' movement across the border and into the strip.

As the most powerful explosions of the war so far lit up the sky, Gallant thought through his invasion strategy, which had been discussed with Prime Minister Netanyahu and the rest of the war cabinet. He had spent years mapping out this plan, hoping he'd never have to use it. The action was fully choreographed—but it would also require decision-making on the fly.

His strategy was based on a simple idea: Hamas could be highly effective when deployed in a hard ring, but it suffered from tactical weakness. As Gallant put it, "very strong in the shell, weak inside." So, with jets and drones clearing a path for the advancing forces, Israel would begin to penetrate Gaza from the north, and eventually from the south. Westward and very close to the sea, Gallant knew that the area was not well protected. From both ends, Israel would approach the Al-Shati refugee camp on the beach in Gaza City. Then, one to three days later, Israeli forces on the eastern side of Gaza would cut westward across the strip.

His goal was to hit the initial Hamas battalions hard and try to destroy what structure they had on the outskirts of Gaza City. The operation to fulfill that goal was finally about to begin.

*   *   *

Meanwhile, as Yonat and I stood on the hill, we wondered what we should say about the obvious increase of intensity in the bombardment. Our bosses had been calling for days to ask when the ground invasion would begin. Everyone could guess; nobody knew; and as a news organization, we had to be prepared.

Yonat reached out to someone in the IDF. All we could get was that this was a raid. It didn't sound like a raid, though.

So as I sent updates on social media and on live TV each hour, we were scrupulous in our reporting. The world was watching and waiting for what would come next, and I selected my words with care.

Social media update. Just want to give you an update here near to the Israel-Gaza border . . . Now, the Israelis have explained what they say is happening tonight. They say they are expanding the raids into Gaza, meaning there will be Israeli troops inside the Gaza Strip conducting operations. This is not, according to the Israeli military, the larger anticipated ground operation. Again, we have to just report what we know here. And this is a very fluid situation. So that's the information that we have.

I also continued reporting live, multiple times an hour. Just as at the beginning of the war, some of the live hits were literally ten times longer than normal. "It's been incredibly difficult for the troops and civilians," I was starting to report, when a huge blast rocked the ground behind me.

"That was a huge air strike," I continued. "They're using this hill to scope out much of the area and also correct their fire. That's how close we are to Gaza, bringing you this story."

With no announcement that the ground invasion would now begin, journalists didn't know exactly when they should be close to Gaza. It was a game of chance and timing. Tonight, as on the morning of October 7, I was one of the only international correspondents providing live updates from this location, and as I sent them out, other outlets picked up my reporting. The *Times of Israel* live blog ran this headline: "Fox News Correspondent Reports on Sounds of Machine Gun Fire Near Gaza."

In another hit, I reported real-time information from inside Gaza, using updates from Nael: the Israelis had cut communication to the strip, a near-complete blackout of phone and internet. But some, like Nael, had international SIM cards that could pick up signals from Israeli or Egyptian towers.

Behind me, large blasts lit up the sky, and users on X posted screenshots of my eyes—how wide they would become after a big explosion. While we work in the field to keep our minds calm, even under fire, it isn't easy. Did it scare you man? one X user wrote. It's cool and natural, but the contrast is funny. He provided before-and-after photos of my face.

"I do want to just give you some new information because my source inside Gaza is texting me as we talk here," I reported. "And I'm just going to read you exactly what he said to me." A loud explosion. Sean, our security team member, had taught me a lot about how to distinguish between the different types of bangs and booms. This time it wasn't an air strike but tank fire. "More tank fire into the northern part of Gaza," I said. "Again, it shows you just how close we are here."

As Nael texted me updates, his tone was notably sad. He grew up in Gaza. He was "Ghazzawi," or "from Gaza," through and through and had spent much of his adult life trying to get the world's attention onto the Palestinian people through storytelling.

"Sound is very big and we're scared," Nael said. "Gaza tonight is alone."

He'd already evacuated farther south, but many hadn't. Some were unable to: they had nowhere to go. Others had special medical needs and it was difficult for them to move. I thought of Nael and the other journalists I know in Gaza.

"We've got to talk about the civilians in Gaza who are innocent bystanders in all of this," I reported. "And they are also terrified tonight. War is such a terrible thing."

*   *   *

As Minister Gallant watched the screens, he saw live feeds of the soldiers moving into Gaza. The Israelis had launched limited raids into Gaza before, to gather intelligence and recover bodies along the border—but this was different. A convoy, kilometers long, was entering the strip from the north.

His troops were in Hamas-controlled territory. They wouldn't be returning for months.

*   *   *

On the hill, there was now no question about what was going on. We heard machine-gun fire battering the air. We saw tracer fire in the distance. We heard asphalt crunching beneath the treads of armored personnel carriers (APCs) driving on the road.

This was it: Phase Two, underway. Nearly three weeks after the massacre, the ground invasion had begun. We would have to do whatever we could to get inside the strip and report on the effects.

13

IN THE HEART OF
THE BATTLE

That night, with Israel's ground invasion of Gaza underway, Raed Mousa, from his house in Rafah, made contact with neighbors in Gaza City who still hadn't left. He had a sister-in-law who had lost her entire extended family in a bombardment. One of his coworkers had lost fifteen family members.

Staying in Rafah wasn't easy either. Around seventy people—nearly all of Raed's extended relatives in Gaza—were living there with him and his wife and kids. The nights were very cold. If you stepped outside, you risked losing your life to a bomb—you had to use the darkness and move fast—and it was hard to sleep amid explosions that might destroy your house and kill your family.

One day, Raed's daughter Danya was in the bath on the third floor when a strike targeted an area right next to the house. On the ground floor with other men, he bolted for the third floor as shrapnel came through the window and almost hit her. With all the women and children screaming, he hugged her and checked for injuries. She was okay—but in that strike, fifteen civilians near their home were killed.

A few minutes earlier, Raed had been checking the water tanks. If he'd still been there, he might have been killed.

So even before the ground war really got underway, Raed had become desperate to get his family out of Gaza. He was working on the O-1 Visa that might get him to the United States—it admits people with extraordinary capacities in medicine, science, arts, athletics, etc. He was planning a new life for his family.

The Egyptians were accepting bribes to get people out. Raed was willing to pay, if he couldn't find another way. Whatever it took.

*　　*　　*

"This is the front line of a ground war between Israel and Gaza," I reported the night of the twenty-seventh as the armored personnel carriers rolled into Gaza and the invasion began. "It will be a bloody urban battle as these Israeli troops enter.

"And even if this is contained tonight to an extended raid inside the Gaza Strip, we are talking about these Israeli troops being immediately engaged. They will not simply roll into Gaza with tanks and APCs. They will face a fierce resistance from factions inside the strip, including Hamas and Islamic Jihad."

Israel would call Phase Two "an expanded raid" into Gaza. In fact it was an invasion, *the invasion*, and we were near the front lines.

Inside Gaza, the night was full of shock and terror. The air strikes, focused on Gaza City and surrounding areas, provided cover for advancing ground forces, who entered from the north and later the east. I tried to establish contact with sources. Sireen and her ten-year-old son, Aden, the Americans stuck in Gaza, were in Khan Younis. Farther north in Deir-Al-Balah, Nael was closer to the bombardment.

In Gaza City, Dr. Abu Warda was still at al-Shifa hospital, still treating incoming patients, as he had been since October 7. "The bombing started all along Gaza," he told me later. "We had a lot of wounded."

As I texted with Nael, I could tell he was concerned. There was an understanding that this night was different. The amount of airpower against Gaza was unlike other nights. I pressed him for information.

He was one of few Palestinians with a connection to the outside world tonight. I was one of the few journalists with a large audience to convey his information to.

What's the feeling tonight inside Gaza? How is it different from other nights? I asked him.

For sure everybody is worried now, it looks some wrong will happen. Especially since they cut the cell phone. Maybe Israel this night will do something big against Shifa hospital, Nael said.

I told him to stay as safe as possible. What else are you supposed to tell someone who is on the receiving end of such fire? How can you reassure your friend that it will be okay?

Just text me if they start the ground operation and from which sides they will enter, Nael said.

* * *

On October 29, two days after the ground invasion began, I was in touch with a good friend of mine, Alex Plitsas, who was trying to get foreign aid workers out of Gaza. During the withdrawal from Afghanistan, Alex had played a critical role in getting vulnerable Afghans out of harm's way once the Taliban took over. I knew he could provide real insight into the situation and conditions that people were facing in Gaza.

Alex: "Still have all those people trapped on the compound in southern Gaza."

"Basically fifty foreign NGO and UN workers."

"Conditions they're describing are absurd."

Trey: "What's it like?"

"They're in Rafah?"

Alex: "They are saying that they are down to emergency water supplies. Their water is turned off. When it was on, it was dirty anyway. Viruses and typical diseases that happen from stagnant water are settling in. A lot of people, vomiting and gastrointestinal issues. They're out of medicines and so they're treating burns with iodine and saline. No post wound care available, out of antibiotics. . . . They thought there was still flour and stuff in the warehouse but it's empty."

Trey: "They're mostly foreign citizens? . . . just waiting to get approval to cross via Rafah?"

Alex: "Yes."

*　　*　　*

More than three weeks into the war, our days were long. The interest among the American audience remained high, and Fox continued to lead the coverage across the industry. Coffee, made by Yoav in a small pot on a gas flame, and cigarettes fueled our days.

Israel had its sights set on Gaza City. The initial push into the strip involved thousands of infantry troops and special forces, supported by the Israeli Air Force, artillery units along the border, and the navy. During the day we watched Israeli tanks move along the border. At night, air strikes illuminated the sky. Taking significant losses, Israel faced resistance from Hamas gunmen ambushing the advancing forces. The last day of October saw fifteen Israeli soldiers killed—the deadliest day for the army since October 7.

In 2014 and 2019, I'd seen war from inside Gaza. In 2021, I'd been among the first journalists to enter the strip after a cease-fire was declared and had met a young Palestinian girl named Nana, from the city of Khan Younis, whose home was totally destroyed.

But her fish survived. That story stayed with me. More than 2 million civilians live in Gaza, things are destroyed around them, and it's a matter of luck as to what or who is left standing and alive.

I thought about Nana and the other innocent Palestinians who have been and will be affected by this war. I also remembered a young Israeli boy we met in May 2023, during that round of conflict between Israel and Gaza. Looking for his ball during a rocket attack, he got caught outside as the sirens sounded. Yonat took him, confused and terrified, to a bomb shelter.

Awareness of the pain on both sides doesn't undermine a reporter's objectivity; quite the contrary. Empathy is necessary to providing clear and objective coverage of conflict. You have to report on the hostages being held in Gaza. You have to report on the al-Shifa hospital patients who can't get anesthesia. On the Palestinian civilians who are digging through rubble looking for their children. On the Israeli families who wish to have funerals for their children but have nothing left to bury.

This will always be a challenging story to cover. Hamas hides among the civilian population, and according to recent polls, it has the support of the majority of Gazan people. How do you square that? And the Israeli response did not protect civilians to the extent that it could have, and, as Prime Minister Netanyahu admitted, it did not successfully reduce civilian casualties. The degree of death and destruction was, objectively, very unbalanced. When asked about that issue, many Israeli officials pointed to the hostages still being held inside Gaza, but we knew it wasn't just the hostages. It's a long-standing Israeli equation: the lives and protection of Israeli soldiers with an objective in Gaza is more important than the civilian Palestinian lives that would be affected.

As one official reminded me, "Israel didn't start this war." And as Palestinian officials have reminded me, Palestinians lived under occupation and blockade for decades before October 7.

*   *   *

In past conflicts with Gaza, Israel had allowed foreign journalists to cross the border independently and report on events and conditions inside the strip. This time was different. Israel had been attacked like never before, and it responded like never before. Publicly and privately, officials asserted that journalists would not be permitted to enter Gaza. I disagree with this notion and believe that full and unlimited access to Gaza should be provided to reporters to cover the realities of war in the enclave. I also found the denial of independent access immensely frustrating personally. I'd spent the past nine years following developments out of the Palestinian territory. In 2014, I'd been the youngest journalist to enter Gaza during the war of that year. Since joining Fox News in 2018, I'd been reporting from the Gaza Media Center in Gaza City.

Now the only way into the strip would be with an army escort. And embeds like that were few and far between. We waited for weeks after October 7 to enter Gaza.

Finally, early on November 3, the call came. A group of three Israeli journalists would be given access to enter Gaza, plus one American outlet: Fox.

"So we've got a last-minute opportunity to go into Gaza with the Israeli military," I told Greg Headen on the phone. It was the middle of the night his time. He asked a lot of questions—and ultimately decided against it. With the sheer number of explosions and the intensity of the fighting going on inside, it was objectively dangerous to operate in that environment.

I tried again via text, once I got more info: "It would be a military embed with the northern division commander in an area where thousands of Israeli troops are controlling the territory and operating. Going in and out. We would be the only international outlet going. I understand if the answer is still no."

"Understood," Headen replied. "Must say no on this one at this stage in ground war. I am reminded what Jay tells me, we have zero margin for error. Sorry, Trey. You'll get in at another point I am sure."

I was disappointed but trusted Headen's judgment. He's never led me down the wrong path and always has my best interests in mind.

Later that day, however, after the Israeli journalists came out unharmed, the military called again about another opportunity, to take place the next morning. This time, CNN and Sky would be going too. I called my best friend, Fin Gomez, the political director at CBS News. He used to work under Headen.

"If you were me, how would you pitch this?"

"Look, man, you know Headen. He's a news guy."

"I know, I know, but I need this embed," I told Fin.

"Give him the info, tell him who is going. You'll get in there," Fin said.

So that's what I did. The situation was no safer—but there was still a rare news angle in play, and on this one we'd have company. Yes, competitors, in a sense, but we're colleagues too, and you feel better sometimes among your own kind. I'd also be able to take our security, Sean.

Headen responded right away. "Do it."

*   *   *

Ron Gabayan, a reservist from the IDF spokespersons unit, gave me the directions. I'd known Ron for years. He was the spokesman who had set up an October 2020 story that we'd done about the completion of the barrier between Israel and Gaza.

Ron said we would need to sign extensive waivers, which basically said that if we were injured or died on the embed, Israel wouldn't be held responsible. We also had to agree to run our footage by the Israeli military censor, a restriction that remains controversial in journalism. I've always held a firm belief on it: I will not budge an inch editorially, but if a legitimate security issue is caused by showing something specific, like an image caught by a screen in an APC, then we can blur it; the same goes for the faces of special forces, who need to remain anonymous. That can be done ethically and transparently.

Plus, I had a plan to get the video to air without having to send raw clips to the censor.

Ron said we'd be given access to an Israeli position south of Gaza City. I sent him my passport—and Sean's. On this embed, like all of them except one where I was able to take two crew members, I chose to take Sean instead of a cameraman. While this was not ideal from a journalism perspective, I made the choice out of respect for my bosses, knowing they would feel more comfortable if I traveled with security.

After two of our colleagues were killed by the Russians in Ukraine, and another seriously injured, I was hyperaware of security risks. Sean was also willing to help wherever needed. When he joined my team, he knew how to shoot RPGs and anti-tank missiles—not video—but he'd picked up the skill quickly. He ended up shooting much of my video inside Gaza.

In addition to the embed documents, I received instructions. "At 11 a.m. tomorrow, at the entrance to the Be'eri community," Ron told me, "you can join Deputy Commander of the 828th Brigade, Lt. Col. Gilad Pasternak," and he included a long bio of Pasternak. Point of contact: Major Nir Dinar.

Weeks before, we'd been at Kibbutz Be'eri, covering the aftermath of the massacre. Now the entrance to Be'eri was to be our launch point for covering Israel's taking the fight into Gaza.

*   *   *

Having set up the embed for the next day, we spent the rest of the day reporting from Sderot. With my old D.C. friend Jeremy Diamond, recently arrived to fill the CNN job, I crammed into the back of the CNN crew car and watched a speech by Hassan Nasrallah, the leader of Hezbollah, broadcast live on Al Jazeera English. Nasrallah described the October 7 massacre as "heroic" and gave a lengthy address about the current situation. There was still daily fire coming from the north; we had to keep an eye on that front. On any day it could escalate to a broader conflict. We needed to stay up to date.

That morning, U.S. secretary of state Antony Blinken had arrived back in Israel for a fourth visit since the massacre. The United States was doing whatever it could to get both tangible and intangible support to its key Middle East partner. The Pentagon had even announced that American drones were flying over Gaza to assist the Israelis with gathering intelligence about the hostages. Now, with the rapidly rising civilian casualty rate in Gaza, coupled with a need for aid among Palestinian civilians, Blinken was meeting with Netanyahu to start exerting pressure on the Israeli leader.

But the secretary also wanted to make clear in his remarks that the United States stood behind Israel and its right to defend itself.

"No country could or should tolerate the slaughter of innocents," Blinken said at a Tel Aviv press conference. "Today we saw additional images, additional footage collected by the Israeli government from video cameras."

He described the killing he saw in the videos. America's top diplomat, clearly affected by the images, spoke with pain in his voice. And less than a month after the massacre, Blinken, like the rest of the world, was still being exposed to new atrocities as evidence was uncovered, gathered, and presented. He laid out a step-by-step plan for what he said would ensure a better future for the people of the Middle East.

First, we need to continue to prevent escalation of this conflict, its spread to other areas and other theaters.

Second, we need to do more to protect Palestinian civilians.

Third, we need to substantially and immediately increase the sustained flow of humanitarian assistance into Gaza, and getting American citizens and other foreign nationals out of Gaza.

Blinken ended his remarks by reiterating the position of the Biden administration: that peace and security can be achieved only through a two-state solution—something the Israeli government and most of the Israeli people disagreed with. Their wounds, and the wounds of Palestinians, were still fresh. Israeli officials told us privately that this wasn't the time to talk about a Palestinian state. They saw such discussion as rewarding terrorism.

The secretary's comments that Friday about peace were made as Hamas was firing rockets at central and southern Israel, and while the Israelis were striking and invading Gaza.

*   *   *

Later that night, both Jeremy and I continued dueling live shots along the border, stopping only for cigarettes and coffee. When rockets or mortars are fired into Sderot, you have ten seconds or less to react and get to safety. And for much of the war, sirens were a multiday occurrence. But this particular day, the day before my scheduled Gaza embed, stands out because of how close to total disaster we came.

I was looking out into Gaza at the city of Beit Hanoun on the same hill we'd been reporting from, preparing to go live on Fox in a few minutes. A group of twenty or more journalists was reporting at the location as well, spread along a ridge. I'd just been talking to Jeremy and his cameraman Matthias Somm, from CNN, who were set up next to our position, when suddenly the usual sirens sounded: "Tzeva Adom, Tzeva Adom."

"Let's go!" I shouted. I sprinted for the armored van, along with my team and the CNN crew. Jeremy and I had just gotten inside when a loud whistle preceded a big explosion, shaking the ground. Matthias was still outside filming on his phone; he captured the rocket impact a couple hundred feet from us. Karl, CNN's security, also still outside, yelled at him: "Get in the fucking bus!"

Other journalists hadn't gotten under cover. The rocket had clearly hit the area where everyone was standing. Sean and Karl jumped out of the van and ran to see if anyone was injured or killed. We all feared the worst.

I grabbed Yaniv and Yoav. We carried the camera gear, trying to keep the shot up and get over to the impact area.

Miraculously, no one was killed or even injured. When the rocket came in, journalists hit the deck, dived into the dirt, or ran to shelter. The impact point was ten feet from where we had set up for so many days, before moving down the ridge to get another angle into Gaza. The rocket sprayed the outside of the school with shrapnel, cutting through the metal fence and cracking a few windows. Sean told me later, "I was sure I was going to find bodies all over." Again, an instance of random timing saving our lives.

Within a minute we were live on TV. I tried to catch my breath under the weight of the flak jacket. I shouted, "Take us now!" as they were tossing to us. The adrenaline was high. Luckily, this vest, a black plate carrier that Sean had sourced for me, wasn't as heavy as my last standard-issue blue one with neck protection, so I was able to speak well.

"Let's go to Trey Yingst," Emily Compagno said.

Over the commotion of journalists and a car alarm beeping, I started to report: "A rocket just slammed into the building right next to where we're at."

It was my first time seeing this scene, so I also had to make sense of what happened and report it in real time. This pacing and multitasking can be challenging under pressure. The windows of some of the media cars were blown out. Others had pieces of shrapnel that went through them like a knife through butter. Some journalists were in their cars, so again it was just by chance that no one died. Firefighters, soldiers, and police officers quickly showed up and got rid of the rocket. The live report was for Fox's *Outnumbered* and lasted for more than ten minutes.

*   *   *

As Ron had said, our embed on November 4 would be with thirty-eight-year-old Lieutenant Colonel Gilad Pasternak, a deputy commander of the 828th Infantry Brigade of IDF Division 36, an experienced warrior, wounded during the war in 2014. It was Gilad who, on October 7, had traveled through destruction from his base at Camp Har Tsavua to organize his brigades in Kissufim and Shufa. Since then, he'd led soldiers in battle as they went after Hamas.

At the entrance of Be'eri, Pasternak spoke with our group before we entered Gaza. I looked into the distance and flashed back to the pile of dead militants we'd seen here weeks before.

The other journalists going in were Deborah Haynes, the defense editor from Sky News, and Jeremy. He and I quickly agreed to help each

other shoot stand-ups and even split shooting b-roll, if needed, sharing the work of getting our stories out. In these tense environments, far less competition among journalists prevails than labels on a TV screen or rankings in ratings might suggest. And with Jeremy, as I've said, I felt none at all.

"It's not going to be comfortable," Pasternak warned us. We'd be crammed into an APC on bumpy paths. It would be very hot. We might die.

Other than that, everything should be just fine.

"What's the level of engagement been on this first road?" I asked.

"First of all, going inside, we don't have certainty for nothing." Pasternak wanted to be clear that we were entering an unpredictable battlefield. Threats could come from any direction; there was real, if calculated, risk involved. "We wouldn't get you inside unless we had a high level of stability and confidence that it's going to be okay."

Deborah asked him what we should do if we take contact—military for "get fired on." Stay inside the APC, Pasternak replied: it's bullet-proof.

I wasn't worried so much about bullets. I doubt any of us were. At the Emanuel base in southern Israel, I'd gotten a look at Hamas weapons that the Israelis had recovered in the south: an arsenal of improvised explosive devices (IED), armor-piercing RPGs, hand grenades, and small arms, some manufactured in Gaza, where I was told explosive factories operate around the clock. And from videos of Hamas and Islamic Jihad battles that week, it was clear they'd killed many Israelis using anti-tank guided missiles and RPGs. One incident in northern Gaza left eight Israelis dead.

"Don't watch that stuff," Sean had told me before the embed. Having worked with rocket systems, he knew exactly the threat we faced; he had briefed me on the trophy protection system, an advanced active protection system that created an invisible shield around the vehicle. The risk is there, he indicated. But that's what we signed up for.

Sean also looked ready to take over the command and engage Hamas

in battle, if it came to that. Sometimes even more than ready—eager. He is a warrior at heart, the type of guy you feel safe with whether in battle or on the streets.

On the twenty-minute drive into the strip, I could tell that some of the soldiers were just as worried as I was. One strike and we were all dead.

Jeremy wasn't all that worried. He chalked it up to my having more combat experience: I'd seen what happens to an APC when it takes a direct hit. Reporting on the front lines of Ukraine, we'd come across many charred remains.

In the back of the APC, Jeremy and I fumbled with SD cards, the memory cards his camera uses, trying to fix the camera he'd been sent into Gaza with. Eventually I changed the setting on his camera and gave him a spare SD card I had in my DSLR photography camera. After years of shooting my own material, I knew my way around.

The APC was so loud, it was hard to think; I didn't put in ear protection because I wanted to be able to follow instructions if we got hit. After that nighttime raid in Tulkarem in September, and reporting with no ear protection in a firefight, the hearing in my right ear still wasn't the same, but I could remember the confusion of not being able to follow commands, and when seconds could make all the difference, I simply didn't like it.

As the APC rolled forward, the crew stopped often to scan the horizon for threats while we watched on the APC's monitor.

The moment we crossed into Gaza, there was a shift in energy. Every juncture, pile, and heap was now a potential trap, a hiding spot for an IED, a tunnel entrance.

* * *

Seconds after we stepped out of the APC at our destination, two bullets whizzed by, and Lieutenant Colonel Pasternak froze mid-sentence.

"Ours?" he asked a nearby soldier. The concern was visible on his face.

Up a mound of dirt and past scattered debris, we met a group of soldiers from Battalion 450: infantry troops, young, eager soldiers who were surprisingly jovial for being in the middle of a gun battle with Hamas. They sat and ate cans of tuna and corn, their rations for the afternoon.

Inside a building, Pasternak introduced us to the battalion commander who was in charge of the sector, Lieutenant Colonel Ron. We were only given his first name. Around him, soldiers rested and talked. Some slept; others read books. This was the zero line, yet they were calm.

"What's happening today?" Deborah asked.

Over bursts of gunfire, Ron said, "Today we go to search a tunnel in the east section over there. We find two tunnels and now we're going to destroy them."

"And what's the gunfire?" Deborah asked.

"We saw some suspects outside."

"How about those booms we just heard. What was that?" I asked.

"Let's go up and we'll explain everything," Pasternak said.

Up a flight of stairs, we reached the rooftop of a building in the Juhor Ad Dik neighborhood, southeast of Gaza City, less than a mile from the border. The neighborhood is just off to the main Salah al-Din Road, running north to south in Gaza. Some of the October 7 attackers launched from here. It's one of the Palestinian areas closest to Israel.

We heard heavy bursts of gunfire and peered over a wall on the edge of the roof. Israeli troops held positions on all sides of the building across the street, engaged in a gun battle with Hamas militants who continued to pop out of the network of tunnels, under Gaza, trying to surprise them. The entrances to these tunnels are hidden all over the place: in civilian houses, in yards, behind sheds. From our vantage point, we couldn't see any of the entrances, not surprisingly, given how they're made. We also couldn't see the Hamas fighters who were firing at the Israelis, but we knew they were there as the bullets whizzed overhead. We stayed low much of the time, trying to avoid the gunfire, doing pieces to camera to include in our reports.

This firefight was characteristic of what Israeli troops were facing inside Gaza: dense, urban warfare in concrete buildings, where it's hard to know where the enemy is hiding and even harder to kill them. The landscape was littered with the remains of structures destroyed by Israeli air strikes.

In the distance: Gaza City, a few plumes of black smoke rising from the skyline.

Loud cracks pierced the air and Jeremy jumped. "Keep your head down," I said under my breath.

"The guys are very much prepared," Pasternak said. "So everything that's moving is suspect. We must say all civilians here are not living here anymore. All of them had brochures from the IDF which told them to go to the south."

He pointed to a golf cart on the side of the house that Hamas had taken on October 7 from a kibbutz just over the border, and to an Israeli flag on a building across the way. The golf cart told the soldiers that the men they were battling had participated in the massacre. This was personal.

Amid bursts of fire, I walked over to a tall blond soldier I'd heard speak English and introduced myself. "Where are you from?" I asked.

"Philadelphia."

"I'm from Harrisburg."

"Ah, no way," he replied, amid another burst of fire. He introduced himself: Jeremiah. He was in the process of making aliyah: the process by which Jewish foreigners move to Israel and become citizens. Some do it for nationalistic reasons, others for religious reasons.

On the roof, I also interviewed Pasternak. Unlike so many of the troops fighting in Gaza, he is not a reservist. This is his full-time job, and long before October 7, he was devoting his life to the cause of protecting Israel.

"This compound was actually one of the compounds built by Hamas," he explained, "inside the population, in order to make front bases, toward Israel. We've seen tunnels here, we've seen mortars here, we've seen missiles here.

"Once we got here, we've had clashes with anti-tank missiles, short-range and long-range. We've seen a lot of sabotage, a lot of booby traps inside houses. We've seen a lot of military infrastructure. And we've seen three tunnels with hundreds of openings all over the neighborhood.

"And we are here to destroy all the infrastructures. You won't be able to do it again in the next war."

"And in one sentence," I asked, "what comes next?"

"The destruction of Hamas."

*   *   *

In the APC riding back to the border, I was counting down the seconds in my head. We crossed into Israeli territory, and I kept counting. I knew we'd be in the clear only when there was some distance between us and the border.

For the drive back to the staging area, I hopped into the front seat of Lieutenant Colonel Pasternak's jeep. Jeremy, Sean, and Deborah sat in the back. I wanted to keep him talking, to get more insight into the mood of the battle and the reality on the ground. The trouble with military embeds is that you are at the mercy of where the army wants to take you and what they want to show you. We needed more information on how the fight against Hamas was actually going.

As we rode, he made his feelings crystal clear. "This is my third war as a soldier," he said, "but this one is at least justified. . . . People won't stop mourning even two years from now. . . . I think the equivalent in America is thirty-six thousand people." He was applying the per capita formula to the Israeli death toll he was working with. The real number is closer to 50,000.

Jeremy asked him, "Do you think commanders and Bibi and every-one is willing to go into Gaza City and clear out Hamas fully?"

"I don't think they have a choice. . . . Yesterday, one of my officers died from a sniper inside. . . . I wasn't able to go to the funeral, so my wife spoke on behalf of me. . . . I'm in charge of five battalions."

The guys we'd just seen were Battalion 450 of the 828th Infantry Brigade. That battalion had lost seven soldiers, the brigade ten. Pasternak told us that those numbers were better than expected: "I think the chief of staff expected much more."

Still, Hamas had by no means been placed fully on the defensive. "This morning," he told us, "two terrorists from the unit that committed the massacre were trying to go through the fence and get into the kibbutzim. This morning!"

"And where was that?" I asked.

"Next to where you got inside."

We processed that.

"I'm glad you told us now!" Deborah said.

14

FRONT OFFICE OR
FRONT LINE?

INSIDE GAZA CITY'S SHIFA HOSPITAL

With Lieutenant Colonel Gilad Pasternak's brigades and many others now on the ground inside Gaza, taking on militants in exchanges of intense fire, the highly anticipated ground war was well underway. Each day, the Institute for the Study of War released maps and research that helped us get a sense of where things stood with the operation. Their updated map showed that Israel had successfully cut the Gaza Strip in half just south of Gaza City—Minister Gallant's strategy—and was now conducting limited operations in the streets of that major population center. Within days of the ground invasion's launch, Israeli forces had achieved the goal of fighting their way to the Mediterranean, though they were still taking contact from Hamas along that line of engagement. They'd also fought their way into the northernmost part of the strip, where clearing operations were underway.

Meanwhile, much of Gaza was still being leveled by air bombardment. Hundreds of bombs were dropped each day, in addition to shelling by navy ships along the coast and artillery units along the border. This attack on all fronts was effectively sustained, causing widespread destruction across Gaza. By mid-November, 40 to 50 percent of buildings in northern Gaza were damaged or destroyed, according to research conducted by university professors Corey Scher and Jamon Van Den Hoek, who used satellite images to assess the damage to Gaza.

International sympathy for Israel in the wake of October 7 was also starting to fade, as images from inside Gaza showed the horror of war up close. Brave Gazan journalists risked their lives to get those images out to the world. According to the Committee to Protect Journalists, more than one hundred of them were killed.

The simple fact was that Israel was quickly losing international support for its war efforts. Israeli officials publicly said there was no "proportional" response to the massacre. They pointed to October 7 and explained that in their view, this battle was for the future of Israel—for the very existence of their state. But outside observers felt differently.

"What is the justification for killing more than twelve thousand Palestinians?" some asked. "Why are hospitals being raided?" others wondered. The numbers were complicated and difficult to independently confirm, not to mention that the Hamas-run Palestinian Ministry of Health didn't distinguish between militants and civilians. Still thousands of innocent civilians were dead already. Anyone who claimed to know specifics was lying. The battlefield was too chaotic to accurately count and identify all the dead. So precisely how many civilians had lost their lives so far?

Some questions couldn't be answered.

*   *   *

As a war correspondent, I rarely get scared. Something about being inside Gaza was different, though. Once inside, there was no turning back.

I'd met the Al-Qassam Brigades of Hamas. These were devout men who were not afraid of death. They have thousands of RPGs and small arms, in addition to more advanced anti-tank guided missiles. They're the type of fighters you really don't want to go up against. For them, dying in battle is the goal. It's honorable to die a *shahid*, or a martyr to the Islamic faith. "Resistance" to what Palestinians see as an occupying power is considered a legitimate, even glorious way to die.

The first time I really felt a cold sense of fear was when I got the news I'd been eagerly awaiting: my second embed, this time deep into Gaza City. On November 13, we learned that CNN had been taken by the Israeli army on an embed to the al-Rantisi children's hospital in Gaza. The army hadn't invited us—and this would be CNN's third embed of the war. We were pissed.

Yonat messaged Lieutenant Colonel Richard Hecht to express our frustration. We'd been tough on the IDF since the start of the war—but also fair. And we had a long relationship with Richard, who, two weeks before the war started, had given us that first foreign embed of a West Bank raid in nearly a decade.

Richard apologized. He said he'd been off when the CNN story got approved. It seemed that Admiral Hagari, Richard's boss and the top spokesman for the military, had put the embed together and left us out. As a consolation, the IDF now offered us a joint embed, the next day, shared with NBC's Raf Sanchez and Sky's Mark Stone, to observe the evacuations of civilians from Gaza City.

We accepted. I was very interested in filming the evacuation corridors and to see Palestinian civilians, even from a distance. Evacuation was a critical part of the story, and it was going largely underreported. Amid the thousands of civilians who were dying, hundreds of thousands were being displaced by the Israeli campaign, innocent people whose lives were uprooted. Aside from my one embed with Pasternak where we were taken to one specific neighborhood and saw only soldiers, I'd been limited to short updates from old friends like Nael. I didn't feel I could do enough from afar to shine light into this very dark place.

The evening before this embed, Raf, from NBC, set up a group chat for him, me, and Mark from Sky. We agreed to pool footage, and Raf would bring his cameraman—the kind of gentlemen's agreement not uncommon in environments like this.

Right before I planned to go to sleep, I got a text from a senior Hamas official. He had news.

In a few minutes, the hospital [al-Shifa, in Gaza City] will be stormed, according to the Israeli occupation's official notification, he texted. Which means a new massacre against patients, casualties, displaced people and medical staff.

"We will report on this development," I replied.

"Please do this urgently," the source added. "To prevent a massacre."

Al-Shifa is Gaza's largest hospital. Originally a British Army barracks, it became a hospital in 1946; the Israelis expanded it starting in the 1980s. I'd reported from Shifa many times, including during the war in 2014, when I waited outside with my DSLR camera at age twenty, filming wounded civilians as they were taken into the hospital for treatment. In 2019, I stood at the gates of the main building as injured and dead Islamic Jihad members were dragged into the emergency room after being hit by Israeli strikes. That time, I was the only international journalist in Gaza after being trapped there when an unexpected war erupted.

Since the outbreak of this war, Israel had spent weeks releasing diagrams of the hospital and Hamas's alleged tunnel network beneath it. That had led to weeks of speculation that Shifa would be targeted, that there might be a days- or weekslong raid.

Now they were actually going to do it.

*   *   *

In his days, now weeks, at al-Shifa hospital, Dr. Abu Warda had gone on treating the wounded hour after hour. With the bombardments, the flood of patients had changed: civilians were now being brought in with wounds from explosives. Thanks to Israel's siege of the strip, the hospital quickly ran low on anesthesia drugs, oxygen, and fuel, though the tide of patients only rose. Doctors, nurses, and other staff were trying to care not just for the host of injured patients but also an entire neonatal intensive care unit, or NICU, full of more than thirty tiny Gazans, recently born. Without power to run the incubators, blankets and aluminum foil kept the babies warm. In this medical catastrophe, images of babies' little bodies and faces, dramatizing the innocence of Gaza's most vulnerable residents, spread around the world.

The Israeli military said it tried to deliver around eighty gallons of fuel to the hospital—enough to fill around four pickup trucks. The IDF said Hamas blocked the delivery. Hamas denied the claim. With the number of dead rising, the hospital morgue didn't have the fuel to stay up and running; without refrigeration, the bodies would rot. Hospital authorities said they buried dozens of people in a mass grave on the grounds.

Then, early in November, the Israeli military sent word to the directors of al-Shifa to evacuate the hospital.

The nurses and doctors, still working desperately and unceasingly to save lives under impossible conditions, didn't want to leave and had nowhere to move all their patients. The United Nations—citing the Hamas-controlled Palestinian Ministry of Health—said that in the face of the order to evacuate, more than six hundred patients remained at the hospital, with hundreds of medical staff, numbers impossible to independently confirm in real time. Doctors Without Borders reported that Israeli snipers were targeting people stepping out of the hospital into the street.

That organization also released a statement on its website:

"The situation in al-Shifa is truly catastrophic. We call on the Israeli Government to cease this unrelenting assault on Gaza's health system. Our staff and patients are inside Al-Shifa hospital where the heavy bombing has not stopped since yesterday." Posted to Doctors Without Borders' X page was a photo of a surgical scheduling board (actually from another hospital in Gaza) on which was written, in green marker: "Whoever stays until the end, will tell the story we did what we could. Remember us."

On November 14, the IDF announced that on the thirteenth, they sent this message to a senior Palestinian health official:

"As we have shown and warned in the past weeks, the IDF has credible intelligence proving that Hamas continues to use the Shifa hospital for military purposes.

"We demand that all military activities within the hospital cease immediately. If Hamas will not do so within 12 hours, Israel will be within its rights under international law to counter these activities."

The fact that the IDF released this statement to the public revealed an intention to take further military action against the hospital. My team and I, along with other journalists, had already been shown that the computer-generated infographic that, according to Rear Admiral Hagari, proved Hamas was maintaining a maze of tunnels and rooms underneath Shifa hospital—that the facility was in fact a command-and-control center.

I'd found the evidence objectively insufficient and had declined to report the claim as fact. U.S. officials, though, leaked it to media outlets. They would also later make clear that they hadn't given Israel any "go-ahead" for conducting an attack on the hospital.

Dr. Abu Warda, having refused to evacuate, had begun to hear frequent shooting outside the hospital—IDF and Hamas in battle—plus heavy bombing in the vicinity. Then, around 2 a.m. on Wednesday, November 15, the Israelis released this statement:

"Based on intelligence information and an operational necessity, IDF forces are carrying out a precise and targeted operation against Hamas in a specified area in the Shifa hospital."

My source in Hamas was right. He was tipped off and then tipped me off.

At the hospital that night, Dr. Abu Warda found that no new wounded patients were coming in. Ambulances couldn't get through. As IDF gunfire drew ever closer, he found himself terribly frightened, and he could sense that everyone in the hospital was too.

Then the IDF entered the hospital.

Later that night, the Israelis released a new statement: "The IDF forces include medical teams and Arabic speakers, who have undergone specified training to prepare for this complex and sensitive environment, with the intent that no harm is caused to the civilians being used by Hamas as human shields."

The IDF claims that the hospital directors asked for a safe route out of the facility, which the military facilitated. Dr. Abu Warda says that three days after entering, the IDF simply ordered everyone to evacuate Shifa.

He moved to al-Ma'madani hospital, also in Gaza City, and continued to treat the wounded.

*   *   *

Wednesday morning, November 15, as Yonat, Yaniv, Yoav, Sean, and I drove in our armored van to a meeting point at Sa'ad junction next to Kfar Aza, Yonat was working the phones. We had the embed scheduled to see the evacuations, and I was ready to go, but Yonat had gotten a call from Keren Hajioff, a longtime contact of ours—the former spokesperson for then–prime minister Naftali Bennett and the friend of my reservist friend Ariel Bernstein. Keren tipped Yonat off that a Shifa hospital embed might be in the works.

The raid had started overnight. The military was considering taking a journalist or two to see what they'd found at the hospital.

Yonat got on the phone with Richard Hecht. After some back-and-forth calls, he offered us a *chance* at the Shifa embed—which meant I had to skip the embed we were headed to, and then just wait, with only a 65 percent chance, Richard said, of going to the hospital. "It'll be far more dangerous," Richard also warned Yonat.

"Give me the phone," I said, then: "Hey, Richard, What's up? What's your sense, how likely is this?"

"Like I said, sixty-five percent, Trey. It's your decision."

I thought for a moment.

"We'll do it."

This embed would be me, Sean, and Yaniv, the cameraman. We sat for a long time on the side of the road at the meeting spot, waiting to see if the embed was a go. We drank mint tea from a local who had set up a café for soldiers. We didn't know what we'd see at al-Shifa: an evacuation of civilians, aid deliveries, weapons, destruction? We didn't know if we'd see anything: the whole embed was up in the air.

And as we waited, and as the hours ticked by, I thought for sure they were going to cancel the opportunity. Soon it was going to get dark. There were too many risks and too many unknowns.

But Sean explained that it would actually be safer to go in at night. He had years of close-combat experience from Afghanistan; I trusted his judgment.

Another issue was convincing the bosses in New York to say yes to an uncertain assignment. I conveyed what information we had to Fox News' Foreign Desk and my bosses in New York, who approved our going on the embed. I told the Foreign Desk to stay in touch with Yonat in case we became unreachable.

We were still drinking tea when Major Liad Diamond from the IDF public diplomacy unit drove by and pulled over.

"Rambo!" That's what I called him. We chatted, and he said, "Conricus is inside. If you get the embed, it'll be with him."

This was good. Jonathan Conricus is the former international spokesman and someone I'd known for years; we'd stayed in distant touch.

But by the time it got dark, we had waited more than five hours. Mentally I was checked out. I accepted the loss of the day. We'd taken a gamble and it didn't pay off. Then the phone rang.

"Yallah, it's happening," Yonat said.

I felt cold and adrenaline surge through me. I'm not sure what it was about this assignment, but I had a bad feeling. I was nervous—scared.

I texted my dad: Will be off the grid for a while. Yonat is available. I didn't want him to be worried when I didn't respond for the next few hours.

Sean, Yaniv, and I arrived at the gathering point at Be'eri. There we met Jonathan and got a briefing, along with a BBC crew also on the embed. He described how Israeli special forces had initially entered the hospital complex on foot and were engaged in a gun battle. He then showed us bags of "intelligence" that included laptops and notebooks that he claimed contained information about the hostages. We couldn't independently verify the information but recorded a brief interview and flipped through the material.

Then we got our security briefing. Going in, we would be taking a new APC called the "Eitan." I felt good about this. This huge, eight-wheeled carrier had a trophy anti-missile system and blast protection on the bottom. It was our best chance of survival if we got hit by an RPG or an anti-tank guided missile (ATGM). And the cabin was much more spacious than the APC we'd ridden in during the earlier embeds, the Namer APC, which Israel had made from the chassis of Merkava tanks.

The special forces we were with were very professional. They remained cool and collected as we drove across the strip. We watched on screens as the forces trained guns upward on windows and rooftops, scanning for ATGM positions or militants with RPGs. The infrared technology gave Israel an advantage. At the center of the screen was a purple cross that helped aim the machine gun positioned on top of the vehicle. Every so often the soldiers would stop and assess before moving forward.

It was dark and quiet outside. Destroyed buildings and debris were everywhere. This was a proper nighttime operation. The acceleration of the APC was often the only noise. In the cabin, a blue light illuminated the faces of the soldiers.

I did a selfie video for social media. "Right now we're with the Israeli military, headed to the heart of Gaza City. They've just taken Gaza's Shifa hospital, where the Israelis say they found weapons and information about the hostages being held inside Gaza."

It wasn't until I saw the Mediterranean Sea on the screen that I breathed a small sigh of relief. I knew the army would have a staging area here, with backup if we needed it. And if we reached the sea, we'd be facing threats from only three sides, not four.

As we rode, Jonathan had his eyes closed, dozing in and out of sleep. Between his naps, we chatted a bit. He had a GoPro camera mounted to his helmet that was rolling. He'd been up for the past thirty hours. I knew the feeling.

At the staging point, we jumped out to switch to another APC, an old Merkava tank that had been converted, like many of the Israeli carriers. I looked around trying to figure out where along the coast we were. It was too dark to tell and I couldn't recognize the buildings. We saw dozens of soldiers, tanks, and vehicles.

I tilted my head up toward the night sky. I was struck by how many stars I could see—zero light pollution. It was beautiful. Around a small fire, troops cooked food.

Entering the other APC, we met a new crew. These guys were younger and seemed less experienced. "Now we're going to the real battle," one of them said.

On a wall in red graffiti: "Never Again," with a Star of David. In the middle of the star: "IDF."

The tension was much higher on the way to Shifa. Instead of driving through the suburbs, we drove through the streets of Gaza City, a complete ghost town. Tall buildings towered above us on either side. We drove north briefly along the sea, then cut in toward the hospital. The APC moved slowly and the gunner was intensely on the lookout for militants. We followed a tank that occasionally engaged targets on the way, and we stopped every block to search for threats.

Inside the APC, I watched the monitors. Seeing everything through a screen made it feel like were in a videogame. Sometimes when the soldier manning the camera thought he saw something, he would zoom in and flip between the filters to search for heat signatures. We drove past destroyed vehicles and what looked like a piece of a tank.

Everyone seemed to be holding their breath, rarely speaking. These roads were not on the front line, they were past it. We were driving through Hamas-controlled territory.

When we finally arrived at Shifa, we had to let the other special forces out to clear the area. This took maybe twenty minutes. I watched the gunner focus in on one window.

A head popped up in the window. I thought the gunner was going to fire. He didn't.

Then he spun the gun around to the street, zooming in on someone with a weapon. Zooming in more, we could tell it was an Israeli soldier. A friendly.

*   *   *

We entered Shifa through a hole blown in the wall of the hospital complex. It was so dark when we got out, I couldn't see my hands.

Jonathan told us not to turn any light on, and we hurried into the compound. I was concerned about snipers here but figured the Israelis had the block at least partially secure.

Walking through the hospital cafeteria, we were weaving in between sleeping soldiers.

"No pictures!" someone shouted.

About fifteen soldiers lined up at the door, us behind them. "Follow the green stick lights and move quickly," Jonathan said.

We stepped out.

I'd been to Shifa before, but never like this. It was so dark that I had little sense of where we were. We were in a courtyard, it seemed? Maybe behind the main building? Gunfire erupted, and as the shots rang, I tried to grab a sound bite from Jonathan, but Yaniv wasn't rolling on the camera. It happens. It's always a fear of mine. These are tense environments to operate in. Knowing that, I shot on my iPhone as a backup. The phone camera does surprisingly well in low light.

After waiting a minute for the BBC crew to catch up, we entered another part of the complex, and Jonathan pointed to a sign above the door. This was Shifa's radiology building. The hallways were filled with debris—no people. The Israelis were taking us here to show us weapons they say Hamas fighters had left in the facility. Behind an MRI machine, we were shown two go bags. Behind a sliding maintenance door, two piles of guns.

On a long table, the Israelis had laid out a map and some Hamas material they claimed to have found. I had no way of independently verifying this information—especially in real time. In my reporting, I therefore attributed everything the Israelis said to the Israelis, and that's as far as I could go. The forces had entered for the first time the night before we did: they said they had checked all the areas for explosives and booby traps; our understanding is that they also photographed what they found. In theory they could have moved things to photograph, or while checking for booby traps. We, of course, didn't touch anything and filmed everything just as we saw it.

I spoke with a soldier, his face covered, who had ridden in the APC with us to the hospital. He said his name was Guy and that he lived in Sderot.

This was Master Sergeant Guy Rozenfeld—the reservist who, on October 7, had left his kids and fiancée with a neighbor in his apartment bomb shelter, headed out on his own for the Sderot police station, picked up four soldiers along the way, and led them into a firefight at the station. "I want to go to their house," he then told his commanders. He'd been fighting the war on Gaza ever since.

Now I got to know him. He talked about his day on October 7, how he put his kids in the shelter and went downstairs with a pistol. "I popped two of them," Guy proudly recalled.

He also talked about revenge. Israeli soldiers usually avoid the subject, but Guy was blunt about his motivations. He thought about his red-haired CrossFit buddy Yotam, begging for help that morning in the chat, kidnapped by Hamas. He told me about his late grandmother, a Holocaust survivor. He told me about one of his fellow soldiers whose brother was being held by Hamas.

*   *   *

After leaving the hospital in the APC, we got back to the evacuation point, and I asked Sean to try the satellite phone—an emergency phone we carry with us that doesn't rely on cell signals but links directly to a satellite. We'd been off the grid for more than four hours. It was dark, we hadn't checked in even once, and we were reporting from contested areas of the Gaza Strip in the middle of the war.

Sean opened the phone and waited. "No connection," he told me.

"Shit. Okay. There's nothing we can do."

As we waited a long time for an APC to take us back, I paced back and forth, back and forth. How I wished I was on a phone call, checking in with our bosses. Then it turned out that the army didn't have an APC lined up. Our only option, it emerged, was to pile into two open-air Humvees with a bunch of young soldiers. Most of them looked barely old enough to be in their country's military, which has a mandatory draft age of eighteen. A few had matching gear; others used Burton snowboard goggles to keep dirt out of their eyes—like the ones I had growing up on the slopes in central Pennsylvania. They acted confident and tough at first, joking around with each other. Then it became clear they had no plan. As they jostled their weapons into place underneath the camo netting above us, they even seemed unsure of who should sit in what seat of the Humvee.

Driving on the dark roads, they showed a lack of urgency. They were making clear mistakes and not fixing them in real time. Turning headlights on, then off, then on again. Not having their weapons ready to fire. Taking uncleared roads, with no air support or armor through areas with large buildings.

Yaniv had handed me a cigarette before we got in the Humvees. I lit it and took a few deep puffs. I wasn't hungry or thirsty. My adrenaline was pumping. And I knew I was right to be nervous: I could tell Sean was uneasy, focusing hard on keeping us as safe as possible in these unpredictable circumstances. It was only by chance that we hadn't hit an ambush or IED.

Suddenly a few mortars flew overhead. Flares lit the sky. We hit a supply route. I saw many other soldiers. We followed their path out.

When we crossed the fence into Israel, I exhaled. We had survived.

I texted my father to tell him I was back in Israel. Last embed for a while, I told him. It was a promise I'd quietly made to myself the moment we crossed back into safety.

Glad you're back, he replied.

Risk-reward doesn't calculate anymore.

Went inside Shifa hospital.

Whoa! he replied.

His enthusiasm was infectious. My deal with myself was shaky.

15

TAKEN TO GAZA

Late one night in early November 2023, Shani Goren and nine other Israeli hostages, adults and children, held by Hamas in a room at Nasser Hospital in Khan Younis, Gaza, were awakened by sounds of pounding footsteps and screaming. The hostages had been in that room a long time, ever since October 23. Now it seemed to Shani that a mob was breaking into the building to lynch them.

She and the others heard rage and hatred from the crowd. The Israeli bombing of Gaza had been steady. The ground war was underway. The group must have been alerted that hostages were being held in the facility, Shani thought. There must have been a plan afoot to drag the hostages out and kill them.

They waited in the dark.

Somehow, that night, the mob was obstructed by the Hamas captors; there was no lynching. But between the prospect of their building being leveled by the Israeli Air Force and the prospect of being executed by Hamas or lynched by angry Gazans, Shani's fear didn't come and go. It could, as it did that night, be compounded and intensified, but there was never a moment of relief.

* * *

Before she was taken hostage, Shani, twenty-nine, was an after-school teacher. During the week, she worked with first- through sixth-graders after their regular classes. On weekends, she spent time with friends and family. On October 7 she was home alone in the community she'd grown up in, and like most residents of Nir Oz, she heard the sirens before she heard the shooting.

Shani called her brother Amit, who wasn't in the kibbutz but was headed for his base. He told her to shelter in place: go to her bedroom and lock the door. The room also served as a bomb shelter, with a metal door. She did, her phone buzzing with WhatsApp messages from the community's group chat.

This didn't seem like a normal rocket barrage. Shani was scared to death.

Amit's partner, Nofar, called her, and Shani, looking on her phone at updates in the group chats, asked Nofar what she was hearing. This was bad—apparently it wasn't only Nir Oz being attacked, but also locations well into the country, as far as central Israel. Nofar stayed on the phone with Shani for about two hours, trying to help her stay calm.

Then, in the distance, she heard cracks of gunfire, and yelling.

They got clearer, closer.

Then Shani could tell that people were inside her house. They approached the bedroom that doubled as a shelter. They did not shoot; they simply opened the metal door from the outside. Shelter doors, built for rocket attacks, not infiltrations, are not normally meant to keep people out and can be easily unlocked.

In the corner, Shani was hiding under a blanket, trembling, trying to stay still. She heard a thud of something hitting the floor: a grenade, tossed through the open door. She braced for a blast, but it never exploded.

Moments later, Hamas stormed the room, yelling. They ripped off the blanket. Four men in military vests held her at gunpoint. A fifth man made an X with his arms. She didn't understand what he meant.

She yelled, "No!"

They tried to take her. She resisted. They got more physical, yelled louder, seized her by the arm, pulled her out of the room. She saw Gazans rummaging through her things. They pulled her out of the house. The sun hit her face. She started screaming—then realized no one was there to hear.

She looked around. No Israelis, only Gazans walking through her neighborhood. The smell of smoke in the air: some houses were on fire. She looked down and saw they had taken her dog. It was being walked by Gazan civilians around the houses of the kibbutz.

One of the men started leading her too, around the neighborhood. It was almost a victory lap, a demonstration, for her benefit, of what they had done to the people of her kibbutz. Hoping to calm herself down, Shani pleaded with the man for a cigarette. He didn't have one, but he got one from a Gazan passing by, who lit it for her.

She took a few puffs, but another Hamas gunman came up yelling at her to put the cigarette out. As sirens blared, she looked around. *There is no kibbutz left*, she said to herself.

Then she saw familiar faces: Doron Katz and her two young daughters, Raz (age four) and Aviv (two), along with Doron's mother, Efrat. Shani's mother and Efrat were neighbors; the families had a long friendship. The Hamas fighters gathered Shani and the other women and girls at the edge of the kibbutz, next to a vineyard, and told them to wait. Glancing into one another's eyes in fear and confusion, they didn't talk much.

A *tuk-tuk*, a motorcycle with a large platform attached on the back, with two additional wheels for support, was waiting for them at the end of a short path. So now they knew. They were being taken.

Rocket sirens sounded again, and almost instinctively the group ran toward a bomb shelter. Hamas fighters followed and as the sirens wailed, demanded they come out. They had no choice but to comply.

They were loaded onto the tuk-tuk. Another woman, Neomit, along with another family—David, Sharon, their daughter Yuli—were loaded on too. It was tightly packed. With everyone afraid to jump off and run, they were driven together toward Gaza.

As they approached the border, about five hundred feet from the fence, beside a field, they heard the roar of an Israeli army helicopter overhead and thought they might be saved.

The helicopter opened fire. Shani ducked and froze. The burst of gunfire lasted a few seconds. She didn't know if she'd been hit or not.

Lifting her head, Shani looked around. She hadn't been hit directly but was sprayed with fragments. The militants had fallen like dominos. Efrat, also hit, died on the spot, next to the tuk-tuk. Her daughter Doron screamed in anguish.

David, Sharon, and Yuli appeared wounded but largely unharmed. David took Yuli in his arms.

Shani had only seconds to take in what was happening. Then she grabbed one of Doron's daughters and Neomit the other and they ran through the field.

Doron was trying to lay her mother's body down and stay with her, but one of the injured gunmen was getting up, and Doron too rushed to the join the running group. Soon, though, they had no choice but to stop. Neomit, the most injured, was covered in shrapnel wounds. Two-year-old Aviv had a bullet wound in her foot.

Shani tied her shirt around the girl's foot, trying to stop the bleeding. They tried to stay low and quiet, watching the flow of people going back and forth between the border and their community.

She saw the Gazans walking her dog on a leash made of rope. They were taking it across the border. She wanted to yell, but she knew she couldn't. She watched her dog disappear into the strip.

Another tractor was rolling toward them, loaded with Hamas fighters. Neomit recognized it from where she worked: the kibbutz garden's tractor. Shani recognized one of the gunmen; he'd been in her house. The group tried to avoid being seen and even considered running, but the children and the wounds made that hard to imagine.

They'd been spotted. A man jumped off the tractor, came toward them, and grabbed little Raz. Everyone got up—except Neomit, who was covered in blood. She played dead. Shani was the last person loaded onto the tractor, terrified that resuming the journey into Gaza would attract another attack by Israeli helicopters.

Neomit lay there until the tractor drove away and then crawled back toward the kibbutz.

The tractor rumbled once more down the path. Dead bodies were scattered on the ground. Shani saw burned tanks, Gazans walking freely with loot . . .

Soon she was inside Gaza. A few hours ago she'd been sleeping in her bed.

*   *   *

As the group entered the strip, people were cheering and screaming. Someone hit Shani on the back. In the chaos, they were pulled off the tractor and shoved into a car. It drove off.

Having arrived at a building somewhere on the outskirts of Khan Younis, they were taken inside. The building seemed bigger than a house, more like a makeshift command center; militants were sitting around. The hostages were put in a small room with two beds, an air conditioner, and a TV, which was on. Al Jazeera Arabic, Shani thought. It showed video taken from Israeli channels. They saw video from Sderot: gunmen in the city in a pickup truck. They saw video of militants coming in on hang gliders.

They'd already understood that the attack was widespread—but to see the videos on the news was different. Israel was under attack. They were hostages of Hamas. And having grown up along the Gaza border, they knew what this meant. War would follow.

After some time, gunmen entered the room and gave the group some food and clothes. The women were told to change into conservative clothing and to wear hijabs.

Since Shani wasn't related to anyone in the group, the gunmen singled her out and started taking her out of the room. But Doron said, "No. She is with me."

She'd just seen her mother die. But this was Doron, Shani thought: a caregiver, protecting the people around her. Having infiltrated Israel, killed people, and taken hostages, the fighters seemed to feel that separating these two Israeli women would be challenging. They obliged the request.

Shani, Doron, and the two girls were taken out of the building and put in a car with two civilians: a man driving, and a woman, her face covered. They were driven to a civilian home. They could tell they were close to the border, in Khan Younis, not far from Nir Oz. Inside, they were left in a room with couches, a toilet, a sink.

The man came in. Speaking in Hebrew, he asked for their names and ID numbers. He didn't reveal his name, but he told them that he knew Hebrew because he had worked in Israel and said they could call him *haver*: "friend" in Hebrew. Both his son and his wife were nurses, he assured them, so they would be taken care of, and now the wife and son came in with a sewing kit and iodine. They stitched up a wound on Doron's back. The wife brought them snacks and fruit.

The adrenaline was starting to wear off. *This was real.*

*   *   *

The next day, the man came in and told them that at least 150 survivors from Nir Oz were in Eilat now. Shani felt he was trying to show them some humanity.

They would stay in that house for two weeks, supervised and managed mostly by women. The days were long. Doron and Shani, terrified themselves, tried to keep the girls distracted by making up stories. They were fed *maqluba*, a local rice dish, which, because of stress and anxiety, they could barely eat. They heard the Israeli Air Force bombing. Shani worried that the house would be hit in a strike.

They also heard the rockets going out from Gaza. The wail of ambulances passing on main streets outside.

Shani had been diagnosed with PTSD from a previous incident. She asked for cigarettes. They gave her five per day. Then they cut it back to three. Trying to stay clean and hygienic, they showered with the toilet's bidet. They wanted to survive. With all they were going through, they knew that for hostages, their situation was not as bad as it might be.

But things can change.

*   *   *

One day at 5:30 a.m., the man came in with his son and woke them up. He was in a hurry, rushing around. "Get dressed," he said. "Let's go."

Shani, Doron, and the two girls were walked downstairs and out of the house into a street full of people. They walked for ten or fifteen minutes, passing dead bodies and dead horses on the road. Blending into the crowd, they didn't dare try to run, didn't think about escaping: they didn't have anywhere to go.

Soon they arrived at Gaza's Nasser Hospital, on the west side of Khan Younis, a medical facility normally used to treat civilians. At the entrance, the men separated them.

Shani was brought into an office full of Hamas militants, then taken to a room on the second floor with a small sink, a hospital bed, four benches, and a mattress. It was 6:30 a.m., and three people in the room were sleeping under blankets.

As the three awoke, Shani saw that they were friends from Nir Oz, the Munder family. Ruti, Keren, Ohad, who were grandmother, mother, and son. They all embraced, and the first thing they did was try to piece together what information they had. Like Shani, the family had been held in a house before being brought here, and they'd had a radio. They were able to tell Shani more about the attack; Shani told them what she'd seen on the TV screen on the first day.

Later that day, another hostage was brought in: Yaffa Adar, eighty-five and frail. They gave Yaffa the hospital bed. And when Shani was taken to the toilet, she ran into Eitan Yahalomi, a twelve-year-old boy she knew from the kibbutz; he'd been in her after-school program. When she came back from the toilet, Eitan was waiting outside their room. Someone in his room had had to use a bin to go to the toilet, so they were letting the room air out, and Eitan came into Shani's room.

He told Shani that at the beginning, he'd been held by himself for a total of two weeks.

Shani said, "Don't worry, you are with me now. Everything will be okay." Eitan said he was with Erez Kalderon—another of Shani's students—in another room. At first she assumed that they must be with Erez's mom or dad, but the boys, she learned, were alone.

When Hamas came in and started to take Eitan away, Shani screamed at them. She'd just promised Eitan she would take care of him. If they took him, she might never see him again. She made a scene. She cried, demanded they bring him back—and eventually both Eitan and Erez were brought in to stay with Shani.

*　　*　　*

Ultimately, ten people would be held in that room, from October 23 to November 23.

The hostages had to look out for each other. Camaraderie developed quickly. Ruti had some cards; they also had paper and pencils. They passed the time making cards and games. At night they would be given food for breakfast: a box with three small pitas, some halva, spreadable cheese, a tomato. Between 2 and 7 p.m. each day, they would get rice and sometimes meat.

To get anything else—water, or a trip to the toilet—you had to knock on the door. Sometimes it would take an hour or more to get a response.

On the one hand, they felt safer than they had before. On the other hand, they lived in constant terror of the bombing. There was a window, with a curtain. They were ordered not to look outside. But sometimes they did.

One day, Shani saw Aryeh Zalmanovich, an eighty-five-year-old hostage she knew from Nir Oz, rolled down the hallway on a stretcher, hooked up to machines. The Israeli military would later confirm that Aryeh died in Hamas captivity.

The adults also continuously worried about being lynched. There was that night when the mob broke in. Another night like that might come at any time.

16

NOWHERE IS SAFE

While Shani and the other Israeli hostages were being held in Gaza in painful suspense, Gazan civilians were suffering under the air and ground assault. My team and I witnessed the aftermath on the daily wire video coming into our feeds from the Associated Press and Reuters, as well as on the horrific videos circulating on social media. Displaced, bombed, running out of places to go, low on resources, the Palestinians were facing true hell on earth.

Those who heeded Israel's commands to move farther south believed they would be spared from the bombing campaign. They weren't. Hospitals ran out of anesthesia, forcing surgeons to operate on patients who were awake. Morgues overflowed, leaving people to bury loved ones in mass graves. And the air strikes and artillery shelling were so relentless that bodies remained under the rubble of neighborhoods. They still lie entrenched there today.

I worried about Nael. He was out of Gaza City, but still in danger. I thought of the countless Palestinians I knew in Gaza from my years of reporting there. The kids I met at a day camp south of Gaza City in 2021. The people I talked to outside al-Shifa hospital in 2014. The journalists I broke bread with in 2019.

Who among them was still alive? What had this experience been like for them? I kept these questions in mind as I reported. It was critical that the world understand the pain and suffering being inflicted on the Palestinian people.

With no end in sight, Gazan families were scrambling to find any relatively safe place to go.

*   *   *

Mohammed Al Aloul, a journalist born and raised in Gaza, worked for Turkey's Anadolu Agency. He was bringing up his young family in Al-Maghazi, a refugee camp in the central part of the strip, about eight miles south of Gaza City.

The Palestinian refugee camps were established and developed by the United Nations Relief and Works Agency for Palestine Refugees (UNRWA) in Lebanon, Jordan, Syria, the West Bank, and Gaza in the aftermaths of the 1948 Arab-Israeli War and the 1967 Six-Day War. In both wars, Palestinians fled or were pushed out of their homes; many of them and their descendants—about a third of registered Palestinian refugees—still live in the camps today.

In Gaza, the camps look different from what you might imagine. They're not literal camps filled with tents, as in rural Syria, but full apartment blocks: small cities within cities. One of eight such camps in Gaza, and among the smaller, is Al-Maghazi, where Mohammed and his family lived, home to tens of thousands of people.

Mohammed considered his life both typical and beautiful. Each day he would sit with his children, holding his one-year-old while talking with the others. Besides little Adam there was Ahmed, thirteen; Rahaf, eleven; Kenan, seven; and Qais, five. He wanted them to follow their dreams. He imagined them becoming engineers, doctors, journalists.

On October 7, he was sleeping in his house while his children were getting ready for school when they heard the explosions and rockets. It made Mohammed think of the Day of Resurrection, when, according to Islam, a cosmic trumpet blast will announce the rising of the dead for eternal judgment, commonly known as Judgment Day. Rockets were outgoing from every direction. Mohammed told his kids not to leave the house and headed to the roof of their building to begin his reporting, taking photos and videos.

Back inside, he told his family that, given the intensity of the rocketry, there must have been a targeted assassination of a Hamas official by the Israelis. Then he headed out to meet up with other journalists in Gaza City, and for the next ten days straight, he reported from there and elsewhere.

His family was on his mind. Mohammed had been injured in 2021 by an Israeli missile; the Al-Aloul family knew just how precious life was. He spoke over WhatsApp with his family every day he could, and his kids urged him to come home. As a Palestinian and humanitarian, he felt a duty to cover this war like any other war, to convey it, give the picture, do his job. As a father, he was torn.

After ten days, Mohammed went home, with a plan to work from there and travel to various spots to report as the war developed. His family was overjoyed to see him. He'd told them all to stay home at their apartment inside the Al-Maghazi refugee camp; it was safer. He wore a blue press vest, and his younger kids spotted him as he arrived and ran up to hug him.

Seven-year-old Kenan looked in his eyes. "Daddy, leave work. Don't go to work, Dad. We are afraid for you."

He felt guilty each time he left to do his job.

Meanwhile, the population of Al-Maghazi had swelled quickly. The Israelis were steadily attacking Gaza City; the Israeli army had ordered evacuations. The civilian population, desperate for refuge, fled in search of safety. Many sought shelter in the camp.

On the night of Saturday, November 4, Mohammed was working with other journalists about twenty minutes from home in the city of Khan Younis, at Nasser Hospital, the facility where, unbeknownst to Mohammed, Shani and other Nir Oz hostages were being held. Editing a video, he was chatting with colleagues about the difficulties of the work and being away from family during the war, when his phone rang.

"Mohammed, where are you?" It was a friend who also lived in the Al-Maghazi camp.

"In Khan Younis. What's happening?"

"Call your family. There is a bombing next to them."

Mohammed called his wife. No answer.

He tried his brother. No answer.

* * *

Moments earlier, a huge blast had shaken the ground in Al-Maghazi. The Israelis had targeted a building in the refugee camp. It felt like an earthquake.

The explosion reportedly damaged or destroyed seven buildings in the surrounding neighborhood. Casualties were rushed to the Al-Aqsa Martyrs Hospital. For many it was too late.

Others were pinned under large piles of rubble, their fate unclear. With no heavy equipment available, civilians spent hours digging for their loved ones by hand. The Hamas-run Palestinian Ministry of Health would eventually report forty-seven deaths. It was a number the Israelis did not dispute.

That night, making desperate calls, Mohammed learned that his building had become collateral damage of the strike. A building filled with families. His family, everything to him, nothing collateral about it. He said he was going to drive toward Al-Maghazi, but his colleagues stopped him.

Driving on Gazan roads at night was incredibly dangerous. He risked an Israeli strike targeting his car.

"I stayed up all night praying and praying to God," Mohammed later recalled, "and praying for mercy and praying that one of my family members would be a survivor.'"

Over the course of the night, new information came to him by phone. His wife and baby had survived the blast and were alive.

Then he received a photo of his five-year-old, Qais, at Al-Aqsa Martyrs Hospital. He was dead, a *shahid*, as the Quran calls someone who dies fulfilling their obligations under Islam. Then came confirmation that two of Mohammed's brothers were also dead.

Mohammed called the hospital. His oldest son, Ahmed, was there and being treated, and when the sun rose on November 5, Mohammed rushed to the hospital to search for his family, still wearing his blue press vest, along with a black and red hat. There he learned that Ahmed too had died in the night. In a tent piled with bodies in bags, Mohammed dug for his other missing children, Kenan and Rahaf. He opened the bags of unidentified bodies, looked at them, closed the bags, kept looking.

When his father and some friends arrived at the hospital, Mohammed was carrying the bodies of Ahmed and Qais shrouded in white cloth, and weeping.

*   *   *

When Mohammed went home to continue searching for Kenan and Rahaf, what he found was a pile of concrete and debris. He couldn't believe it. Everything was gone—the home he'd spent so many years living in no longer existed.

People were trying to dig through the rubble. With no tools to help in the search for their loved ones, they clawed at the gray concrete slabs to no avail. Mohammed got on his hands and knees trying to find his children, his nephews, his friends. By the time a single orange backhoe arrived to help with the search, it was too late for most.

Mohammed returned to the hospital, to the bodies of his two other children. He found he could do nothing but pray. In total, eleven people from Mohammed's immediate and extended family were killed in the strike, including three of his brothers and his sister, and three of his brother's children. Eleven out of the more than 9,500 deaths reported at the time by the Hamas-run Gaza Health Ministry, which doesn't distinguish between civilians and militants.

Mohammed's story—losing four of his children—is by no means unique. The Israeli air campaign had decimated entire neighborhoods, killed entire families, maimed civilians. And that was only the beginning.

"The Israeli army said, 'We made a mistake in bombing Al-Maghazi camp,'" Mohammed told me, and I could hear the pain in his voice, sent over WhatsApp, translated from Arabic by a journalist contact of mine in Gaza. "What does 'I made a mistake' mean? . . . Thank God, they were all martyrs. They were peaceful citizens with displaced people.

"I will never forget—not today or in a hundred years."

17

"HE'S ALIVE!"

On the seventh, near the Gaza border, I had crossed paths with my friend Itay Eliyahu, a reservist IDF operations driver, driving a Humvee in a column—I told him to be safe and keep his head down. After the attack, Itay's unit was stationed in a barn in a kibbutz in southern Israel: a mobile combat team of jeeps and Humvees, they get called in when other units need backup. In the early weeks following the attack, after dealing with what had happened to their lives, their families, their country, Itay and his unit spent all their time training. Everyone knew that Israel would invade Gaza; it was never a matter of if but when. The local community was helpful, letting the soldiers shower in their homes, giving them food.

Soon the unit was moved to the north—along the border with Lebanon. Itay spent three weeks there. Then they were called back down to the Gaza border, where they spent a week going in and out of the strip in their backup role, as needed.

Ultimately, with the invasion underway, they spent fifty-five days inside.

* * *

Two months before, Itay's life had looked a lot different. On the night of October 6, the last night of Sukkot, he was out drinking with his friends at Teder, a bar in Tel Aviv, next to my apartment, until 4 a.m. On

Saturday morning, Chloe, his fiancée, woke him up in a panic, rushing into the room. "There are missiles—alarms are going off in Tel Aviv.'"

Itay shrugged it off: a normal part of living in Israel. His bedroom, like many, doubles as a bomb shelter. He rolled back over, but Chloe persisted. "No, no, this is different," she said.

He got up and put on a shirt, went into the living room. The TV was on, and he saw the white trucks barging into his country. He understood right away. This was war. He sat down and watched. *Get your shit ready*, he told himself. *It's just a matter of time before I get called.*

He went to grab his vest and magazines from his closet and began cleaning and preparing the gear. Within an hour, he had shaved and was ready. At 11:27 a.m. he got the call from his 2855th Battalion commander, serving as the officer on duty in the 55th Paratroopers Brigade that morning. Itay was to round up the troops as an operations driver and report immediately to the Bilu base in the city of Rehovot, just south of Tel Aviv.

That's where all of the *yamaheem* are stored: reserve supplies. *All the stuff*, Itay thought, *reserved for doomsday in Israel.*

His dad picked him up at the apartment and dropped him off at the base. But while Itay had expected his whole reserve unit to be there, they weren't. This was weird. He never did anything without his team. And things were a mess: no gear for him, no ceramic plates—the component that blocks bullets—to put in his plate carrier.

He had gathered what ammunition he could and was sitting filling magazines with bullets when a commander approached and told him to drive some soldiers south. "I don't even know who these soldiers are," Itay protested. "I'm not going to war without my *tzevet*!" His team.

"That's not what we're doing right now," the officer said. "You're going to drive them as fast as possible down south."

It wasn't a suggestion. It was an order.

Driving toward the front lines, with soldiers and a commander he didn't know, Itay had no idea what to expect. He didn't know if he could count on his new comrades. Reservists: they might not have picked up a gun in a while.

His concerns were borne out when, ten minutes away from the base, Itay heard a pop.

"What the fuck was that?" he said. One of the soldiers had accidently discharged his weapon.

Any other day, they would have pulled over, stopped the car, filed a report. Today the commander said, "Just continue driving. Don't even look back."

*   *   *

So Itay drove. Sometimes slowly—he was trying to avoid burning cars and dead Israelis. Other times fast—so his soldiers wouldn't be ambushed. He was only beginning to realize: *all hell has broken loose.* Driving between bodies, he thought it looked like a scene from a Hollywood movie, not Israel.

How was this real? How could Hamas be in Israel? Where was the rest of the army?

At about 4 p.m., they arrived at the entrance to Kibbutz Kfar Aza. It was filled with Hamas gunmen—so the guys he'd driven jumped out of the Humvee. Itay was to stay with the Humvee; they told him they'd be back to check in thirty minutes, and they ran into battle.

He waited. Hours went by, with no sign of his new crew. At 2:30 a.m., a heavy barrage of rockets and mortars rained down on his position. He took cover with a few other soldiers who had been waiting nearby. The fire kept coming in. He saw the fear in the young soldiers' eyes and tried to calm them.

He didn't know what to do next. He had no orders, no commander, no directions.

When the rocket and mortar fire let up, Itay slept on and off on the side of the road, a firm and dry place with some cover near the entrance to a sewer. The next morning, he found two of his friends among the soldiers, and they decided to drive toward Be'eri to look for Hamas militants there.

That night, back in Kfar Aza, exhausted after searching for Hamas militants and helping collect victims' bodies around Be'eri, Itay was hoping to get some sleep. Battles were ongoing, but there were enough reinforcements now that he felt he could finally rest.

But someone came running toward the group of soldiers he was with. "We need a medic! Is anyone a medic?!"

Itay is the trained combat medic on his team, a specialized expert in Tactical Combat Casualty Care (TCCC). He got up and ran toward the trouble. There had evidently been an incident with Hamas on the border—the details didn't matter to him at this point. An armored vehicle was bringing in the casualties.

Among them was a familiar face: Assaf Danby. Itay had been at his wedding only two months earlier. Now, critically wounded, with two gunshot wounds to the stomach, Assaf was slipping in and out of consciousness.

Itay began providing care. "I'm with you," he told Assaf. "I know you. I was at your wedding. You're going to get through this."

Suddenly Assaf's eyes were wide open. "Listen," he said. "Don't tell Sharon," his wife. "Don't tell Sharon. Don't tell Sharon." He said it again and again.

Itay assured him he wouldn't. Assaf's organs were coming out of his stomach, so Itay hooked him up to an IV and gave him medicine to encourage blood clots and help with internal bleeding. Pulling out a pad used specifically for stomach wounds, he worked quickly, focused and calm. He needed to save his friend.

Three days later, he received a text message from Chloe. Did you treat Assaf Danby? she asked.

Holy shit. Is he alive? he texted back. Tell me he is alive.

Assaf had survived and was being treated at the hospital. Itay exhaled.

*   *   *

Itay and the other soldiers spent a few days in and around Be'eri, spending the nights in Kfar Aza. All they wanted was to kill as many of the attackers as they could—"To get the border back," Itay recalled later, "to what it had been before." When they weren't searching for Hamas fighters, they helped ZAKA, Israel's search-and-rescue unit, collect bodies. The work was gruesome. Some people were burned beyond recognition; with others, there were only pieces of their bodies to collect.

Then they went back to Kfar Aza, entered the kibbutz, and joined a unit clearing houses. They were going house to house, clearing one at a time, when two Hamas fighters appeared in the distance trying to leave one of the houses. A brief firefight erupted. The Hamas gunmen were killed on the spot.

* * *

Weeks later, inside Gaza, Itay found some days slow. The unit sat in a house on the outskirts of Khan Younis listening to music on handheld radios and playing Shesh-Besh, an Israeli game similar to backgammon. Itay thought of his family back home. Of his fiancée, Chloe, and his brother Assaf. He was eager to get back to his work in real estate. He planned to take tennis lessons when he got out of reserve duty.

Other days were busy. The unit was called on to provide fire support for units uncovering tunnels, killing and capturing Hamas fighters, taking new territory. They went neighborhood by neighborhood, house by house, expanding Israeli control of the area.

One day an urgent call came over the radio: their battalion was pinned down in a narrow street nearby, taking heavy fire from multiple directions. Help was needed, the mission multilayered: locate the battalion, provide fire support, bring extra ammunition, evacuate any wounded.

As Itay and his unit raced in Humvees toward the battalion's position, they found themselves caught in a street so narrow it was more like an alleyway; the militants were above them. And it was here that they located their battalion, in a scene of sheer deadly chaos, under fire, bullets whizzing right over Itay's head.

To the men pinned down by fire, it seemed that the unit appeared out of nowhere to help. Itay could see the gratitude and sheer relief in their eyes—as if they were actually saying "thank you" to what they saw as guardian angels.

They told Itay one soldier who had been killed needed extracting: Gideon Ilani. Itay had the evacuation stretcher, a folded green cloth with metal rods, and he could see Gideon in the distance. But under the hail of gunfire, there was no safe way to get to him.

Suddenly one of the soldiers, without being ordered, ran through the gunfire to his friend. He didn't want to believe Gideon was dead. Bending down, he felt Gideon's neck for a pulse.

"He's alive!" the soldier yelled. "He's alive!" Without thinking, Itay and his friend grabbed the evacuation stretcher and ran toward Gideon.

Half his face was gone. He'd been shot with an RPG that hit him in the head but didn't explode, and the force had ripped open his skull. As bullets pierced the air around them, they got Gideon on the stretcher and to the waiting Humvee, where an army doctor and Itay started stripping him to begin care. Itay pulled off the helmet. It was filled with blood, and his brain matter seemed to be gushing out.

They needed to get him to the border and onto a medevac helicopter. Through the bumpy, dusty roads of Khan Younis, the Humvee sped forward.

On the way, the doctor decided to conduct a cricothyrotomy: an emergency medical procedure that involves cutting a hole in the throat and inserting a breathing tube. In the bouncing, swaying vehicle, he made the cut and inserted the tube.

There was hope. Once the tube was inserted, Gideon breathed on his own. He was maintaining a pulse. Crossing into Israel, they saw the waiting helicopter, blades spinning. They transferred Gideon, alive, into the chopper.

Later Itay learned that Gideon had died on the way to the hospital. He was thirty-five years old.

18

IN THE TUNNELS

For the first month and a half of the war, my friend Nael was taking care of his elderly parents in Gaza while working part-time as a journalist. Until moving with his family to Chicago a few years before, he'd spent his entire life reporting in Gaza, and having been home visiting on October 7, he saw the war as a crucially important—and terribly sad—story that he just had to tell.

Often, after a nearby strike, Nael went out to shoot video at the scene. Sometimes, when the signal wasn't good enough to send video, he would just report what he saw. He was also providing reports for Swiss media and for other journalists he knew. Nael did all this while making sure his family in Gaza had food to eat and water to drink, daydreaming about his two boys in Chicago and his wife, Nancy, who was expecting their third child.

On November 20 we spoke over text about his situation:

Nael: Let me ask you if I want leave gaza to US through Rafah crossing.
Nael: Because my wife will have new baby next month. We still have time
Nael: Can you ask the US consulate or the Israel's about my case

This is a man responsible for protecting not only my life, on multiple occasions, but also the lives of many Fox journalists who have rotated through the Israel-Palestine beat.

> Trey: For sure. I will find a way to get this done. I have a contact who is working with the state department.
> Trey: *You have a green card right? As a legal permanent resident?*
> Nael: I have Palestinian passport and green card
> Trey: *Can you send me everything?*

Nael sent me a copy of his passport and green card. I told him I'd start working on trying to get him out right away. He said he'd stay in Gaza until the beginning of December to take care of his parents. From that, I knew he was feeling optimistic about his chances of getting out.

I didn't share his optimism. We'd done a lot of reporting on American citizens and legal permanent residents stuck in Gaza. Despite the significant leverage the Americans have over the Israelis and the Egyptians, the U.S. State Department still didn't seem capable of exerting that leverage to get people home. That left vulnerable Palestinians resorting to an Egyptian company, basically a pay-to-play scheme charging $5,000 per person to get out. Or there were private operations, leveraging the influence of well-connected individuals who could get people on the Egyptian list and ultimately out of Gaza.

With no luck calling the U.S. embassy in Jerusalem, I resorted to reaching out to those I knew who deal with extraction, which is finding ways to get people out of conflict zones. I have a long list of people I met in Afghanistan during the U.S. withdrawal and in Ukraine during the war. My first message was to Alex Plitsas, who weeks earlier had told me of his success in getting those foreign doctors out of Gaza.

Trey: Hey bro, question for you. Have you heard anything about Green Card holders/legal permanent residents who want to leave through Rafah?
Alex: *So far it has only been citizens. I'll see what I can find out.*
Trey: Okay thanks. I've got an old friend who lives in Chicago normally, but was inside Gaza when this kicked off.
Alex: *No problem, I just pinged my State Department contact. Also, there's a former poet in residence at Harvard, who has an American son and is stuck. [Jake] Tapper [of CNN] was talking to him.*

Alex had been scheduled to arrive in Israel the week the attack unfolded; we had planned to have dinner on October 10 in Tel Aviv. Like many former military and intel guys, he has a tendency to jump into action when disaster unfolds and help out where he can. Our businesses are similar: it's all about who you know and who your friends are, especially when you're in a bind.

He got back to me soon.

Alex: *Ok, my understanding is that green card holders can exit but they need to get added to the list for the gate. They have to contact the U.S. Embassy in Cairo to do so.*

Cairo? I exhaled in near defeat. Everyone was having trouble getting in touch with the U.S. embassy there. It had been showing no signs of giving help. Especially for a legal permanent resident. A few days later Nael texted me.

Nael: Palestinian embassy in Cairo: The Egyptian Authority will open Rafah crossing for Palestinian passengers' arrival.
Trey: *Great. Will you try to leave?*
Nael: For departure I still need to coordinate with the Israelis.

I asked Yonat to reach out to Coordination of Government Activities in the Territories (COGAT), the Israeli operation responsible for overseeing who and what goes in and out of Gaza. COGAT promised to help. They took Nael's information.

They would never actually do anything.

*   *   *

In the days after the al-Shifa hospital raid, many people claimed that the IDF had planted those Hamas weapons we'd been shown in the hospital—that the facility wasn't in fact being used as a military headquarters by Hamas, and the IDF was staging a scene to falsely show it was.

The weapons had been found in an MRI room, people pointed out online—Hamas media outlets said this too—and since a magnetic resonance imaging machine, when operating, is a giant magnet, no metal can be in such a room.

But this machine wasn't turned on. In any event, we could report only what we'd seen, and that's how we reported it: Was it plausible that the IDF planted those weapons, grab bags, and maps? Sure. Was it the most likely scenario? No. In planting weapons, they would risk that information getting leaked; high-ranking officials would be forced to step down. And accusing any military or government of planting evidence requires a high bar of proof. Our job as journalists is to hold those in power accountable, in this case the Israelis and Hamas; that's why when we'd gone to the hospital, I made sure to ask about the protection of Palestinian civilians, to investigate all competing claims, to ask soldiers involved in the raid what they'd seen and found. I also reported that despite Israeli claims that multiple layers of tunnels underlay the facility, we hadn't been shown any such tunnels.

I pushed for another Shifa embed. If there are tunnels under the hospital, I urged my military contacts, then let's see them. Show us the proof.

On Wednesday, November 22, exactly a week after the Israeli army had taken us to Shifa in the middle of the night, we were offered that additional embed, this time to visit the hospital during the day. Before 8 a.m., we were gathered at Kibbutz Be'eri. It was a chilly morning, but Sean suggested I leave my jacket. After years of work and deployment in Afghanistan, he knew that once things get started, it would be warm, especially with a flak jacket and helmet. He was right.

We went with a group of other journalists. One was ABC's Matt Gutman. When I'd first met him, I didn't think Gutman liked me: he's in his mid-forties, with kids; we're in different stages of life and career. But after going into the battlefield together, we became friends. War has a way of doing that to journalists. Unlike reporting political stories or domestic events, where competition is high, reporting in war zones involves a more basic goal: survive. That can foster cooperation.

While Gutman had brought his cameraman, I'd brought Sean, so Gutman kindly agreed to have his shooter act as a pool camera for us: he would shoot some of my taped reporting; I would have access to the material. Sean and I would also shoot on our small Sony Z-90 camera, both as backup and so that we could get some shots that were different from the ABC reports.

As we approached the border, riding on benches in the back of an open-air army Humvee, black smoke billowed from the area we were about to enter. The Israelis were launching new air strikes against Gaza. This time, though, I was glad to be taking a Humvee for the first part of the journey: the roads had been properly cleared; the ride would give us a firsthand, daytime look at the destruction inside Gaza. The Israeli and Egyptian governments still weren't allowing journalists to enter Gaza alone—they didn't want the world to see the full extent and true devastation caused by the Israeli air and ground campaign—so this was the closest we could get to reporting independently.

At the border, while we waited, we spoke with some of the soldiers we would be entering with; they needed final clearance before we could go inside. There were many D-9 bulldozers in this area, equipment of choice for the Israelis, who use them to build dirt hills for protection from anti-tank weapons, to clear pathways for tanks and Humvees, and to check for roadside IEDs.

We entered Gaza. I could see the tall fence with sensors supposed to alert Israel to infiltration attempts. The Israeli side was covered with circular coiled barbed wire. Five minutes after crossing, we were already at Salah al-Din Road, the main evacuation route for Palestinians looking to travel from the north to the south.

Here I saw Palestinian civilians for the first time since the war began. More than one hundred waited on the road, many holding white flags to indicate that they were noncombatants, others with Palestinian IDs held out in front of them. We could see them only from a distance, but their faces looked tired, their bodies exhausted. I thought of the many Palestinians I'd met over the years, those I had an *iftar* (evening) meal with during Ramadan in Jerusalem, the kids I played soccer with in Gaza. And the journalists who protected me when I was in Gaza, in the earlier wars. Like my friends in Israel, they laugh, love, cry.

The eyes of the Palestinian civilians on the road were filled with agony and despair. Empty of joy, they had seen homes and lives crumble before them; displaced by a war they did not ask for, they were walking many miles southward, in search of a safety that did not exist. Each had just a bag or two, and no assurance they'd ever return home. As we took some video and did a taped report, the moment brought home the human cost of this war. They weren't militants or Hamas fighters; they deserved to be treated with respect and dignity. We watched them move slowly down the long road.

We continued past Israeli positions with tanks and soldiers and observed a catastrophic degree of destruction. Entire blocks flattened. Homes reduced to rubble. Hardly a building not damaged or destroyed. I'd come here, south of Gaza City, in 2021 after the eleven-day war, when we worked on a story about the effects of war on the minds of Palestinian children. Only a few blocks from here had been a day camp with therapy, dance, and play sessions.

We were headed toward the sea on the main supply route that the Israeli military had cut across Gaza. With dust in my eyes and on my face, I started to do a few videos for social media:

Right now we are back inside the Gaza Strip with the Israeli military. When you see it during the daytime, you get a sense of just how widespread the destruction is. So many Palestinians who are displaced will have no homes to return to. . . . The battles rage on inside Gaza. The Israeli air force is still striking targets in the distance. We've seen thousands of ground troops holding territory. . . .

Then, driving north on Al-Rasheed Road along the Mediterranean, I recognized many buildings from riding on this road with Nael. Once more than ten stories tall, they'd been hit from the air and by the shellings and looked like they could collapse at any moment. The road itself was covered in dirt and sand.

And yet I was calm on this drive to the staging area. This time, something about being in a Humvee made me feel safer than I'd felt in an APC. It was true that if we took small-arms fire, we wouldn't have any protection—and Hamas had released videos of their forces using anti-tank missiles to target similar convoys. Still, being able to see made me feel far less claustrophobic.

At the staging area, we jumped out and I looked toward the port of Gaza City. Nael and I had gone there to look at the small fish market and have a coffee by the beach. Now it was debris. Hopping into a waiting APC with Gutman and his cameraman, other journalists, and Major Nir Dinar in charge, I knew the drill. This was the more dangerous part of the journey, deeper into Gaza City. We needed the extra armor.

Now I had that feeling again, in the pit of my stomach: worry about getting hit with an RPG. But Gutman and I talked, and that distracted me. "You seem to have the family-and-work balance figured out," I told him.

"Maybe I'm not the best example to follow," he quipped.

Our small talk was drowned out by the roar of the moving APC. Nir looked tired and rested his head on the side of the vehicle. I watched the screens closely as we moved toward al-Shifa hospital.

Our arrival was less intense than our nighttime arrival a week before. The Israelis had taken the surrounding blocks, and a few tanks and APCs were already outside the facility. Stepping onto the hospital grounds I saw Rear Admiral Daniel Hagari.

"Trey, thanks for coming."

"Sure, nice to see you." While we waited for everyone to gather, I peered down into the shaft of a tunnel uncovered at the edge of the hospital. A long ladder was barely sticking out of the top. The other journalists gathered around to look, and I stepped back. In the distance you could hear gunfire as battles continued in Gaza City.

Hagari showed us a variety of weapons the Israelis said they had recovered from surrounding buildings in the hospital complex. This arsenal was far more extensive than what we'd seen before: dozens of Kalashnikovs, forty grenades, and a drone, among other things. In the distance, we heard the air strikes. Hagari then held up a blue-and-white bag from Kibbutz Be'eri that had been found in the hospital.

"Women and girls were woken up in their beds on the seventh of October. Brutally taken hostage to Shifa hospital in a car. People brought here hostages, not just the ones I showed you in the video," Hagari said.

Now it was time to see the real reasons the Israelis had brought us here. They wanted to prove to us that Hamas was using the hospital grounds for military operations. Next to the internal medicine building—named for its donors, the government of Qatar—the Israelis had dug into the ground and revealed a tunnel. There were no entrances to this tunnel from inside the hospital: to find it, they had interrogated people who worked in the hospital and followed wires that ran underground from inside the building.

A group went in before me, so I passed the time by waiting around this area of the hospital grounds. Climbing a dirt mound, to my surprise, I saw Palestinian civilians sheltering at the hospital. I was pulling out my phone to take pictures and video when a soldier called to me, telling me I couldn't film them.

"Sorry," I said. "You can't tell me what I can and can't film."

A young Palestinian girl dressed all in pink looked shell-shocked as she stared into the distance, clutching a white teddy bear, a water bottle, and a bag of bread. Next to her was an old woman, likely her grandmother, in a dark purple hijab. These people had survived nearly two months of war and had seen horrible things unfold before their eyes. I wanted to go speak to them, but the soldiers wouldn't let me, and I needed to be ready for my turn to enter the tunnel and start reporting: the mission for the day.

Still, I documented what I saw and used it in our report. Behind them, a UN worker in a blue vest and helmet crossed from one building to another, flanked by a doctor in teal scrubs and a white coat, Israeli soldiers standing nearby. Patients were still being treated at al-Shifa hospital; others were sheltering there, despite the facility's having run out of resources and supplies. Around one thousand Palestinians were estimated to be still in the complex.

When it was my turn to enter the tunnel, one of the soldiers said I could take my protective gear off since it would be very hot and cramped underground. I declined. Descending, I looked left to see a soldier with his weapon raised and a light shining down a long tunnel.

"Yamina," he said to me. Right, the direction, in Hebrew. So I turned right, following Gutman. Off the tunnel, we entered a large room, tiled, as in the hospital. Yet the soldier guiding us said that this room did not have an entrance to the building; we wondered if this could once have been a hospital basement. I'd seen similar tile in a hostage video released earlier in the month.

"Is this part of the hospital?" Gutman asked.

"It is not a part of the hospital," the soldier said.

As we continued reporting underground, it was clear this tunnel had been constructed like the Hamas tunnels we'd seen on video: wide enough for only one person, concrete walls on either side, concrete arched roof. When an Israeli air strike nearby shook the ground around us, it felt like a small earthquake, and all I could think about was the tunnel collapsing. In these environments, death feels closer.

After what felt like forever, we made it back aboveground. Hagari decided to take us to another area, a few blocks from the hospital, next, where the body of a nineteen-year-old corporal, Noa Marciano, had been discovered. This wasn't part of the original plan. Hagari had enough rank to make in-the-field decisions, and we were eager to see as much as possible.

Before we walked, I made a video with a point I wanted to make in my reporting.

"As we report here from Gaza City, we should also talk about Palestinian journalists. Dozens have been killed since this war began. Others, forced to evacuate to the south. It is critical that all journalists are protected amid this war and we should highlight the hardworking Palestinian journalists inside Gaza."

Heading to the next location on foot, we came upon a moving tank whose turret swung around as the soldiers with us yelled at it to stop. I don't think it had seen us walking. Turning the corner, looking down a street filled with debris, I saw a UN bus, stopped. People were inside. They were evacuating to the south.

I knew this would be our only opportunity to speak with Palestinian civilians.

So after we filmed at a location where the body of a hostage had been discovered, we stopped by the bus, and I tried to talk with an older man inside. He spoke only Arabic. The army was trying to hurry us along, but we needed this sound, the voice of people directly affected by the war. Under the pressure, I was forgetting how to ask questions in Arabic. I always had a few prepared, in case I was in this situation, so I ended up introducing myself and just asking how the man was.

Then I got to a younger man named Mohammed, putting the microphone up to the open window of the bus. "Peace be upon you. My name is Trey," I told him in Arabic. "I'm a journalist with Fox News."

He spoke some English. "It's our home anyway. It's our country." I could see the pain and sorrow in his eyes. "It has been destroyed. So, it's our country after all."

Before we left for the staging area, I talked with Hagari on camera. "The Israeli military has faced criticism for raiding Gaza's al-Shifa hospital. With what you've found," I asked him, "was it worth it?"

"I think it was a professional operation. We're now seven days here. Not a single shot was fired inside the hospital, hitting a doctor, a patient or a civilian. Not one."

We followed a tank on our ride to the staging area and learned from the soldiers in the APC that for weeks they'd had to sleep in the vehicle for safety, ten soldiers to one APC. Twelve of us were crammed inside; I couldn't imagine sleeping.

Once we got out, I saw a fighter jet overhead, returning from a bombing mission. It launched flares to avoid being shot down. Back in the Humvees we drove on a different road, which seemed to take longer. A large plume of black smoke guided our trip out. The Israelis had launched another air strike along the border, and something was on fire.

We passed a row of large trucks. "Mines!" Sean pointed out. That's what the truck was carrying. "Wonder where they'll place them." Similar mines had been used to blow up buildings across Gaza. The Israeli military often faced criticism for that—and on at least one occasion, tragedy, when an early detonation killed Israeli forces.

Back in Israel, the military censors, two young women, active in the army so around nineteen, demanded that we give them all of our video for their review.

I told Yonat to let me talk to them. "We've been through this before," I told them. "No screens and no faces of special forces—we aren't agreeing to anything else. You will see in our final piece, we are not showing sensitive information."

"We need to see, though. Also, did you take any video on your phone?"

"When I have that camera?" I pointed to the camera. I didn't answer the question.

Finally I convinced them they didn't need to see all of our material, and I whispered to Yaniv, who was driving, "Let's go." I didn't want to give them time to change their minds.

Right before we left, they asked if we could get a picture.

They'd been following me on Instagram.

19

CEASE-FIRE

Shani Goren and the other Nir Oz hostages were still being held in the crowded room in the Nasser Hospital in Khan Younis. They'd survived the mob's break-in—the near lynching. Now it was late November, nearly a month since their arrival in the room.

Then, on Wednesday the twenty-second—the day I saw al-Shifa hospital again—Hamas moved part of the group into another room in the facility, just Shani and the two boys Eitan and Erez, with no explanation. In their new room, they met some Nir Oz residents they hadn't seen since the first awful day of the killing and kidnapping, people Shani had no idea if she'd ever see again.

A Hamas fighter in civilian clothes had charge of this group. Shani asked him why they had been moved, and he told her there was a cease-fire.

She felt some relief. Yet she also thought she knew why she'd been moved. Those left in her first room, she sensed, were the ones being released; she wouldn't be among the first to come out of Gaza.

She was right. After three days in the new room, she was moved to yet another room, this time with Erez but without Eitan. The people left in her former room were released. This was the system: if you were moved, it wasn't your day. Shani was now dreaming of being home with her family and losing hope of ever being in a group chosen for release.

Two days later, she was moved to still another room, where she met Liat Atzili, an American citizen whose husband had been killed on the seventh, and a woman named Ilana Gritzewsky. Liat said, "Today we are getting released."

"If I'm in this room," Shani said, "no one is getting released."

Days passed amid the cease-fire. She was still in Gaza.

*   *   *

On Thursday, November 23, the main spokesman for Qatar's foreign ministry, Majed al-Ansari, held a press conference in Doha to publicly confirm details of the cease-fire agreement, which would involve the release of certain Israeli hostages in Gaza and certain Palestinians detained by Israel. Al-Ansari explained that before the process would move forward, they still needed to confirm the names on lists coming from both sides. That done, at 4 p.m. the next day, the release would begin.

I'd been reporting extensively on the ongoing efforts of the Qatari government to broker a cease-fire deal. After spending months in Doha during the U.S. withdrawal from Afghanistan, my sources in the Persian Gulf region got way better. I used these contacts to gather details about the agreement and report them to our audience.

Israeli officials had also been leaking hostage-release information to Israeli media. Thirteen Israelis—twelve women and girls and a nine-year-old boy, Ohad, who had marked his birthday in captivity—were to be released to the Red Cross inside Gaza. We gathered that twelve of the hostages that would come home on the first day were from Nir Oz—from which we'd reported in the aftermath and knew as Yoav's brother's kibbutz. They would be driven to the Egyptian border. There the Israeli intelligence agency, Shin Bet, would confirm their identities; then they would proceed into Egypt to be transferred home. The Palestinian detainees in Israel would meanwhile be released to East Jerusalem and the West Bank.

Early Friday, at 7 a.m., the Gaza Strip fell quiet for the first time in nearly seven weeks. No fighter jets flying overhead, dropping large payloads. No thuds of outgoing artillery. No incoming rocket sirens. It seemed too good to be true, and the world watched and waited to see if the first group of hostages would really be exchanged. If so, the region would get four days of quiet, with the possibility of an extension.

That morning, I spent hours deleting comments on my Instagram and blocking accounts spamming my page there and on X. Our video of the Palestinian who had been arrested while we were visiting the Nova Festival site had gone viral. Thousands of people were accusing me of faking the video and saying the man was a crisis actor. Amid the boiling information war, anytime one side found something they thought they could call wrong with a report, they were jumping on it.

Just before lunchtime on Friday we arrived at Hatzerim Airbase, east of Be'er Sheva in the Negev Desert of southern Israel, where some of the released hostages were to be driven or flown, depending on their condition, from the release point in Egypt. We wanted a glimpse of them, and from a coverage standpoint, it was a gamble where to go to catch the best glimpse. Some journalists chose to report from the Schneider Children's Hospital in Petah Tikva, where some hostages would be sent. Others went to the Kerem Shalom Crossing, a junction of Gaza, Egypt, and Israel. Others, like us, went to the air base.

As we watched, white ambulances in a line were checked by a guard and entered the base. Two helicopters flew overhead. Given the sensitivity of the transfer and the lack of information on the hostages' conditions, a variety of contingency plans were clearly in place.

The transfer proceeded as planned. In addition to the thirteen Israeli hostages, twelve Thai captives who had been working in southern Israel on the seventh were released. Forty-nine days after first being taken into Gaza, these twenty-five people were free. With the transfer underway, the Red Cross released a statement: "In its role as a neutral intermediary, the ICRC over several days will transfer hostages held in Gaza to Israeli authorities and ultimately their families, and transfer Palestinians detainees to authorities in the West Bank, to be reunited with their families." The statement underscored the fact that the Red Cross had not been involved in the negotiations.

Video released from inside Gaza revealed how these exchanges went. The Israeli girls and women were paraded again through the streets before cheering and whistling Gazans, then put in Red Cross Toyotas with the famous white-and-red flags. Civilians surrounded the jeeps, jeering, screaming, and recording with their phones, some hitting the windows with sticks and open palms.

From the air base, we went live. "Reports do indicate those thirteen hostages are now in Egypt," I reported just after 6 p.m. local time.

After 8 p.m., images started coming out of the West Bank as the Palestinian detainees arrived there, twenty-four Palestinian women and fifteen Palestinian teenage boys from the Ofer prison. Their bus was surrounded by chanting people. On top of the bus, a man waved two Hamas flags. One of the Palestinian women released, Roda Abu Agamiya, came up to a journalist in the crowd and yelled, "We are the sword of Mohammed Deif."

She was referring to the number two Hamas official, one of the masterminds of the October 7 massacre; Agamiya herself had reportedly been jailed for trying to recruit Palestinians to join the militant group Popular Front for the Liberation of Palestine. The moment reminded me of a quote from former Israeli prime minister Yitzhak Shamir: "The sea is the same sea and the Arabs are the same Arabs," Shamir said in 1996 after the Oslo Accords were signed. For Palestinians, resisting Israeli occupation is in their blood. Many would rather be jailed or killed than live under a blockade or occupation.

Life in the West Bank is dismal for the majority of Palestinians, and they see Israel as the main problem. That's why so much popular support prevails for Hamas and its military wing. The current ruling West Bank party, Fatah, is largely unpopular: civilians think it is wildly corrupt and doesn't represent their interests. Both accusations are true. If elections were held today, Hamas would take the same kind of control over the West Bank that it has over Gaza.

That night, an event in the West Bank illustrated just how tense things were in the Middle East. Images started circulating online showing two men accused of being collaborators with Israel. The men were killed, dragged through the streets, and hanged from an electrical pole while a crowd cheered and took videos; the bodies were then thrown in the trash. The message sent by the Palestinian militant factions was clear: working with Israel, especially during the war, would have deadly consequences.

*   *   *

By Saturday, November 25, however, Israel was seeing images of hope for the first time since the war began. Families reuniting in hospital hallways. Tight embraces that people thought might never come.

The day also gave new insight into how the hostages had tried to interpret the small bits of information they'd been able to get when inside Gaza. A clip circulated online from Israel's Channel 12 showing a released hostage, Ruti Munder, telling her family she already knew her son Roi was dead, killed on October 7: she'd learned it from the radio.

That proved that family members going on Israeli radio channels and speaking about their loved ones, just hoping someone in Gaza would hear, had been successful in some cases. Other hostages, who hadn't known the fates of their loved ones, were overjoyed to be released only to learn that family members had been slaughtered.

The second day of hostage releases was delayed, as reports indicated Israel was putting immense pressure on Hamas and threatening to resume the campaign against Gaza if the deal didn't move forward, but after a few tense hours, the process resumed. Thirteen more Israeli hostages came out, this time with four Thai nationals. In the group was Emily Hand, an Irish-Israeli girl whose father had been interviewed by CNN's Clarissa Ward when he thought she'd been killed. The incident further clarified how hard it was to get clear information in the early days of the war. A heartbreaking interview made its way around the world, only for the man to find out his daughter was alive.

The following days proceeded mainly as expected. Some of the smaller agreements within the deal were also being fulfilled: more aid going into Gaza; Israel keeping the airspace over Gaza empty during agreed-upon times.

And the deal ended up being extended: two days' further cease-fire for twenty more hostages.

*   *   *

If anyone had reason to be broken by the events of October 7, and by the long and harrowing captivity that followed, it was Chen Almog-Goldstein, an Israeli hostage released on Sunday, November 26. In her home at Kfar Aza, she'd seen Hamas gunmen shoot her husband, Nadav, in the chest, leaving him mortally wounded, and watched her eldest daughter, Yam, bleed out after they shot her in the face. Then Chen and her three younger children had been hustled into a car and driven to Gaza.

And yet she wasn't broken. Chen came out of Gaza with a mission.

Something had happened to her. It had begun almost right away, in the car on the way to Gaza. At the border, when the car stopped, the gunmen got out and loaded bodies into the trunk, which was open to the passenger area. Chen told the kids not to look.

She also assured them they would be okay. Her terror and grief were turning to purpose. She made a decision. For her children, she had to stay strong.

*   *   *

Her time in Gaza would severely challenge Chen's courage. It had taken them seven minutes to get to Gaza. It would take seven weeks to get home.

They were held, at first, not in civilian homes, like many of the others, but down in the tunnels. That first day, Tal, her youngest son, having not cried so far, saw the tunnel entrance and burst into tears.

Imprisoned underground in the hands of the organization that had murdered her oldest daughter and husband before her eyes, Chen did everything she could to keep the children calm. At one point, she saw two female Israeli soldiers who were being held underground in the tunnels—they seemed terrified, and she tried to calm them too.

It was hard to breathe. The sand of the tunnels got in their mouths and eyes, and the air was heavy. The ground shook with the Israeli bombing campaign.

And they kept being moved. First to an apartment aboveground, then another apartment, where they stayed for weeks, then a supermarket, then a mosque, then another apartment, then back into a tunnel. For each move, Chen and her daughter Agam were dressed in traditional Islamic clothing, with hijabs covering their hair. The first time, they looked at each other and started crying. The clothing not only concealed them—it felt like an effort to steal their identities.

Through it all, there was constant bombing, no electricity, early sunsets, and long nights. Soon Chen could distinguish between types of strikes.

Their closest call was after their overnight stay in the supermarket. The next morning, having slept behind the shelves, they heard huge bursts of gunfire right outside, like a jackhammer, combined with bombing from above. As the gunfire got closer and closer, the four of them hid under a mattress they'd found on the floor.

We've survived so much, Chen thought. *Now it is over.*

But the guards jumped on top of them. Hostages were Hamas's bargaining chips. With their own bodies, the guards shielded Chen and her kids from the explosions and the gunfire, and when the fighting died down outside, the guards told them to breathe, to relax.

How can we relax? We just almost died.

She had a number of conversations with her captors. She was worried that if Hamas was losing the war, an order would come down suddenly to execute all hostages. Sometimes she asked the guards whether, if given that order, they would kill her and the kids.

"We will die first," one of the militants assured her. "Or at least die together."

*   *   *

Brought back down into the tunnels in late November, Chen started to feel new hope—but also new anxiety. There was talk of a cease-fire. Nobody knew what would really happen. Hope for relief amplified the suspense.

In the last tunnel where she and the kids stayed, Chen met up with two female hostages—the soldiers she'd met in the tunnels at the beginning of their captivity—and four other women. They told her what they had experienced. Chen was horrified, yet again.

They told her the guards had subjected them to sexual assault. There were patterns involved. In a moment of weakness, when a hostage was overwhelmed by fear, grief, and anxiety, a guard would approach as if to comfort her, then start caressing her, touching her upper body. There were even worse stories—incidents of sexual demands made at gunpoint.

Chen had once been a social worker. She knew this was unfathomable trauma. She offered the women what comfort she could, though she knew there wasn't much she could do for them now.

She also made a promise to herself. She saw these women as strong. She also saw them as needing a voice to speak on their behalf, bear witness to what they'd suffered. Chen had seen her husband and eldest child slaughtered. At this moment she still didn't know if she and her surviving kids were really about to be released. Still, she promised herself: if she did make it out, she would be a voice for these strong, abused women.

Chen would keep her promise. After her release, she spoke in media interviews and at rallies. She didn't want the world to forget Black Saturday, the darkest day of her life.

*   *   *

On Sunday morning the team and I went to report for the first time from Hostages Square in Tel Aviv. The area had been set up as a makeshift memorial for those kidnapped by Hamas. Civilians held events there to keep the world's attention on the most important thing to them: their family members and fellow Israelis.

Just after lunchtime, we were having coffee outside the public library facing the square when Yoav rose from his seat. His brother Gil was walking up to us. Between Yoav's working around the clock and Gil's no longer having a permanent home, this was the first time they'd seen each other since October 7.

They embraced with a strong hug. After their reunion, Gil came to speak with us. Having almost been murdered by Hamas in his own home, he still looked like he was in shock. But he smiled and told me he was thankful to be alive.

In Tel Aviv for the first time in a long while, I took a rare day off and went to my apartment. I wanted to get some sleep that night. Along with the PTSD symptoms—those aural hallucinations, where you hear bombing, sirens, rockets at full volume, which seem anything but imaginary—my nightmares had been getting worse. They took many forms now. Me and the crew trapped in Gaza, with no Israeli escorts, filming the war, only to be taken by Hamas. Hamas raiding my home in Pennsylvania—and we have no weapons, no way to protect ourselves . . .

That night, hoping to clear my mind for sleep, I left my apartment and took a long walk around Tel Aviv. I wandered with my headphones on, listening to "Take a Moment to Breathe" by normal the kid. I choose this song whenever my mind is in a bad place—when I was reporting in Ukraine, it helped a lot.

An hour and a half passed quickly. Just after 11 p.m., finally relaxed, my guard down, I was able to exhale. I was cutting through my neighborhood, with very few people out, when right next to my building, I glanced up and froze. Panic shot through me.

A long tunnel stretched out in front of me. Nobody was around, just this Gaza tunnel—the kind I had been in. I whipped off my headphones. In confusion, I walked toward the tunnel.

The panic soon faded. I'd reached the Suzanne Dellal Centre, a theater and dance studio next to my house. The tunnel was real. It was an art exhibition protesting the capture of the hostages and calling for their release. I walked in. The tunnel was built to perfect scale; it even had dirt on the floor. At the entrance, people had signed messages for the hostages and drawn Israeli flags.

*   *   *

Shani's day did come at last. She was removed, but this time for release.

It didn't go the way she'd imagined.

In her latest room at the hospital, Hamas-linked civilians undressed her and Ilana—Liat had to stay—to be sure they weren't taking letters or information or documents. Given a bag with clothes, the two were told they were going home. Escorted through the building, they saw that it was filled with Palestinian civilians, some wounded and receiving care, others sheltering from the Israeli bombs. They were ushered into a waiting car.

But the car wasn't taking them home.

"You are going to the tunnels," the driver said.

The tunnels? Given blindfolds, Shani's hope turned to despair and fear.

"To meet Sapir Cohen," the driver added. Shani had no way of knowing that, as part of the cease-fire negotiations, Hamas had categorized which hostages would be released together, and at what time.

The car arrived at the backyard of a civilian house—an entrance to the tunnels. Blindfolds removed, they climbed down a ladder, following a man with a flashlight into a narrow corridor. Then they climbed down another ladder. The corridors were so narrow that they had to go single file.

People in the tunnels sleep during the day and stay awake at night. During the day, a lot of people are passing through, mostly Hamas fighters changing positions. These humid, damp, underground mazes are also used as jails, guarded by Hamas gunmen. Some hostages are kept in larger communal rooms, some in cells. Shani couldn't tell exactly how deep they were going—but it was deep. They walked for about thirty to forty minutes.

Finally they arrived in one of the communal rooms far underground. Here were Sapir Cohen, David Cunio, Eitan Mor, and Ofer Calderon. They too had been moved into this area; it was being used both as a staging area for the hostage release and a holding area for adult men like David, Eitan, and Ofer, who wouldn't be released as part of the current agreement. They all spent the night there.

They had been asleep for a while when a man came in, a GoPro camera attached to him, and woke them up. "Do you want a cigarette, or do you want to go home?" he asked Shani.

"I want to go home," she replied.

"Five minutes." He told them to prepare a pita for themselves.

Sapir, Ilana, and Shani were escorted into a corridor; the rest stayed behind. They walked, and in a different part of the tunnel they picked up another woman on the list for release, Nili Margalit. They kept moving.

Emerging from the tunnel, Shani blinked in the light. *It might be finally happening*, she thought.

Yet nothing was clear. The four women were put in a car and driven for what felt like an hour, then switched to a different car. They were outside Nasser Hospital—back again. They waited there for four hours.

While they waited, Hamas was getting into uniforms—they even asked Nili to help them tie their green bands on their heads. They normally don't dress like this. Hamas fights the Israeli army with RPGs and machine guns and dresses as civilians since they want to blend in—except when they're trying to look to the world like a legitimate army.

Dressed up now, they started taking pictures of each other. Then, as the hostage group still waited, they brought in two others, Bedouins they had kidnapped. This was all taking a long time, Shani thought. She was more and more afraid that something would go wrong.

But after still more waiting—five more hours—they were driving again, and heading south.

They arrived in Rafah. Here they saw the white Red Cross jeeps. And yet until they entered Egypt at the Rafah Crossing, Shani couldn't breathe.

After fifty-five days as a hostage of Hamas, she was free.

In Israel, she and the group were driven to Hatzerim Airbase. There she was met by her brother Amit; she hadn't spoken to him since the morning of October 7. Then she was flown to Wolfson Medical Center, where the rest of her family was waiting for her.

"My life hasn't changed yet," she told me, "because my friends are still in Gaza." The experience has given her life new meaning—but with the war ongoing, and hostages still inside, the nightmare never ends.

Chen's heart, too, was still with the hostages. "What we experienced and went through in Gaza, and now," she explained. "You are a refugee, displaced—a displaced person in your own country."

"We are ready for the eighth of October to start," Shani said.

*   *   *

While some of the Israeli hostages were getting out of Gaza, Nael was still stuck there, and he was getting desperate to find a way out. COGAT had been no help, but finally, on November 30, he was able to get directly in touch with the U.S. consulate himself. But it was a red herring. False hope.

He texted me:

I already spoke to the US consulate and gave them my details to put my name at the list. The sound was good and they told me to follow the list's from tomorrow.

I asked him for a confirmation email, and he sent it to me. It was from the U.S. State Department's "Task Force Team."

Dear Nael,
    Thank you for calling us today. You do meet the criteria to be included in the list of names and so we will move forward with the details you provided. If any additional information is needed, we will reach out to you. If your name is published on the official, online crossing list, you should be permitted to exit Gaza and enter Egypt on any day as long as the crossing is open.

The email had a link to a Facebook page where the list would be published. It sounded so easy.

It wasn't. By early December, Nael's name still wasn't on it.

Out of ideas, I reached out to a friend whom I can only describe as an operator. I knew he would find a way to get it done and I'm protecting his identity so that he can help others in the future.

I was determined to help Nael. I made sure my bosses were in the loop. My conversation with my friend started a process, and three months later, after a multiperson and intense effort, Nael would arrive home in Chicago.

*   *   *

In total, 105 hostages were released during the cease-fire including 81 Israelis. Yet some who should have been released in those first groups were still in Gaza. One was Noa Argamani, twenty-six, seen in the October 7 video, her face contorted with fear as she was taken to Gaza on a motorcycle.

Early on Friday morning, December 1, 2023, Hamas failed to provide Israel with the promised list of hostages to be released that day. Despite reports that it would be extended for an eighth day, the ceasefire collapsed exactly a week after it began. Within hours, Israel and Hamas were back at war.

20

TO START REPORTING

The beginning of the cease-fire had been announced in words, but the end was proclaimed with rockets and bombs. Just before 6 a.m. local time, a single rocket was fired toward Sderot. Sirens sounded as the rocket was intercepted by the Iron Dome.

Soon sirens were sounding throughout southern Israel, and just after 7 a.m., black smoke rose from Gaza City in the aftermath of an Israeli air strike. The war had picked up right where it left off.

The Israeli military released a statement: "Hamas violated the operational pause, and in addition, fired toward Israeli territory. The IDF has resumed combat against the Hamas terrorist organization in the Gaza Strip."

The Qataris, who had brokered the cease-fire and were scrambling to contain the fighting, released a statement of their own: "The State of Qatar expresses its deep regret at the resumption of the Israeli aggression against the Gaza Strip following the end of the humanitarian pause, without reaching an agreement to extend it. The Ministry of Foreign Affairs confirms that negotiations between the two sides are continuing with the aim of returning to a pause."

But it was too late.

The feeling among officials and many other Israelis was that these battles would have to continue for months—in a limited way even for years. Hamas consists of a political wing and a military wing that includes militants who fight a complex guerrilla war while hiding behind civilians. More than 130 hostages remained in the strip. Even if Israel officials had been willing to end the war that very day, they never would have been willing to leave their citizens behind enemy lines. Entering a new phase of fighting, the Israelis now expanded operations in northern Gaza and began dropping leaflets in Khan Younis, Gaza's second-largest city, telling Palestinians to evacuate farther south.

*   *   *

With war raging again inside the strip, my team and I jumped back into action and resumed reporting along the border. With rockets soaring overhead, we based ourselves in Sderot, and as in the first days of the war, we jumped into the car and chased down the impact sites. We had gotten into such a strong routine that we could arrive with the shrapnel still smoking. Next to one house, I picked up a few pieces of the twisted metal and held it in my hand for a taped report—like taking a hot potato out of an oven, I had to keep moving it in my hand to avoid getting burned.

Eager to keep the attention of my new, younger audience, I also continued to provide updates on my social media accounts. On one social media video, "You can see here the amount of rockets that were just intercepted overhead," I said, pointing to a clear blue sky crisscrossed with streaks of white smoke. "These came from the Beit Hanoun neighborhood in the northern part of Gaza. An indication that fifty-eight days into this conflict, Hamas and Islamic Jihad have maintained their ability to fire rockets from the northern part of the Gaza Strip."

Day and night, air strikes pummeled the area across the border. With surveillance over Gaza now so widespread, Israel could often immediately target positions while rockets were still being launched. They were also dropping thousands of bombs in northern Gaza to hit anything they deemed a reasonable target. The word *reasonable* is up for interpretation.

*   *   *

Master Sergeant Guy Rozenfeld, who had fought Hamas at the Sderot police station the morning of October 7, was back in Gaza. I'd met him when he was serving in the raid on al-Shifa hospital. He had survived so far, but he knew how things go. It was impossible to predict anything.

His main focus was still on going after Hamas, his motivation linked to the seventh. He thought about his friends killed that day and wondered what had happened to those taken into Gaza, hostages like Yotam Haim, the red-haired drummer who had begged him and others for help that horrible morning in the CrossFit chat.

One afternoon in Gaza's Shejaiya neighborhood, infamous to Israelis for intense Hamas resistance in close urban quarters, Guy sat with soldiers and platoon commanders of the Golani Brigade, exhausted from the fighting. The next day, at the same location, the Golani troops were ambushed, and in hopes of preventing Hamas from taking the injured and dead into the tunnels, additional Israeli forces came to help and were ambushed too. Guy had been there less than twenty-four hours before. Men he'd just sat with were dead.

It's all luck. That's what Guy had come to believe. He was eager to keep fighting.

*   *   *

Dr. Raed Mousa did get himself and his family out of Gaza shortly after I aired a story about his situation.

Having left the house in Rafah, thanks in part to American extraction specialists who wish to remain anonymous, and in part to an O-1 Visa, for those with valuable skills and achievements, the Mousa family now lives in Erie, Pennsylvania.

"People lost everything," he told me of those left behind. As a doctor, he's especially conscious of the medical disaster ongoing in Gaza, where "if anyone is injured . . . and their injury is more than a scratch, they will die.

"The only thing keeping them alive," he says, "is the hope of a ceasefire."

*   *   *

Sireen Beseiso and her son Aden also got out of Gaza. They're home in the United States, back in Salt Lake City, Utah.

Sireen has strong opinions about the conflict—some of them even extreme. Regarding the released hostages, she told me she thought they'd been well treated. "The hostages went on the news saying [the captors] brought a doctor every two days . . . they were very nice, they didn't rape them, they made sure they were safe.

"Who bombed them?" she went on. "The Israelis, the IDF soldiers bombed them. To be honest, in that moment, I said I'd rather be underground with Hamas, safe, than being in my own home in Gaza, being blown up."

When it comes to the October 7 attack itself, she sees the motivation as understandable. "If you have a cat or a dog in your own home and you put them in a cage and you can't take them for a walk or give them treats or treat them good, what will happen in the end? They're going to attack you. It's the same. They're keeping Gazan people inside a cage."

In her "they," however, Sireen includes Hamas leaders. "I'm against them. They're living their life in Qatar, in hotels, fancy schools, fancy restaurants, and people, they're dying in Gaza." She doesn't envision a peaceful future. "Seeing all these kids suffer and live through this, how would we know they're not going to be all resistance [fighters] someday," she said.

*   *   *

Most in Gaza, even among the better off, can't leave. Every day that the war raged on, and Israeli air strikes continued, the death toll of Palestinian men, women, and children rose. Thousands and thousands more were left critically injured. In the few hospitals still undamaged, doctors were wholly overwhelmed, facing the staggering, impossible challenge of providing effective care to an endless stream of desperate patients, without even the most basic resources. For all the horrific injuries Dr. Abu Warda has seen and treated since the war began, it was an event in December that devastated him.

On the evening of the eighth, he was watching the news on his phone in the big building in Gaza City where he and his entire extended family lived when a bomb hit the building and turned it to rubble. Without light and help, the survivors couldn't dig through the debris to locate the others. Dr. Abu Warda felt he could do nothing for his family. He was "just watching, helpless," he told me. In the morning, he said, when they began to find the dead, they discovered that thirty-one people from his immediate and extended family had died in the blast, including his uncles and his grandfather. Others were hospitalized in the ongoing medical disaster.

"They bombed our home without any reason. . . . We are not Hamas," he reminded me. "We are not Fatah." He sent his wife and daughter to shelter in a school in the north of Gaza.

"I don't remember any day after this day," he says. And of October 7: "We lost everything from that day."

Yet he's back at a Gazan hospital now, al-Ma'madani, treating patients as best he can. We're both thirty years old. What different lives we live.

* * *

It was mid-December when Lieutenant Colonel Gilad Pasternak's radio crackled with an update: "We have three terrorists eliminated."

This was in that infamous Shejaiya neighborhood in Gaza City, where Israeli troops spent days battling Hamas fighters holding the buildings. They'd even sent a K-9 unit into a building only to see Hamas kill the dog.

Gilad ran to his commander with the news, though something felt off. Three would be a lot of Hamas fighters to find and kill at once. Hamas was no longer organized as in the early days of the war. Single fighters more often engaged Israeli troops, using RPGs and small arms.

When Gilad and his commander arrived at the scene, soldiers reported that an Israeli sniper had shot and killed two of the men where they stood. One of the dead men was shirtless. Both had shaved heads. A makeshift white flag lay beside them. The third man, at first only wounded, had managed to retreat into a nearby building. He yelled for help—in Hebrew—then reappeared, and a soldier shot him dead.

The soldiers had decided to leave the two where they lay and remove the third man's body. Gilad and the soldiers tried to revive him, but it was too late, and there was nothing they could do.

This young man didn't fit. He didn't look Palestinian. His red hair. His skinny yet athletic body. They had a bad feeling that they had killed a hostage.

Gilad's commander decided to send all three bodies to Israel, just to be sure, and while they waited for word, Gilad and the soldiers, investigating the scene, found a white sheet with "SOS" written in food stains. The military had seen this sign before; it was presumed to be a Hamas ploy to draw them into an ambush.

In the evening, they received news even more distressing than they'd feared. All three of the men they had killed were Israeli hostages. Gilad felt worse than at any other time during the war.

Gilad didn't know Yotam Haim—the man from Kfar Aza, now accidentally killed by Israeli soldiers—but Guy did. Having pleaded for help in the CrossFit chat on the morning of October 7, Yotam had been taken hostage, and had survived captivity, until the moment he faced the Israeli army in the Shejaiya neighborhood of Gaza City.

*   *   *

"It was a tragic tactical mistake," Defense Minister Gallant told me later.

On receiving reports of the hostage killings, Gallant had made the three phone calls to the families himself. "I told them I am responsible," he said to me. He told the chief of staff to see what had to be done to avoid future events like this.

He also understood the difficult situation the soldiers were facing. "In these moments," he told me, "you have to know what your goal is and concentrate on achieving it."

*   *   *

My friend Itay, the medic, got married. I attended the wedding.

Mali, the police officer wounded at the station in Sderot, has been working ever since her release from the hospital.

Ron, the IDF soldier who said we'd meet on the beach in Gaza, was injured by Hamas mortar fire but survived. Gilad Pasternak, the lieutenant colonel in charge of five battalions—he told me "people won't stop mourning"—is still fighting the war. Jamil Faris, the reservist I met on a tank, now works at the front desk of the hotel that we report from in Tel Aviv.

And in December, Chaim Peri, the seventy-nine-year-old peace activist, taken by Hamas from Nir Oz, appeared in a hostage video. His son Lior had said that if he could only speak to his father, he would tell him, "Hold on, we're coming. We're doing our best."

But in June 2024, Chaim Peri would be pronounced dead.

*   *   *

In December, I got a rare day off and decided to go home to Tel Aviv and—first—sleep, and then try to be a normal human. Walk around. See a friend or two. Have Thai noodles at a spot down the street.

On my way back from eating, I walked past a sweet black street cat that looked like one that my friend Hamdah and I had saved the day before the war started and named Beanie. The cat was a reminder of the simple things—a connection to a reality that, after being consumed by war for weeks, I now found I craved.

Back at my apartment, sitting on my couch, I was finally able to decompress. I closed my eyes and thought about all we'd witnessed. The weeks blended and collapsed and it seemed just yesterday that I'd been here, in the apartment, waking to a call from Yonat telling me something was happening . . .

Was it all just a bad dream?

I wished.

Air raid sirens suddenly sounded across the city. I opened my eyes.

It wasn't my imagination. It was true. Tel Aviv was under attack again.

And I was heading out to my balcony again, cell phone in hand, to start reporting.

EPILOGUE

THERE IS NO PEACE HERE

The war between Israel and Hamas continues today. After the cease-fire collapsed on December 1, weeks of battle turned into months of war. The winter months brought with them more death and destruction. Rocket fire from Gaza continued, as did Israeli air strikes across the strip, with Israeli ground troops eventually reducing their presence but never fully leaving the enclave.

The year 2024 was ushered in by red-alert sirens sounding across Tel Aviv as rocket interceptions replaced fireworks in the Israeli skies above. Most of the other international correspondents across the industry took time off for the holidays to see family and reset. I wanted to keep going. In January we were back inside Gaza with the Israeli military, still unable to enter independently and report with freedom of movement. Back in an APC, driving along bumpy paths into the southern city of Khan Younis, I had the same concern about being hit by an RPG or anti-tank missile—only this time, I was far more exhausted. The adrenaline of the early days of the war was replaced with lethargy. Like finishing a marathon, only to be told you now have to run back on the path you arrived on.

Into the tunnel network beneath Khan Younis we climbed and crouched. We saw where hostages had been held, in concrete cells with iron doors. This was by far the most extensive tunnel system I'd entered in Gaza. It reminded me of tunnels we'd see along the northern border back in 2019, dug by Hezbollah. Advanced, expansive. A maze under a city.

For the American audience, interest in the war between Israel and Hamas remained high. There was an understanding that this was now the longest war in Israel's history and that daily fire would continue on the southern and northern front. Red-alert notifications on our phones were more common than text messages or emails.

*   *   *

At the end of January, our team got a visit from the very top of Fox News: the executive chair of Fox Corporation, Lachlan Murdoch; the CEO of Fox News, Suzanne Scott; and the president of Fox News Jay Wallace. They were joined by Vice President Greg Headen and London Bureau Chief Dragan Petrovic. This trip was not meetings and suits but a visit to the front lines of the conflict as it raged in the distance.

We drove past the spot where we'd reported that fateful morning of October 7 and headed to the Erez Crossing, where Hamas militants had broken into Israel. Wearing flak jackets, we toured the area and met with Rear Admiral Daniel Hagari before visiting the community of Kfar Aza.

I found that Lachlan, Suzanne, and Jay were all deeply interested in learning about the story firsthand, to understand the history unfolding before our eyes. With no camera crews filming the interactions, no reporters in tow, they stopped and spoke to people affected by the massacre. To a couple in Kfar Aza, who had returned to their home in an area along that Gaza border where mass murder took place. To soldiers who told them what the war was like. They had questions about the civilians of Gaza. They cared. It's refreshing to know that we work for real humans who are kind and empathetic about the stories we cover.

*   *   *

No other hostages had been released since the November cease-fire agreement, although in February two hostages made it out of Gaza alive, following a daring rescue mission conducted by the Israeli army and intelligence services. Ongoing negotiations hosted by Qatar and Egypt often made progress but then failed to come to fruition, due to hard-line demands by Hamas and Israel.

I continued to speak with Israeli officials, including Defense Minister Yoav Gallant, as well as to senior Hamas officials. I wanted to keep our coverage well rounded, to talk both about the suffering and rising death toll of Palestinian civilians and about the hostages who remained in Gaza.

*   *   *

The October 7 attack had set off a chain reaction that included months of attacks from Iranian proxies across the Middle East: Palestinian militants in Gaza and the West Bank, the Houthis in Yemen, Hezbollah in Lebanon, Iran-backed Shia militias in Iraq and Syria, and finally the Iranian regime itself.

The brazen attack by Iran came about after an Israeli air strike targeted a building in Damascus, Syria, killing seven members of Iran's Islamic Revolutionary Guard Corps (IRGC), including Brigadier General Mohammad Zahedi. Zahedi was responsible, in part, for smuggling Iranian weapons to proxies in the region, including Hezbollah. Targeting a building next to the Iranian embassy was meant to send a message of deterrence, but it resulted in the first direct attack against Israel from Iran in the country's history.

A situation that was already hot now hit the boiling point. The question was when, not if, Iran would respond. And it did. On April 13, news broke that a swarm of drones was headed from Iranian territory toward Israel. It would take them hours to arrive.

Sean and I spoke about the situation, understanding that Iran could decide to launch cruise and ballistic missiles along with the drones as they got closer. That's exactly what they did. We stood from our live position in Tel Aviv, watching interceptor rounds from Israel's Arrow Defense system soaring through the sky. It was surreal to be standing in Israel as the country was under such a large-scale attack. One hundred twenty ballistic missiles, 170 drones, and 30 cruise missiles, according to the Israeli military. This was a moment for the history books, and we reported accordingly, staying up all night in team coverage to keep our audience updated.

The vast majority of the incoming fire was intercepted outside Israeli territory by an informal coalition of Israel's allies, including the United States. Some of the missiles that made it to Israel were shot down by air defense systems. There were no deaths and just one critical injury in Israel.

But the story isn't about how successful the attack was. The story is that the equation in the Middle East has now changed forever.

By March, Gaza's al-Shifa hospital once again became the focal point of the conflict, with Israeli forces launching another raid against the facility. This raid was more extensive and lasted for nearly two weeks. The Israelis say they killed more than two hundred gunmen during the operation, which completely destroyed the hospital.

*   *   *

Nael is in Chicago, where he drives for Uber to support himself and his wife and kids. Once there's a cease-fire, he wants to go back to Gaza and see the rest of his family again.

"I saw footage of Gaza City. That made me cry," Nael told me. "I can't believe that they destroyed the whole of Gaza City. That is a tragedy."

It has occurred to me again that the war will continue indefinitely, a sense that Hamas will never be destroyed. You can't destroy an ideology, a people who have been raised with the idea of resistance always in mind. In the middle of May, the team and I drove toward the Gaza border, just south of where we'd stood on the morning of October 7, to report from Netiv HaAsara. More than 220 days after the massacre, it was as if the war hadn't played out. Israeli ground troops were once again operating in northern Gaza. Air strikes targeted buildings in front of us. Rockets soared overhead. The team and I ran for cover as red-alert rocket sirens sounded: "Tzeva Adom" "Tzeva Adom." But something was different now. So much time had passed.

On Saturday, June 8, four hostages were rescued in an IDF operation in central Gaza. Among those freed was twenty-six-year-old Noa Argamani—seen on video on October 7, taken into Gaza on the back of a motorcycle. According to the Hamas-run Palestinian Ministry of Health, nearly three hundred Palestinians were killed during the raid, mostly civilians, in order to rescue the four Israelis. As always, we had no way to confirm the specific number, but videos of dead women and children circulated online; there's no doubt that many civilians were killed during the operation. The ratio continues to be disproportionate—a source of significant disagreement between supporters of Israel and supporters of Palestine.

Diplomatic efforts to end the war continued, but as of late July, they remained unsuccessful. Israelis meanwhile began bracing for the possibility of a broader war with Hezbollah in Lebanon.

* * *

When I think back to that first day, one of the things that's still with me is how close my team and I were to death on that fateful morning, when we stopped to report at the intersection. If we'd kept going, if we'd driven just a minute further and arrived at the next intersection, we would have found ourselves right in the midst of the carnage, under attack by Hamas gunmen.

I've played out the scenario in my head countless times.

Would I have tried to reason with the gunmen before they killed me? Would I have tried to explain in Arabic that I was a journalist? Would they have murdered me anyway?

I think about it a lot.

October 7, 2023.

ACKNOWLEDGMENTS

I owe so many people thanks and acknowledgment for getting me to the place in my career where I can travel the world telling stories. I've devoted the past ten years of my life to the craft, and along the way a lot of people have supported me and made this dream possible.

Starting with my father, Jerry, who sacrificed everything to make sure we had the best childhood possible. You taught me first how to treat people and build bridges, then traveled with me around the world as my cameraman, producer, and agent. You stood with me in Ukraine in 2014, filming reports with me that only a few dozen people would watch. Eight years later I returned on my own to report for an audience of millions. I've never forgotten your belief in me, before anyone else.

And to my late mother, Debbie, I wish so dearly that you were here to read this. Thank you for teaching me empathy and communication. I am a better human and journalist because of your many lessons. Your kindness lives on through me and Aly. And to Aly, my twin sister, I admire your adventurous approach to life. You inspire me to live more each day.

To my late grandmother, Mary Margaret, who instilled a sense of wanderlust in me from a young age and took me to every corner of the globe, and to my living grandmother, Bobbi, who at ninety-five teaches me each day the true meaning of life, thank you.

A huge thank-you to my extended family, including Aunt Karen, Uncle Tom, Aunt Bonnie, Uncle Dale, Uncle Howie, Mindy, Uncle Dick, Aunt Maryanne, Aunt Leslie, Stacy, Blake, Caleb, Grant, Emma, Anna,

Mariya, Jared, Kensi, Pete, the Katz family, and the Belz family. I appreciate each of you for your love and support.

I'd also like to express my gratitude for my friends. The people who have stood by me through life. To Fin and Sarah, Jeremy, Raf, Joey, Andrew, Paul, Rico, Hamdah, Shahriar, Nick, Carla, Alex, Johnny, Anthony, Kaitlan, Tim, Erez, Jacob, Harry, Melissa, Mikey, Dana, Jana, Sophia, Chloe, Dani, Itay, Assaf, Trevor, Evan, Justin, Zach, Alexander, Chelsea, Brianna, Dominick, David, Tyler, Ford, Remi, Matthias, Gavy, Katie, Sarah, Alex, Oliver, Brian, Neil, Neri, Roey, Bill, Matt, my brothers in Beta Theta Pi, and so many others. And of course, my mentor and friend, J.C. Bua and his wonderful wife, Michele.

I also remain indebted to my professors at American University, Bill Gentile, Margot Susca, Terry Bryant, and W. Joseph Campbell. Along with so many others who believed in me, like my high school teachers Charlie and Annie Masters.

When I think of whom to thank at work, the list is too long to write. The countless producers, cameramen, and technical staff who make our work possible. Thank you.

Thank you to the Murdoch family, CEO Suzanne Scott, President Jay Wallace, Fox Books and Fox Nation President Lauren Petterson, Executive Vice President Kim Rosenburg, Executive Vice President Scott Wilder, Executive Vice President Tom Lowell, Senior Vice President Sharri Berg, Vice President Greg Headen, Vice President John Sylvester, Vice President Gary Schreier, foreign desk editor Thomas Ferraro, DC bureau chief Bryan Boughton, London bureau chief Dragan Petrovic, and the entire executive team.

A special thank-you to the media relations team led by Irena Briganti, including Caley Cronin and Ali Coscia. You have gone above and beyond to make sure the world knows about our work. It's greatly appreciated.

To my team in Jerusalem past and present, including Dudi, Yonat, Yaniv, Yael, Yoav, Ronen, Uri, Eli, Ibrahim, Karen, Dana, Dvora, Achinoam. And to all of the anchors and correspondents at Fox who support my journey.

And to our security teams from SEPAR, including Sean Nolan, Dane Kenny, and many others, we appreciate your keeping us safe.

Benji, my friend, I look up to you and am proud to know you. Thanks for inspiring all of us to be better people. I admire your courage and tenacity.

Pierre Zakrzewski and Oleksandra "Sasha" Kuvshynova, I think of you both often. We continue to do this work in your honor.

To the *Black Saturday* team from Harper Collins and United Talent Agency, I'm thankful to work with such professional and thoughtful individuals. Lisa Sharkey, Maddie Pillari, Mandi Ogle, and Alexandra Von Zedlitz, your excellence and professionalism helped this book come to life. I'm grateful to have you.

To the entire marketing and production teams. And to so many others who helped to create, produce, and market this book.

At United Talent Agency, of course, Byrd and Eric, who believed this book could come to life after our first call as I reported under fire on the Gaza border. And to Steve, Luke, Andrew, Jason, Emily, and Josh.

And to my agents, Adam Leibner and Carole Cooper, thank you for believing in me and caring so much about my success. I'm lucky to have both of you in my life.

NOTES

PROLOGUE

2   a Palestinian territory: "Doctrine of Hamas," Wilson Center, October 20, 2023, https://www.wilsoncenter.org/article/doctrine-hamas; "Hamas Covenant 1988," Avalon Project, https://avalon.law.yale.edu/20th_century/hamas.asp.

3   blockaded by Israel: "Israel and the Occupied Territories," U.S. Department of State, https://www.state.gov/reports/2016-report-on-international-religious-freedom/israel-and-the-occupied-territories/israel-and-the-occupied-territories-the-occupied-territories; Abraham Bell, "International Law and Gaza: The Assault on Israel's Right to Self-Defense," Jerusalem Center for Public Affairs, January 28, 2008, https://jcpa.org/article/international-law-and-gaza-the-assault-on-israel%E2%80%99s-right-to-self-defense/.

3   Hamas had warned that such a visit: "Rocket Launched from Gaza at Israel after Threats over Ben Gvir's Temple Mount Visit," *Times of Israel*, January 3, 2023, https://www.timesofisrael.com/rocket-launched-from-gaza-at-israel-after-threats-over-ben-gvirs-temple-mount-visit/.

CHAPTER 2: "WE ARE AT WAR"

17   at more than thirty locations, more than 3,000 Hamas fighters: "IDF Estimates 3,000 Hamas Terrorists Invaded Israel in Oct. 7 Onslaught," *Times of Israel*, November 1, 2023; "Hamas' Attack Is a Staggering Failure for Israel's Intelligence and Security Forces," NPR, October 9, 2023, https://www.npr.org/2023/10/09/1204577965/israel-intelligence-security-hamas-gaza; "Where Was the Israeli Military?" *New York Times*, December 30, 2023, https://www.nytimes.com/2023/12/30/world/middleeast/israeli-military-hamas-failures.html.

18   "I can hear gunfire": "Resident of Southern Town Says Terrorists Roaming the Streets," *Times of Israel*, October 7, 2023, https://www.timesofisrael.com/liveblog_entry/resident-of-southern-town-says-terrorists-roaming-the-streets-she-can-hear-gunfire/.

18   "There are wounded here": "Resident of Kibbutz Infiltrated by Terrorists Sends Whispered Plea for help," *Times of Israel*, October 7, 2023, https://www.timesofisrael.com/liveblog_entry/resident-of-kibbutz-infiltrated-by-terrorists-sends-whispered-plea-for-for-help-please-send-troops/.

20   At about 8 a.m.: Interview with Defense Minister Yoav Gallant, April 12, 2024.
21   more than 100,000 rockets and precision-guided missiles: "Hezbollah Hiding 100,000 Missiles That Can Hit North, Army Says," Associated Press, May 13, 2015, https://www.timesofisrael.com/hezbollah-hiding-100000-missiles-that -can-hit-north-army-says/; "Hezbollah: What Is the Military Power of Iran's Ally in Lebanon?" Reuters, April 16, 2014, https://www.reuters.com/world /middle-east/lebanons-hezbollah-what-weapons-does-it-have-2023-10-30/.
21   Hamas had taken credit for the operation: "'March toward Palestine': Hamas Releases Mohammed Deif Speech from October 7," *Jerusalem Post*, March 27, 2024.
21   around 3,000 rockets were fired into Israel: "As War Grinds on, Israel Sees Sharp Drop in Rocket Attacks from Gaza," *Times of Israel*, November 13, 2023, https://www.timesofisrael.com/as-war-grinds-on-israel-sees-sharp-drop-in -rocket-attacks-from-gaza/.
22   Operation Al-Aqsa Flood: First learned by the author from Nael Ghaboun, October 7, 2023, confirmed the same day by Hamas officials.
26   "we are at war": "'We Are at War,' Netanyahu Says, after Hamas Launches Devastating Surprise Attack," *Times of Israel*, October 7, 2023, https://www .timesofisrael.com/we-are-at-war-netanyahu-says-after-hamas-launches -devastating-surprise-attack/.

CHAPTER 3: MOMENTUM

36   198 Palestinians had been killed and more than 1,600 injured: "Hamas-Run Ministry in Gaza Says 198 Palestinians Killed since Start of Terror Group's Assault," *Times of Israel*, October 7, 2023, https://www.timesofisrael.com /liveblog_entry/hamas-run-ministry-in-gaza-says-198-palestinians-killed-since -start-of-terror-groups-assault/.

CHAPTER 4: THE WORLD WOULD BE WATCHING

40   Israel formally deployed its first group of troops: "Where Was the Israeli Military?" *New York Times*, December 30, 2023, https://www.nytimes.com /2023/12/30/world/middleeast/israeli-military-hamas-failures.html.
42   Hamas had also strategically targeted: "How Hamas Broke through Israel's Border Defenses during Oct. 7 Attack," *Washington Post*, October 27, 2023, https:// www.washingtonpost.com/world/2023/10/27/hamas-attack-israel-october-7 -hostages/; "How Hamas Used Small Commercial Drones in Its Attack," *Jerusalem Post*, October 15, 2023, https://www.jpost.com/israel-news/article-768485.
43   Just after 5 p.m.: Briefing by Rear Admiral Daniel Hagari, October 7, 2023.
44   active fighting continued: "Hamas Surprise Attack out of Gaza Stuns Israel and Leaves Hundreds Dead in Fighting, Retaliation," Associated Press, October 7, 2023, https://apnews.com/article/israel-palestinians-gaza-hamas-rockets -airstrikes-tel-aviv-11fb98655c256d54ecb5329284fc37d2.

CHAPTER 5: THE BATTLE IN SDEROT

48   around 200 Israelis were dead and more than 1,000 injured: "Hundreds of Israelis and Palestinians Are Dead after a Surprise Attack from Gaza," NPR, October 7, 2023, https://www.npr.org/live-updates/israel-gaza-war.

48   believed to have around 15,000 total rockets: Background briefing by an Israeli intelligence official, 2022.

53   "Last night, the Security Cabinet": "Security Cabinet Approves War Situation," Israeli Ministry of Foreign Affairs, https://www.gov.il/en/pages/security -cabinet-approves-war-situation-8-oct-2023.

53   the first since the Yom Kippur War in 1973: "Israel Officially Declares War for 1st Time Since 1973," *Times of India*, October 8, 2023, https://timesofindia .indiatimes.com/world/middle-east/israel-officially-declares-war-for-1st-time -since-1973-as-death-toll-mounts-to-600/articleshow/104261182.cms.

53   300,000 reservists were called up: "Israel Drafts 300000 Reservists as It Goes on the Offensive," Reuters, October 9, 2024, https://www.reuters.com/world /middle-east/israel-drafts-300000-reservists-it-goes-offensive-2023-10-09.

54   Israel needed to enter Gaza on the ground, now: Interview with Defense Minister Yoav Gallant, April 12, 2024.

66   killing thousands in the process: "The Science Is Clear. Over 30,000 People Have Died in Gaza," *Time*, March 15, 2024, https://time.com/6909636/gaza-death-toll/.

CHAPTER 6: "THIS TIME WILL BE DIFFERENT"

68   120 rockets toward Ashkelon and Ashdod: "October 9, 2023—Israel-Hamas War News," CNN, October 9, 2024, https://www.cnn.com/middleeast/live-news /israel-hamas-gaza-attack-10-09-23.

69   "I have ordered a complete siege": "Defense Minister Announces 'Complete Siege' of Gaza," *Times of Israel*, October 9, 2024, https://www.timesofisrael .com/liveblog_entry/defense-minister-announces-complete-siege-of-gaza-no -power-food-or-fuel/.

77   confirmed Israeli death toll now above 900: "Israelis Wounded Near Lebanon Border as Death Toll Reaches 900," *Haaretz*, October 9, 2024, https://www .haaretz.com/israel-news/2023-10-09/ty-article-live/at-least-700-israelis-killed -2-000-wounded-over-130-held-hostage-in-gaza/.

80   "Israel is at war": "Statement by Prime Minister Benjamin Netanyahu," October 9, 2023, Israeli Ministry of Foreign Affairs, https://www.gov.il/en/pages /statement-by-prime-minister-benjamin-netanyahu-9-oct-2023.

80   Thirty-two American citizens were killed: "At Least 32 Americans Were Killed in Israel," *Washington Post*, November 3, 2023, https://www.washingtonpost .com/world/2023/10/11/americans-killed-israel-names-victims/.

CHAPTER 7: HAMAS IS HERE

91   Videos later showed various instances of bodies: Israel Defense Forces, https://x.com/IDF/status/1721779346791125036.

CHAPTER 8: KIBBUTZ BE'ERI'S HOUSES OF HORROR

95   Hamas claimed they had dozens of hostages: "Hamas Captures Hostages as Israelis Share Photos of Those Missing," CNN, October 8, 2023, quoting Al-Qassam Brigades spokesman Abu Obaida, posting on Telegram, October 7, 2023, https://www.cnn.com/2023/10/07/middleeast/hostages-hamas-israel -gaza/index.html.

106 She told the press the same thing: IDF Investigation Clears Commander of Killing Civilians in Kibbutz Be'eri Tank Attack," *Jewish Chronicle*, April 3, 2024, https://www.thejc.com/news/israel/idf-investigation-clears-commander-of -killing-civilians-in-kibbutz-beeri-tank-attack-pja31a8a.

CHAPTER 9: AN INFORMATION WAR

114 Gallant reportedly arrived at a determination: "Biden Convinced Netanyahu to Halt a Pre-Emptive Strike Against Hezbollah," *Wall Street Journal*, December 23, 2023, https://www.wsj.com/world/middle-east/how-biden-averted-a -second-front-by-convincing-israel-not-to-attack-hezbollah-on-oct-11 -e14a0a3b.

123 forty beheaded babies: "Kfar Aza Massacre: Hamas Beheaded Women and Babies," 124News, https://www.youtube.com/watch?v=8iibO7SHbgo.

CHAPTER 10: THE ARMY ISN'T COMING

128 On October 20, the first two hostages were released: "Two Hostages Released by Hamas are Judith and Natalie Raanan," NBC News, October 20, 2023, https://www.nbcnews.com/news/world/two-us-hostages-released-hamas -rcna121446; "Hamas Releases Two American Hostages from Gaza after Qatari Mediation," Al Jazeera, October 20, 2023, https://www.aljazeera.com /news/2023/10/20/hamas-releases-two-american-hostages-from-gaza.

129 Eighty residents were kidnapped: "'We Are Officially Hostages,'" Associated Press, December 5, 2023, https://apnews.com/article/israel-hamas-war-news -hostages-0c14750240138853a70e38b0c09ef157.

136 Hamas had brought manuals: "'Top Secret' Hamas Documents Show That Terrorists Intentionally Targeted Elementary Schools and a Youth Center," NBC News, October 13, 2023, https://www.nbcnews.com/news /investigations/top-secret-hamas-documents-show-terrorists-intentionally -targeted-elem-rcna120310.

CHAPTER 11: "WE'LL MEET ON THE BEACH IN GAZA"

143 over 3 percent of the population was called upon to fight: "Israel's Massive Mobilization of 360,000 Reservists Upends Lives," *Washington Post*, October 10, 2023, https://www.washingtonpost.com/world/2023/10/10/israel-military -draft-reservists/.

148 around 1,400 people, with 250 held in Gaza: "Israel-Hamas War News," CNN, October 16, 2023, https://www.cnn.com/middleeast/live-news/israel-news -hamas-war-10-16-23/h_5b2bc7a10400bc271f9f39fdb98cb528; "What Is Known About Israeli Hostages Taken by Hamas," AJC Global Voice, February 26, 2024, https://www.ajc.org/news/what-is-known-about-israeli-hostages-taken-by -hamas.

149 They targeted remote machine-gun positions: "How Hamas Attacked Israel's Communications Towers," *New York Times*, October 10, 2023, https://www .nytimes.com/2023/10/10/world/middleeast/hamas-israel-attack-gaza.html; "Failure at the Fence," *Frontline*, PBS, November 2023, https://www.pbs.org /wgbh/frontline/documentary/failure-at-the-fence/transcript/.

149   Fox is the top-rated cable news network: "Fox News Channel Makes Cable News History as the First Network to Mark 22 Consecutive Years at Number One," Yahoo Finance, January 30, 2024, https://finance.yahoo.com/news/fox-news-channel-makes-cable-190400374.html.

151   Israel was still only using 30 percent of its airpower: Interview with Defense Minister Yoav Gallant, April 12, 2024.

CHAPTER 12: THE GROUND INVASION BEGINS

153   500 to 600 Americans were still trapped in Gaza: "Americans Remain Stuck in Gaza as U.S. Evacuation Deal Falters," *Washington Post*, October 124, 2023, https://www.washingtonpost.com/world/2023/10/14/gaza-americans-rafah-border/.

155   Israelis claimed they hit 320 different targets: "IDF Says It Hit 320 Hamas and Islamic Jihad Terror Targets in Gaza over Past Day," *Times of Israel*, October 23, 2023, https://www.timesofisrael.com/liveblog_entry/idf-says-it-hit-320-hamas-and-islamic-jihad-terror-targets-in-gaza-over-past-day/.

156   800 Palestinians had been arrested across the West Bank: "IDF Says 800 Palestinians Arrested in West Bank Since Start of War," *Times of Israel*, October 23, 2023, https://www.timesofisrael.com/liveblog_entry/idf-says-800-palestinians-arrested-in-west-bank-since-start-of-war/.

157   the heroic story of Aner Elyakim Shapiro: "Staff Sgt. Aner Elyakim Shapiro, 22: Unarmed, He Fended Off 7 Grenades," *Times of Israel*, October 18, 2023, https://www.timesofisrael.com/staff-sgt-aner-elyakim-shapiro-22-unarmed-he-fended-off-7-grenades/.

CHAPTER 13: IN THE HEART OF THE BATTLE

177   laid out a step-by-step plan: "Remarks, Antony J. Blinken, Secretary of State, Tel Aviv, Israel, U.S. Department of State, November 3, 2023," https://www.state.gov/secretary-antony-j-blinken-at-a-press-availability-40/.

CHAPTER 14: FRONT OFFICE OR FRONT LINE?

191   NICU, full of more than thirty tiny Gazans: "Premature Babies Are Evacuated from Embattled Hospital in Gaza," *New York Times*, November 19, 2023, https://www.nytimes.com/2023/11/19/world/middleeast/premature-babies-al-shifa-hospital-gaza-evacuation.html; "Under Bombardment, Gaza Medics Fight to Save Patients with No Power, Water or Food," *Guardian*, November 12, https://www.theguardian.com/world/2023/nov/12/under-bombardment-gaza-medics-fight-to-save-patients-with-no-power-water-or-food.

191   targeting people stepping out of the hospital: "Urgent: Patients and Medical Staff Trapped in Hospitals under Fire in Gaza," Doctors Without Borders, November 11, 2023, https://www.doctorswithoutborders.org/latest/urgent-patients-and-medical-staff-trapped-hospitals-under-fire-gaza.

192   "As we have shown and warned": "IDF Demands Military Activities in Shifa Cease," Israel Defense Forces, November 14, 2023, https://www.idf.il/en/mini-sites/hamas-israel-war-24/war-on-hamas-2023-resources/idf-demands-military-activities-in-shifa-cease/.

192   "Based on intelligence information": "IDF Forces Are Conducting an Intelligence-Based Precise Operation," Israel Defense Forces, November 14, 2023, https://www.idf.il/en/mini-sites/idf-press-releases-regarding-the-hamas-israel-war/november-23-pr/idf-forces-are-conducting-an-intelligence-based-precise-operation-in-a-specified-area-in-the-shifa-hospital/.

CHAPTER 16: NOWHERE IS SAFE

212   Palestinian refugee camps were established and developed: "Palestinian Refugees," United Nations Relief and Works Agency for Palestine Refugees in the Near East, https://www.unrwa.org/palestine-refugees.

214   damaged or destroyed seven buildings: "Comment by UN Human Rights Office Spokesperson Seif Magango," Office of the High Commissioner, United Nations Human Rights, https://www.ohchr.org/en/statements/2023/12/comment-un-human-rights-office-spokesperson-seif-magango-continued-bombardment; "Gaza Health Workers Pushed to the Limit amid Airstrike 'Carnage,'" UN News, https://news.un.org/en/story/2023/12/1145077.

CHAPTER 18: IN THE TUNNELS

224   vulnerable Palestinians resorting to an Egyptian company: "Some Gazans Are Paying Tens of Thousands of Dollars to Escape with their Families," NPR, March 1, 2024, https://www.npr.org/2024/03/01/1235355010/some-gazans-are-paying-tens-of-thousands-of-dollars-to-escape-with-their-familie.

CHAPTER 19: CEASE-FIRE

237   "In its role as a neutral intermediary": "ICRC Teams Begin Multi-Day Operation to Reunite Hostages," International Committee of the Red Cross, https://www.icrc.org/en/document/israel-and-occupied-territories-operation-reunite-hostages-detainees-families-deliver-assistance.

238   One of the Palestinian women released: "Released Palestinian Prisoner Investigated for Inciting More Terror," *JNS*, November 27, 2023, https://www.jns.org/released-palestinian-prisoner-investigated-for-inciting-more-terror/.

247   In total, 105 hostages were released: "What Is Known about Israeli Hostages Taken by Hamas," *AJC*, February 26, 2024, https://www.ajc.org/news/what-is-known-about-israeli-hostages-taken-by-hamas.

CHAPTER 20: TO START REPORTING

250   More than 130 hostages remained in the strip: "How Many Israeli Hostages Still Held after 6 Months," *Newsweek*, April 8, 2024, https://www.newsweek.com/how-many-israeli-hostages-still-held-6-months-gaza-1887290.

ABOUT THE AUTHOR

TREY YINGST is the chief foreign correspondent for Fox News Channel. Since joining FNC in the summer of 2018, Yingst has reported from Ukraine, Afghanistan, Pakistan, Iraq, Lebanon, Gaza, Israel, Jordan, Turkey, UAE, Bahrain, Qatar, Morocco, and France, among other locations. In 2024, Yingst received the prestigious George Weidenfeld Prize, presented by Axel Springer, for his frontline war zone reporting. He's been named to the *Forbes* magazine 30 Under 30 list and *AdWeek* magazine's "Young Influentials" List, in addition to having profiles written about his work in *Vanity Fair* and *Variety*. In 2023, Yingst had an exclusive sit-down interview with Ukrainian president Volodymyr Zelenskyy. He's also interviewed Israeli prime minister Benjamin Netanyahu and leadership from Hamas. Yingst has a bachelor's degree in journalism from American University in Washington, D.C., and graduated magna cum laude from the honors college. While at American University, Yingst cofounded the media outlet News2Share, with which he was reporting from hotspots around the world at the age of twenty.